WHERE TO STASH YOUR CASH LEGALLY

OFFSHORE FINANCIAL CENTERS

OF THE WORLD

Fourth Edition

Robert E. Bauman, JD

SOVEREIGN OFFSHORE SERVICES LLC.
(The Sovereign Society)
98 S.E. Federal Highway, Suite 2
Delray Beach, FL 33483
TEL: 561-272-0413
Website: http://www.sovereignsociety.com
Email: info@sovereignsociety.com

WHERE TO STASH YOUR CASH LEGALLY

OFFSHORE FINANCIAL CENTERS OF THE WORLD

Fourth Edition

Robert E. Bauman, JD

About The Author

Robert E. Bauman, JD

Mr. Bauman, legal counsel to The Sovereign Society, served as a member of the U.S. House of Representatives from 1973 to 1981. He is an author and lecturer on many aspects of wealth protection. A member of the District of Columbia Bar, he received his juris doctor degree from the Law Center of Georgetown University in 1964 and a degree in international relations from the Georgetown University School of Foreign Service in 1959. He was honored with GU's Distinguished Alumni Award in 1975. He is the author of *The Gentleman from Maryland* (Hearst Book Publishing, 1985), and the following publications of The Sovereign Society: *The Complete Guide to Offshore Residency, Dual Citizenship & Second Passports* (7th ed. 2009), *Swiss Money Secrets* (2008), *Panama Money Secrets* (2005), *Forbidden Knowledge* (2004), and *The Offshore Money Manual* (2000). He also served for nine years as founding editor of *The Sovereign Society Offshore A-Letter*, an Internet e-letter received daily by more than 200,000 readers worldwide. His writings have appeared in *The Wall Street Journal, The New York Times, National Review* and many other publications.

Author's Comment

For almost two decades, I have been researching and writing about offshore financial matters, including tax havens, asset havens, offshore banking, asset protection trusts, international business corporations, family foundations, limited liability companies and about the state of the offshore financial world.

Even though I had earned a degree in international relations, a law degree, and served eight years as a member of the U.S. House of Representatives, when I began this work I quickly discovered how little I knew about the "offshore" world.

My limited acquaintance with "offshore" had created the erroneous impression that most of us harbor after too many Hollywood movies and TV shows. There, the offshore world was depicted in the sensational shorthand of numbered bank accounts, sinister con men and fraudsters, money launderers, drug kingpins and corrupt foreign politicians taking bribes on tropical islands.

More recently, tax-hungry politicians from high-tax welfare states and their global leftist allies have mounted false attacks on the offshore world. They seek to portray tax havens as sinkholes of tax evasion, drug money, terrorist cash and they have even made the preposterous claim that tax havens caused the global recession.

The truth about "offshore" is far different.

But finding the truth for the first-time offshore adventurer can be a frustrating, discouraging task and, if you get burnt, a very short and unpleasant journey.

The offshore world offers Americans few tax savings, certainly not as many as slick promoters claim. That's because American citizens and resident aliens are taxed on their worldwide income, while most other nations only impose taxes on earnings within their own national territory. But going offshore does offer tax deferral and, most of all, in this lawsuit-happy age, it offers ironclad asset protection and far more financial privacy (and, yes, secrecy) than can now be found in the United States and many other major countries.

That's what this book is all about — legal ways to save on taxes, protect your wealth, invest and grow your money, and find financial privacy — and peace of mind.

I will tell you the who, what, why, when and where of the offshore world — based on my personal experience, and that of the many experts we work with across the globe; the same trusted professionals you'll find listed here for your own use.

Welcome to the offshore world.

ROBERT E. BAUMAN, BSFS, JD
AUGUST 2009

TABLE OF CONTENTS

WHERE TO STASH YOUR CASH LEGALLY

OFFSHORE FINANCIAL CENTERS OF THE WORLD

CHAPTER ONE

A Safe Haven Offshore = Peace of Mind

SUMMARY: The reasons for using an offshore haven; the ways and means of moving your assets and wealth offshore to a tax-free or low-tax jurisdiction; places where you can invest with maximum profitability, minimum taxes and much greater financial privacy.

Like it or not, vast technological changes have created a new world economic structure.

It's a global system that offers huge financial opportunities based on instant communications, interlinked databases, electronic commerce and digital cash flows. And, in many ways, it has shifted power from the monopolistic policies of the high-tax nation state to the beleaguered individual citizen, greatly increasing personal financial freedom and the chance for profit. In turn, this new freedom has caused a reaction by grasping governments everywhere, trying desperately to keep control over their citizens and eager to know what we are doing, especially with our finances.

As part of Big Brother's plans to control its citizens, political leaders in major nations have attempted to use the global recession that started in 2008 as an excuse to attack and curb offshore financial activity. They, along with their allies in the media, have sought to portray tax havens as secretive places where crime and tax evasion is rampant. Even more ridiculous, they blamed offshore financial centers for somehow causing the economic downturn that, in fact, was caused by their own unwise economic policies.

Small wonder many people don't have a clue about what "offshore" actually means, nor are they aware of the major global financial revolution that has taken place. This book goes beyond the clues and reveals the secrets. It tells you the truth about offshore financial activity and tax havens, and how to profit offshore and what you can do to reap the benefits.

By now, most people understand the meaning of the huge advances in computer and software technology and the vast expansion of the Internet. With smart phones, Twittering and Blackberries buzzing, today's economic news travels fast. Insider information is no longer confined to Wall Street and the City of London. Waves of news and rumors ripple daily through world time zones and stock markets as 24/7 television covers events live — an example of the irresistible technological advances that have forced a totally new operational reality on financial and banking systems.

In many respects, all this constitutes a government bureaucrat's worst fear: millions of cell phones and computers linked worldwide, electronic banking and online investment accounts, "smart card" money, easily available email encryption; free communications, all of it mostly unmediated by governments. An astute observer put it this way: "You get untraceable banking and investment, a black hole where money can hide and be laundered, not just for conglomerates or drug cartels, but for anyone."

You can see why government bureaucrats, especially the tax collectors, are frantic. The potential freedom of this new world money system runs counter to all the Big

Brother control-freak, socialist policies that have bled tax-payers and crippled prosperity for most of the last century. That official fear of losing control is what spurs the incessant attacks on offshore financial centers.

As the world now understands, the government is doing all it can to stifle these liberating trends. But I believe they will fail.

WHY GO OFFSHORE?

Until relatively recently, most people thought "personal finance" meant checking and savings accounts, home mortgages and auto loans. Even now, with widely available international offshore mutual and hedge funds — many of them successful even in the face of world economic turmoil — relatively few investors take advantage of global diversification. Here are some of the reasons to go offshore:

1. Investment diversification. Many of the world's best investments and money managers will not do business with U.S. citizens directly. They have made the choice that it is easier to do business with the rest of the world than it is to comply with the draconian rules of the U.S. government. By going offshore, you can gain access to these U.S.-restricted investments. Less than 2,000 foreign securities are traded on U.S. markets, representing a tiny percentage of the securities traded on other world markets. The only practical way to buy these offshore shares is through a foreign bank or broker.

2. Higher returns. There are opportunities in traditional financial markets, such as offshore mutual funds and London-traded investment trusts, which offer much higher returns than are generally available in U.S. markets. For example, the United Kingdom-based Ecofin Water & Power Opportunities Capital Investment Trust, a split-trust, has gained 592% over the last five years in British sterling, or 474% in U.S. dollars.

3. Currency diversification. Investors wishing to stabilize their portfolios can protect their wealth against the falling U.S. dollar by simply holding other currencies (such as the Japanese yen or Swiss franc). While U.S. investors can purchase foreign currencies through a few U.S. banks, offshore banks generally offer higher yields, lower fees and lower minimums. Foreign currency opportunities are plentiful, such as earning nearly 13% on the declining U.S. dollar versus the euro in one recent year. For decades, the U.S. dollar has been losing value in relation to stronger currencies. In 1970, a U.S. dollar would purchase 4.5 Swiss francs. Since 1971, the franc has appreciated nearly 330% against the U.S. dollar.

4. Safety and security. Twenty years ago, the United States experienced a wave of bank and savings and loans failures at a rate unmatched since the Great Depression. In 2008-2009, a government-prompted U.S. housing crisis in subprime mortgages and unregulated derivative investments combined to produce another American banking crisis that again recalled the experience of that same Great Depression of the 1930s. Saving many of the major U.S. banks required trillions of taxpayer dollars in bailouts and, at this writing, the end is not yet in sight.

In contrast, the offshore banks I recommend in these pages were not, and are not, exposed to risky investments, such as subprime mortgages, Third World debt and highly leveraged derivative investments. Indeed, we take pride in the fact that for a decade we have warned against using certain offshore banks, such as UBS of Switzerland. Our recommended banks are well capitalized and conservatively managed — and they do welcome American clients at a time when many offshore banks do not.

5. *Asset protection.* Lawsuits have reached epidemic proportions in America. If a creditor gets a judgment against you in the state where you live, that judgment may be easily enforced. In contrast, if you invest or bank in a suitable jurisdiction — Switzerland, for instance — you can be configured financially to be essentially judgment-proof. The prudent use of offshore havens provides U.S. persons with a greatly enhanced ability to protect assets from the threat of lawsuits, civil forfeiture, business failure, divorce, foreign exchange controls, repressive legislation, lengthy probate and political instability. Going offshore largely avoids the vast U.S. asset-tracking network, which permits private or official investigators to easily identify the unencumbered assets of a potential defendant.

6. *Financial privacy.* Many people want protection from the prying eyes of business partners, estranged family members and identity thieves surfing the Internet. And financial privacy can be the best protection against frivolous lawsuits that end with big judgments — if you don't appear to have enough assets to justify the time and expense of an attack in a plaintiffs attorney's mind, you won't be seen as an easy target. Simply put, assets you place "offshore" are off the domestic asset-tracking "radar screen." The United States is one of the few nations lacking a federal law that protects bank or securities accounts from disclosure except under defined circumstances. Many disclosures that would be illegal in other countries, either under international agreements such as the European Privacy Directive, or under national laws guaranteeing financial secrecy, as in Switzerland or Panama, are commonplace in the United States.

The advantages I described above have especially strong application when it comes to placing assets offshore.

Increasingly, the financially well informed are becoming comfortable with offshore bank accounts that also can be used as investment vehicles. But the use of more complicated offshore techniques, such as the international business corporation (IBC), a foreign-based asset protection trust (APT), a private family foundation or a limited liability company have been ignored for the most part. While these methods take a bit more time and effort, they can greatly enhance your choice of financial strategies and their effectiveness. In these pages, I explain these proven strategies and show you how you can use them.

One more thought: perhaps you might consider relocating your personal residence offshore in a tax haven nation that welcomes foreigners with tax exemptions and special privileges that make life easier and less complicated. I will explain which nations, such as Panama and Belize, offer such inducements and how you can take advantage of them.

Privacy as a Human Right

For citizens of the United States, discussion of the issue of personal and financial privacy must start with the fact that under the draconian terms of the 2001 PATRIOT Act, financial privacy in the United States is dead and gone. The government now has the power to obtain financial information in secret about anyone — and to confiscate your wealth.

Small wonder that many millions of Americans do business offshore to take advantage of strong privacy laws in places such as Switzerland, Panama, Singapore, Austria and Luxembourg.

Of course, the usual cry by those who advocate ever-increased government surveillance of not just our finances, but every aspect of our lives, is the old saw: "If you aren't doing anything wrong, what do you have to hide?"

It is absolutely wrong to characterize this debate as "clean money versus dirty cash" or "security versus privacy" or, now the latest, "banking stability versus global recession."

Privacy is an inherent human right, and a requirement for maintaining the human condition with dignity and respect. The real choices are personal freedom and liberty versus government control of our lives and fortunes.

Tyranny, whether it arises under threat of terrorist attack, alleged solutions to banking problems, or under any form of unrelenting domestic official scrutiny, is still tyranny.

Liberty requires security without intrusion — security plus privacy. Widespread surveillance, whether by police or nosy bureaucrats, in whatever form it takes, is the very definition of a police state.

And that's why we should champion privacy, both personal and financial, even when we have nothing to hide.

Having said that, I must acknowledge that the world now lives in an era when terrorism is a major concern of almost every nation. Official anti-terrorism policies are expressed in a host of national laws that severely curtail financial and personal privacy. These laws were originally premised on fighting drugs and combating money laundering and other crimes. But these laws have all but abolished any personal or financial privacy — at least for those accused or suspected of crimes of any nature. Governments now have much greater powers in deciding who is "suspect" and the list of crimes based on paperwork or failure to report grows ever longer.

But please understand: for the average offshore investor or person otherwise financially active offshore, there is little to fear from anti-crime laws that compromise privacy. So long as you obey the financial reporting laws and tax obligations imposed on you by your home nation, you will remain in the clear. Professional advice will help and protect you in this essential education.

I will repeat in these pages an important reminder — the financial privacy and bank secrecy laws of many other nations are still very much stronger than those in the United States. In America, the PATRIOT Act and other draconian laws essentially have abolished the right to privacy. Privacy laws in other countries can be a definite advantage for you — and an added legal shield for your financial activities.

INVESTMENT PROFITS OFFSHORE

For more than a decade, the trend has been towards foreign investment. In 1980, less than 1% of U.S. pension fund assets were invested abroad. By 2009, that figure had risen to 26%. In addition to pension funds, mutual funds and stock purchasers, banks bought into emerging markets in a very big way, especially European and Japanese banks.

"When history books are written 200 years from now about the last two decades of the 20th century," former U.S. Treasury secretary, Lawrence Summers, now a chief aide to U.S. President Barack Obama, told *The New York Times*, "I am convinced that the end of the Cold War will be the second story. The first story will be about the appearance of emerging markets — about the fact that developing countries where more than three billion people live have moved toward the market and seen rapid growth in incomes."

Of course, that optimistic comment came well before the global recession of 2008-2009 in which emerging market stock values sank along with those in other world markets. Even so, after bruising global downturns in past history, the U.S. economy usually has led the world back to growth, but developing countries could be the engine that powers future recovery. As of this writing, despite fears in early 2009 that they would be among the biggest victims of the financial crisis, emerging market giants like China, India and Brazil were set to rebound strongly in 2010, the Organization for Economic Cooperation and Development predicted, even as Europe, the United States and Japan lagged behind in their recovery.

As historian Professor Niall Ferguson noted: "The globalization of finance played a crucial role in raising growth rates in emerging markets, particularly in Asia, propelling hundreds of millions of people out of poverty."

Cross-border investments have proven profitable, despite temporary setbacks. What used to be tagged "Third World" investment funds have become the more appealing "emerging market funds."

The global economy of today is very different from that of past times. As depressed as it may be, finance and technology still dominate the economic scene. On a typical business day, the total amount of money moving in just the world's foreign exchange markets is over US$6 trillion, and that is a mid-2009 figure. That's more than 20 times the 1986 daily total of $270 billion. The volume of foreign exchange trade has increased by roughly 160 times in the last 30 years.

The fires of the global credit crisis that first appeared as a wisp of smoke in a corner of the U.S. mortgage market turned into a global firestorm that cut through the housing, bond, and stock markets. Between 2007, when the crisis started, and mid-2009, U.S. households alone suffered a $13 trillion drop in the value of their financial and housing assets.

But before the 2007-2009 crash, investment capital exploded worldwide. In 2006, mutual funds, pension funds, and other institutional investors controlled over US$30 trillion, 15 times the comparable 1980 figure.

Boom and Bust

With $9.6 trillion in assets, the U.S. mutual fund industry remained the largest in the world at year-end 2008. Nevertheless, total net assets fell $2.4 trillion from year-end 2007's level, largely reflecting the sharp drop in equity prices experienced worldwide in 2008. Investor demand for mutual funds slowed in 2008 with net new cash flow to all types of mutual funds amounting to $411 billion, less than half the pace seen in 2007.

Once autos, steel and grain dominated world trade, but more recently trade in stocks, bonds and currencies has replaced them. In 2005, for the first time, the value of world merchandise exports exceeded the $10 trillion mark and commercial services exports increased by 11% to $2.4 trillion.

Those rosy numbers did not last. In 2008, total world trade dropped by almost 10%, the largest decrease in any year since World War II.

Regardless of boom or bust, what we must remember is that wealth has become stateless, circulating wherever the owner finds the highest return and the greatest freedom. In other words, cash without a country.

From 1970 to 2009, spending by investors in industrialized nations on offshore stocks increased more than 200 times over while national capital markets merged into one global capital market. As stock markets close in London, they open in New York and as American exchanges end the day on the U.S. west coast, markets in Hong Kong, Singapore and Tokyo come to life.

Unfortunately, this same interconnected global market also helps to spread economic downturns faster than the speed of the swine flu virus. In the global recession of 2008-2009, investors, banks and funds in many countries lost cash and value because of unwise foreign investments in so-called "toxic" unregulated subprime mortgages, stock swaps, derivatives and other esoteric investment vehicles, the value of which is now a major question — and a major problem. In May 2009, Standard & Poor's 500 Index was down 44% compared to October 2007.

AVOIDING ROADBLOCKS TO PROSPERITY

At a time when some politicians are demanding more government regulation, few realize that information about most offshore investments, profitable or otherwise, is denied to U.S. persons who want to invest offshore. Cumbersome rules and regulations imposed by the U.S. government on foreign investment funds drive their fund managers away. Unwilling to waste time and money on bureaucratic registrations, most offshore funds will not even do business with anyone who has a U.S. mailing address.

As Professor Ferguson said: "It is more than a little convenient for America's political class to blame deregulation for this financial crisis and the resulting excesses of the free market. Not only does that neatly pass the buck, but it also creates a justification for . . . more regulation. The old Latin question is highly apposite here: Quis custodiet ipsos custodes? — Who regulates the regulators? Until that question is answered, calls for more regulation are symptoms of the very disease they purport to cure."

This global economic integration continues despite outdated U.S. laws that hinder offshore activity and hobble American investors. One of the main obstacles remains restrictive securities legislation. Any "investment contract" for purchase of a security sold in the United States must be registered with the U.S. Securities & Exchange Commission (SEC) and often with similar state agencies. This is an expensive process. The U.S. also requires far more stock disclosure by sales entities than most foreign countries, burdening the process further with U.S. accounting practices that differ from those used abroad.

International fund managers are practical people who keep their eyes on the bottom line. Many correctly calculate that operating costs in the U.S. would wipe out any possible profit margin. Ironically, many mutual funds and hedge funds with top performance records are run from offices in the U.S. by U.S. residents, but do not accept investments from Americans. To avoid SEC red tape and registration costs, investment in these funds is available only to non-U.S. persons.

Fortunately, there are ways for U.S. citizens to get around these government obstacles. In these pages, I explain how you can access such offshore investments, legally and safely, using offshore entities such as a trust, a limited liability company, international business corporation, or even a private family foundation, located in a haven nation.

EXODUS OFFSHORE GROWS

Much of the revolution in world economies occurs as an escape from leech-like national tax systems that financially prop up dying welfare states. People in ever-greater numbers are seeking to move to countries where hard work is rewarded, not punished by wealth confiscation — places where business is free to make its own decisions, without regulatory predators hovering over every attempt at free enterprise.

The United States offers a good example of this growing emigration trend. *U.S. News & World Report* estimated that each year three million U.S. citizens and resident aliens leave America to make new homes in other nations. Admittedly, this surprising number of three million people leaving must be compared to the millions clamoring to get in from even more restrictive nations.

But there's a huge difference in the economic status of these two groups. Those seeking admission are, by and large, poverty-stricken persons desperately trying to better their lot with new lives in the Promised Land. They'll settle for low paying jobs, welfare, free education for their kids and U.S. government-subsidized housing and health care.

Those seeking to escape the growing tyranny aimed right at them by the United States government are typically wealthy people. One estimate is that the loss of three million people annually equals a loss of 2% of the national workforce and $136 billion in income. And it is this gusher of fleeing people who take with them the lion's share of the U.S. tax base. These are the very people who pay for all of those programs the new immigrants covet.

Increasingly, the problem is that the wealthy perceive, and correctly so, that they are under attack by their own government, so they are taking the only rational option left open to them. They're taking their wealth and leaving.

Look back on multiple government attacks on wealth during the last decade and you will find an outline of U.S. congressional legislation that has all but abolished domestic financial privacy, reversed the burden of proof forcing the accused to prove his own innocence, allowed billions of dollars of property confiscation by police civil forfeiture fiat — all wrapped in the U.S. flag held high in the phony wars against drugs, money laundering and, the latest ruse to gain limitless government power — anti-terrorism. And America now has in President Obama a leader who wants to "spread the wealth around."

But, as they say about human beings, "Old habits die hard." Despite the occasional financial excursion abroad, human nature dictates that most folks prefer to make and save money at home. We tend to be comfortable with the familiar and less threatening domestic economy of our home nation. In 2009, only 74 million (about 26%) of Americans had passports (and another million Americans living near the Mexican and Canadian borders had "passport cards") — yet this was the highest percentage ever.

TAXES DRAIN WEALTH

People who move some or all of their assets offshore simply recognize the present reality — that government at all levels is engaged in the systematic destruction of hard-earned wealth. It's what I call the "Nazification" of the economy. That's certainly true in the United States, the United Kingdom and too many European Union (EU) nations. Sadly, in ever greater numbers, Americans must look to a select list of foreign lands for the kind of economic freedom once guaranteed by the U.S. Constitution — and even these "tax havens" are now under attack by major nation tax collectors.

The tax collectors know that the most talented citizens of the U.S., U.K., EU and other welfare states are deserting, setting up financial shop where they and their capital are treated best. What has been called the "permeability of financial frontiers" now empowers investors instantly to shift vast sums of money from one nation to another and from one currency to another. Tyrannical politicians are eyeing possible curbs on these financial freedoms too.

Lovers of freedom see in these developments the potential for liberation of "the sovereign individual" — the courageous person who declares independence from "decrepit and debilitating welfare states," as *The Wall Street Journal* described them. (For more about this concept, see *The Sovereign Individual* by James Dale Davidson and Lord William Rees-Mogg, [Simon & Shuster, 1997] an excellent book that explains the mass exodus of wealthy people from high-tax nations.)

No wonder the U.K. Revenue and Customs, the U.S. Internal Revenue Service and other tax hounds are worried. In Europe "undeclared" (and untaxed) income is nearly 13% of Europe's combined gross domestic product (GDP), up from 5% in the 1970s. In the somewhat freer U.S., the underground "black market" economy accounts for over 8% of GDP. That means billions of dollars slipping through the eager hands of the taxman.

Why the growing black market? Confiscatory taxes, exorbitant labor costs, over-regulation — all failures of big government. All things bureaucrats love.

DIMINISHED PRIVACY IN THE DIGITAL AGE

In many ways, life in modern America and the U.K. parallels the chilling description of life in the ultimate totalitarian state foretold in George Orwell's famous novel, *1984*. In part, we have ourselves to blame. Although we claim to value freedom and privacy, too many of us willingly surrender personal information piecemeal, until we stand exposed to the world.

Those who conduct their financial affairs with reckless openness make the work of government snoops easy. As you read this, corporate and government computers hum with detailed binary facts about you and your family. Nothing is sacred: health, wealth, tax and marital status, credit history, employment, phone calls, faxes and e-mail, travel, eating and reading habits, even individual preferences when cruising the Internet are recorded.

In an age of digital cash, interconnected databases, electronic commerce and instant worldwide communication, no area of financial activity offers more pitfalls than personal and commercial banking. Once considered discreet and honorable, banks and other financial institutions have been forced to become a U.S. version of Big Brother's Thought Police. This dubious role American banks serving as spies was intensified when the U.S. government gave them billions in bailout funds and took over partial management.

Case in Point

The U.S. government has created secret databases with hundreds of thousands names gathered from unknown sources, supposedly to expose "potential terrorists." This is accomplished with technologies such as "data mining." Included is the "no fly" list that bars selected Americans from travel. This process has stripped Americans and others of their privacy and exposed to them to the stupidity of error-prone bureaucratic analysis.

Sadly, in today's world, you need to conduct your financial affairs with the utmost privacy, caution and discretion. In this book, I will discuss concrete legal and practical steps you can take to guard against being victimized by a government run amok.

Action Summary

To protect your privacy and wealth, consider taking the following steps:

1. Establish an offshore bank account in a tax-free, privacy-oriented, financial-friendly nation. When done correctly, your cash will be secure from almost all U.S.-based claims. But first, carefully investigate any foreign bank you consider using.

2. As part of your overall estate plan, create your own offshore asset protection trust, limited liability company or private family foundation to hold title to specific assets.

3. Precisely document all financial transactions so that you always have ready proof that your activities are legal.

4. Educate yourself about and comply with, all laws, rules and regulations concerning reporting of your financial activities to government agencies.

5. Before you act, consult an experienced professional attorney and/or accountant and find out the U.S. or other tax implications of your plans.

6. Get a firm and reliable estimate of the cost of what you are planning, both at the start, upon implementation and for the first few years of operation.

CHAPTER TWO

Creative Offshore Financial Strategies

SUMMARY: In this chapter, you'll learn specific strategies for offshore living, residency, second citizenship, investing, bank accounts and conducting your business for maximum profit and the greatest tax savings. And I'll tell you about U.S. reporting requirements for offshore financial activity.

Later in these pages, I will explain which jurisdictions and countries qualify as the best tax and asset havens for fulfilling your personal wealth and estate management goals. (I use the phrase "jurisdictions and countries" because some places are independent nations, while others are colonies of the United Kingdom.) After reading this chapter, keep in mind the strategies I describe here as I explain the individual offshore tax and asset havens where they are used.

Before I get to geography and specific places, let's consider several personal, financial and business strategies you can employ offshore, once you choose your own tax or asset haven. These varied strategies can be used individually or in combination, as your situation requires. But each one is fully legal and each has been used by many thousands of people worldwide — with highly satisfactory results.

Later in this book, when I discuss individual jurisdictions that are tax havens and/or asset havens, I'll tell you in which of these havens these strategies are best employed.

One or all of these may be just the financial strategies you are seeking.

STRATEGY 1: A HOME BASE IN A TAX HAVEN

For those who choose to leave home and live in foreign country, places that qualify as tax havens can provide better living and greater profits. While eventually you may consider obtaining citizenship in the land of your choice, the first step is to qualify to become a resident officially approved by the government. (Keep in mind that once you become a citizen of a country, you are no longer an exempt "foreigner" and become subject to taxes and other laws.)

Interestingly enough for those who live in foreign countries for long periods, scientists have found a link between creativity and living abroad. *The Economist* magazine reported on a study by academics at the Kellogg School of Management that showed better problem-solving skills in 60% of students who were either living abroad or had spent some time doing so, whereas only 42% of those who had not lived abroad demonstrated such skills.

A second test found that those who had lived abroad were more creative negotiators. And even when researchers discounted the possibility that creative people were more likely to choose to live abroad, the link between creativity and foreign life held true, "...indicating that it is something from the experience of living in foreign parts that helps foster creativity."

The authors of the report supplied no great detail as to why living abroad should stimulate the creative juices, but their conclusion contains the most likely rationale: it may be that those critical months or years of turning cultural bewilderment into concrete understanding may instill the ability to "think outside the box."

Even though U.S. persons (citizens and permanent residents) are taxed on their worldwide income, there are many attractive places to live where taxes are reduced on business activities, or where business may be totally tax-exempt if conducted offshore. These hospitable places exempt foreigners who live there from taxes because they only levy taxes on income earned within their borders, under what is known as a "territorial" tax system.

Personal income tax rates in many major welfare states are now 50% or higher. This crushing burden of combined social security taxes, capital gains taxes, net worth taxes, wealth taxes and inheritance taxes, has prompted many to seek low or zero tax havens where they can make a new home tax-free.

Many countries provide tax incentives to qualified foreigners who become new residents. Qualifications include a good health condition, a clean record with no past criminal acts, a guaranteed sufficient income and enough assets so that you won't need a job in the local market.

However, it isn't easy to find a haven offering both low taxes and the high quality of life, including a wide range of amenities, excellent medical facilities, easy residence requirements and a warm climate, all within easy reach of major American or European cities.

But a few countries come fairly close to the ideal I described.

For instance, a foreigner living in **Italy** who receives a fixed income from foreign bonds pays only a flat 12.5% tax. Inheritance taxes are at a very low 4% rate. A foreign resident who is employed in Italy pays tax only on income earned within the country. A "tax credit" is granted for taxes deducted outside Italy. Unfortunately, for most other types of income, taxes in Italy are quite high. In 2009, the income tax rate for an individual ranged between 23% and 43%.

The Mediterranean island nation of **Malta** is one of the most attractive locations for foreigners looking for a warm climate, as well as low taxes. Permanent foreign residents enjoy a privileged tax status, with only a 15% tax charged on income remitted from outside to Malta, subject to a minimum tax liability of about US$5,000 per year. To obtain permanent residence, one must show proof of an annual income of about US$24,000 or capital of about US$360,000. Although a residence permit entitles you to live in Malta, you don't actually have to spend any minimum length of time there. This is particularly useful if you are away for long periods.

The **Republic of Panama** offers one of the most attractive locations for tax advantaged residence in the Americas. It has a special pensionado program for foreign retirees providing tax-free living with substantial discounts on the price of many goods and services. Under its territorial tax system residents pay no tax on income earned outside Panama. Under several different immigration programs tailored to attract them, foreigners may acquire residence as a financially independent person/retiree or as an investor. The Central American country of Belize also offers a special program for foreign retirees much like that in Panama, with zero taxes and other incentives.

For people of great wealth, **Austria**, **Switzerland** and **Singapore** are among the nations with special immigration and tax arrangements for foreigners who wish to live or retire there. It's fair to say that there are countries in many parts of the world where individual arrangements can be made for tax-advantaged residence.

If you are looking for a place to do business offshore or to make a new home, the haven that will meet your needs can be found. It's out there waiting for you and I'll help you find it.

STRATEGY 2: DUAL CITIZENSHIP

Let's say you have decided to establish a new residence in an offshore tax haven. Now you may want to consider acquisition of dual citizenship and with it, a second passport. Dual citizenship simply means that a person is officially recognized as a citizen of more than one nation. Under U.S. law, this status is fully legal, and it is legal under the laws of many nations.

A second passport, quite literally, could save your life. In some cases, a government may block its citizens from traveling internationally. If it becomes necessary for you to leave and you have only your home country passport, you're stuck. That's because your passport is the property of your government and the government can seize a passport at anytime.

At the very least, having a second nationality and passport is a hedge against unexpected events. The dual status gives you the option of residing in another country away from home where there may be tax advantages. But as I said, those tax advantages are of limited benefit to U.S. citizens who are taxed on worldwide income, without regard to where they physically reside.

You may be able to acquire a second nationality and passport based on your ancestry, by marriage or because of your religious affiliation. If you don't qualify on these grounds, your principle option for obtaining citizenship is through establishing residence in your chosen country for a required period of time (usually 5 years) or by obtaining citizenship by investment.

Citizenship by investment, also called "economic citizenship" describes the granting of citizenship by a sovereign country in exchange for a financial contribution to that country or for an investment in a business, real estate, or government designated project in that country.

In recent years, the number of economic citizenship programs has dwindled down to only two. The several programs that did exist were criticized for allegedly helping international organized crime and even terrorists. Such sensational charges were largely false, but they led to the termination of citizenship by investment programs in Ireland, Belize, the Cape Verde Islands and Grenada.

St. Christopher & Nevis and the **Commonwealth of Dominica**, both small island nations in the eastern Caribbean (what used to be the British West Indies), are now the only two countries that promote legal citizenship by investment programs. In Austria, it is also possible, under certain conditions, to obtain citizenship without prior residence based on a substantial investment, but this is done on an individual basis and is rarely granted. Each of these programs requires that applicants pass a rigorous screening process.

St. Christopher & Nevis

The St. Kitts & Nevis (the nation's popular name) passport program enjoys an excellent reputation and it offers visa-free travel to British Commonwealth and many other countries.

Under their current citizenship-by-investment rules, to qualify for St. Kitts & Nevis citizenship, an investment of at least US$350,000 in designated real estate, plus additional government and due diligence fees are required. Alternatively, a cash contribution can be made to the Sugar Industry Diversification Foundation in the amount of US$200,000 (for a single applicant). The charitable contribution is an easier route for most applicants, because of the set cost and avoids further expenses associated with owning real estate in a foreign country. In either case, you don't have to live in St. Kitts or Nevis to secure your second citizenship, so buying real estate could just be an additional burden if you're not interested in spending time there.

Under the official contribution options now in effect, there are four categories:

- Single applicant: US$200,000 investment required, inclusive of all fees

- Applicant with up to three dependants (i.e., one spouse and two children under the age of 18): US$250,000

- Applicant with up to five dependants (i.e., one spouse and four children): US$300,000

- Applicant with six and more dependants: US$400,000

In each category, the total amount includes all government and due diligence fees.

The real-estate option requires the purchase of a condominium or villa from an approved list of developers with a minimum investment of US$350,000. Transaction costs add 10% to the purchase price, i.e. at least US$35,000 and likely US$50,000 or more, as real estate prices are now at a relatively high level in St. Kitts & Nevis. Add government fees of US$35,000 for a single person.

At this writing in late 2009, the rumor is that St. Kitts & Nevis may soon double these fees, so if you're interested, move now.

Processing time for charitable contribution applications takes up to three months and dual nationality is permitted with no residency requirement. Using the real estate option lengthens the average processing time from four to 12 months or longer. The real estate cannot be re-sold until five years after purchase.

COMMONWEALTH OF DOMINICA

In the Commonwealth of Dominica, there are two options for obtaining citizenship by investment: a Family Option requiring a US$100,000 payment, plus US$25,000 for each additional child under 25 years old and a Single Option requiring a US$75,000 payment. Application, agent and registration fees total approximately US$17,000. You must also travel to Dominica for an interview. With registration and professional fees of about US$15,000 added to the basic figure, applicants can anticipate a total cost of at least US$107,000 under the single option and US$132,000 for the Family Option before adding additional children under age 25.

REPUBLIC OF AUSTRIA

In Austria, you may qualify for citizenship if you make a substantial investment that creates jobs. There is no "program" as such and few cases are approved. An equity investment of approximately US$1 million is normally required, along with application and legal fees of approximately US$250,000. This rarely granted Austrian passport offers the only possibility to obtain a "first world" passport through investment, and one that offers the additional right to live, work and travel in all 27 countries of the European Union, since Austria is an EU member state.

Since citizenship by investment remains politically controversial within each of these two countries, these programs could be suspended or terminated at any time. If you are interested, now is the time to act. In the event these programs are changed or abolished in the future, those persons who already have acquired passports will be able to retain them.

For more information about the three economic citizenship programs I described you can contact:

- Mark Nestmann, President, The Nestmann Group, Ltd. 2303 N. 44th St. #14-1025, Phoenix, AZ 85008 USA; Tel.: (602) 604-1524 Email: assetpro@nestmann.com; Website: http://www.nestmann.com

- Henley & Partners AG., Mr. Christian Kälin, Executive Director, Kirchgasse 24, 8001 Zurich, Switzerland; Tel.: +(41) 44 266-2222; Email: chris.kalin@henleyglobal.com Website: http://www.henleyglobal.com

Strategy 3: Expatriation — The Ultimate Estate Plan

Expatriation has been called "the ultimate estate plan." It is a legal, step-by-step process that can lead to the legal right for a U.S. person (citizen or resident alien) to stop paying U.S. or other national income taxes — forever.

In sum, it requires professional consultations, careful planning, movement of assets offshore and acquisition of a second nationality. When that's done — and done exactly right — you must leave behind your home country and become a "tax exile" with a new established domicile in a low or no tax jurisdiction. And, for U.S. citizens, this unusual plan requires, as a final step toward tax freedom, the formal relinquishment of citizenship.

Is this a drastic plan? You bet it is.

And in truth, there are many other perfectly suitable offshore strategies that I recommend that can result in some tax savings that don't require anything as dramatic as expatriation. These include international life insurance policies, annuities, and offshore investments made through retirement plans. But for U.S. citizens and long-term U.S. resident aliens ("green card holders") seeking a permanent and legal way to end their obligation to pay U.S. taxes, expatriation is the only option.

Blueprint for Ultimate Tax Avoidance

Individuals have been leaving their own native lands to seek opportunities elsewhere since the dawn of humankind. But it has only been since the development of the modern nation-state and taxation by some nations, such as the United States, on the worldwide income of their citizen-residents, that this process called "expatriation" has taken on significant tax freedom consequences.

One of the first tax advisors to appreciate the potential tax savings of expatriation was my friend and colleague, Marshall Langer JD, a leading international tax attorney.

Langer is the respected author of several major international tax treatises, but also the daring creator of a now out-of-print book, *The Tax Exile Report* (1992). This title gained international notoriety when the late U.S. Senator Daniel Patrick Moynihan (D-NY), red-faced and angry, waved a copy of the book at a televised Senate hearing, denouncing it as "…a legal income tax avoidance plan." (Note that the senator said *"legal"* — and indeed, it is.)

In explaining why expatriation is so attractive to wealthy Americans (and others), a few years ago a Forbes magazine article gave the compelling arithmetic: "A very rich Bahamian citizen pays zero estate taxes; rich Americans — anyone with an estate worth US$3 million or more — could pay 55%. A fairly stiff 37% marginal rate kicks in for Americans leaving as little as US$600,000 to their children." Even though U.S. estate taxes were temporarily reduced since then, an even more impressive part of the Langer plan is the ability to escape American income, capital gains and other taxes.

When it comes to expatriation, however, Americans face a unique burden. Unlike almost every other nation, with one or two exceptions, U.S. citizens and long-term residents cannot escape home country taxes by moving their residence to another nation. The only way to leave U.S. taxes behind is to end their U.S. citizenship or resident alien status.

THE NEW REFUGEES

Becoming a "tax exile" by choosing to expatriate is not without problems. In America, expatriation to avoid taxes has been a hot political issue for the last 20 years.

The original source of the controversy over expatriation was a sensational article in the November 24, 1994 issue of *Forbes* magazine, entitled "The New Refugees." Filled with juicy details (famous names, luxury addresses, big dollar tax savings), the story described how clever ex-Americans who became citizens of certain foreign nations, legally paid little or no U.S. federal and state income, estate and capital gains taxes.

Ever since, expatriation has been a favorite "hot button" issue kicked around by the American news media and "soak-the-rich" politicians. Indeed, President Barack Obama made offshore financial activity by U.S. individuals and companies an issue during his successful 2008 presidential campaign.

It's understandable why politicians keep this political football in play. To the average uninformed U.S. taxpayer, expatriation seems like just another rich man's tax loophole. Before *Forbes* raised the issue, few people had even heard of the concept of formal surrender or loss of U.S. citizenship.

Taken together with the controversy over U.S. companies having offshore affiliates or re-incorporating offshore to avoid U.S. corporate taxes (both legal at this writing), politicians have found in expatriation a convenient straw man that they can beat unmercifully. Former President Bill Clinton's Treasury secretary, Lawrence Summers, now Obama's top White House economic advisor, went so far as to call tax expatriates "traitors" to America. He was forced to apologize for his hyperbole.

THE RIGHT TO END U.S. CITIZENSHIP

As a national political issue, expatriation is hardly new.

In the bitter aftermath of the U.S. Civil War (1860–1865), Congress hotly debated the status of people in the southern states that formed the Confederacy. Ultimately, Congress decided "rebels" who swore allegiance could again become U.S. citizens. The "Expatriation Act of 1868" formally recognized that all Americans do have a right to give up their citizenship, if they so choose.

A century later, in the Foreign Investors Tax Act of 1966, Congress again decided to make an issue of expatriation. In that Act, lawmakers tried to impose onerous taxes on exiting wealthy Americans who relinquished their U.S. citizenship "with the principal purpose of avoiding" U.S. taxes, a highly subjective intention that was virtually impossible to prove. The IRS couldn't prove such "intent" and didn't even try.

The lengths to which American politicians will go to penalize supposed tax expatriates is demonstrated by a never-enforced provision of U.S. law, enacted in 1996, which permits the U.S. Attorney General to bar from returning to the United States anyone who renounces their U.S. citizenship to avoid American taxes. In this manner, Congress lumped individuals exercising their legal right to avoid taxes with narcotics traffickers, those with communicable diseases such as HIV and terrorists.

Amidst the political furor, thoughtful experts criticize what they see as a much broader and dangerous U.S. anti-expatriation precedent. They point out that these laws involve not only retaliatory government acts against resistance to high taxes, but pose possible human rights violations guaranteed by others' laws and even by the Human Rights Charter of the United Nations. It is worth noting that the U.S. Supreme Court has repeatedly affirmed the right of U.S. citizens to end their citizenship, as well as the right to enjoy dual citizenship.

In reality, this political frenzy probably reflects collective envy more than any sense of patriotism by Americans or their congressional representatives. Expatriation is not as serious a problem as some pretend since fewer than 800 Americans, rich or poor, formally give up their citizenship each year. Most expatriates give up their U.S. citizenship because they are returning to their native land or marrying a non-U.S. citizen, not to avoid taxes.

SAVE MILLIONS OF DOLLARS, LEGALLY

Amidst the controversy, until 2008 there were very substantial tax savings for wealthy U.S. citizens who were prepared to end their citizenship. While only a handful of very rich Americans legally expatriated, the list included some prominent names:

In 1962, the late John Templeton, respected international investor, businessperson and philanthropist, surrendered his U.S. citizenship to become a citizen of The Bahamas. This move saved him more than US$100 million when he sold the well-known international investment fund that still bears his name and many millions more in estate taxes when he died in 2008.

Billionaire mutual fund magnate Sir John Templeton (he was knighted by Queen Elizabeth in 1992), made a controversial decision. He decided to renounce his U.S. citizenship after moving his home to The Bahamas, where there is no estate or income tax or investment tax. He became a British and a Bahamian citizen and lived tax-free in The Bahamas until his death in 2008. Interestingly, Templeton's investment record improved markedly after he stopped worrying about the tax consequences of his investment decisions. As a result of tax-free compounding, Templeton was worth several billion dollars and, at death, he was one of the world's wealthiest men. However, Templeton did not necessarily recommend that other investors follow his lead and switch allegiance to a tax haven such as The Bahamas. (It's almost impossible for an American to become a Bahamian citizen today.) But, Templeton strongly recommended that smart investors should take full advantage of tax-deferred vehicles such as a life insurance, annuities, self-directed pension plans and offshore business.

Other wealthy ex-Americans who took their formal leave from America included billionaire Campbell Soup heir John ("Ippy") Dorrance, III (Ireland); Michael Dingman, chairman of Abex and a Ford Motor director (The Bahamas); J. Mark Mobius, one of the leading emerging market investment fund managers (Germany); Kenneth Dart, heir to the billion dollar Dart container fortune (Belize); Ted Arison, head of Carnival Cruise Lines (Israel); and Fred Kreible, millionaire head of Locktite Corporation (Turks & Caicos Islands).

THE LAW TODAY — A U.S. EXIT TAX

While all those former U.S. citizens I just named were

able to escape American taxes, they did so in the past —
but they probably could not do it again today.

That's because on June 17, 2008, President George W.
Bush signed new anti-expatriation legislation, Public Law
No. 110-245, unanimously passed by Congress under the
misleading title of "The Heroes Earnings Assistance and
Relief Tax Act of 2008," also called the "Heroes Act." (I'll
just call it *the Act* from here on.)

The Act dramatically changed the former income tax
regime applicable to both U.S. citizens who expatriate
and long-term U.S. residents (e.g., "green card holders")
who decide to end their U.S. residency (the Act calls both
groups collectively *covered individuals*).

Much of this law has little to do with expatriation
since it provides increased benefits for U.S. armed forces
veterans. But because the rules of Congress require that
all new spending programs be accompanied by a source
of revenue to pay for them, the anti-expat tax crowd in
Congress jumped at the chance to wrap their long-time
tax nostrums in the American flag.

The new expat tax supposedly will finance the millions
needed to pay for veteran's benefits, but few believe that
to be true. A study by the Congressional Budget Office
guessed that the law might net the government up to
$286 million over five years.

This expat "exit tax" — because that indeed is what
it amounts to — had been the devout wish of liberal,
left-wing Democrats for a decade or more. In 2008,
Democrat Rep. Charles Rangle of New York, then chairman of the powerful, tax-writing House Ways and Means
Committee, slipped this horrendous tax restriction into

the popular military pension/pay bill, (without hearings or public notice). President George W. Bush, the great tax cutter, signed it into law without so much as a whimper.

TOTALITARIAN TAXES ON "COVERED INDIVIDUALS"

In advocating an exit tax, the political left has adopted policies very similar to those of Hitler's Nazis, apartheid South Africa and the Communist Soviet Union. Each of these totalitarian regimes in their despotic days fleeced persecuted departing citizens (Jews, gypsies, political dissidents) with similar confiscatory taxes.

In fact, this Act probably violates protections in the U.S. Constitution that guarantee the right to voluntarily end U.S. citizenship and the right to live and travel abroad freely, although I seriously doubt that any wealthy expatriate would ever waste money on a court challenge once they have gone.

Under this law a person who is a "covered individual" falls within the clutches of the Act expatriation provisions if, on the date of expatriation or termination of U.S. residency, (i) the individual's average annual net U.S. income tax liability for the five-year period preceding that date is $145,000 or more (for 2009 adjusted for inflation); (ii) the individual's net worth as of that date is $2 million or more; or (iii) the individual fails to certify under penalties of perjury that he or she has complied with all U.S. federal tax obligations for the preceding five years.

Of course, if you're lucky and don't now fit within the above definitions, this new law may offer a very real opportunity to escape U.S. taxes as you become more prosperous in the future. (More about that, and what might be a very good no-tax deal if you qualify, in a moment.)

EXCEPTIONS

There is an exception in the Act for those who have dual citizenship and became U.S. citizens by accident of birth, either because they happened to be born in the U.S., or born to a U.S. parent and subsequently lived in the U.S. for only a limited time.

Covered individuals under items (i), (ii) or (iii) above, have two limited exceptions that avoid taxes under the Act. They won't be taxed if they certify compliance with all U.S. federal tax obligations and either: (i) were a citizen of the United States and another country at birth if, (a) they are still a citizen and tax resident of that other country and, (b) they resided in the U.S. for no more than 10 of the 15 taxable years prior to expatriation or giving up long-term residence; or (ii) they renounce U.S. citizenship before the age of 18-1/2 if they were not residing in the U.S. for more than 10 years before the renunciation or the termination of long-term residency.

In scanning random examples of the official U.S. State Department expatriate lists I mentioned above, it seems that a high proportion of those listed are probably green card holders, hardly wealthy, who are returning to their country of birth. In other words, most persons who chose formally to end their American status are not very rich tax evaders, but rather folks whose assets and tax bill are well below the amounts the new Act states.

Of course, the official list of expatriates doesn't include

those who simply move to another country and gradually sever their ties with the U.S. Technically, these people are still subject to U.S. taxes, but if they give up their claim to U.S. Social Security or federal pension benefits, it is difficult for the IRS to find them. This Act may well increase that number.

CONFISCATION BY TAXATION

There was a time in the United States when tax rates on the very top earning individuals approached 90% or more. The Reagan tax revolution brought those rates down to more reasonable, upper 30% levels.

But under the Act covered individuals are taxed enormously under new Code Section 877A (the called a "mark-to-market tax"). This vindictive tax taxes all assets as if the person's worldwide assets had been sold for their fair market value on the day before expatriation or residency termination. The Act allows an exemption of $626,000 (for 2009) of the gain as adjusted for inflation in future years.

This phantom gain will presumably be taxed as ordinary income (at rates as high as 35%) or capital gains (at either a 15%, 25%, or 28% rate), as provided under current law. In addition, any assets held by any trust or portion of a trust that the covered individual was treated as owning for U.S. income tax purposes (i.e., a grantor trust) are also subject to the mark-to-market tax.

No doubt many people caught by this tax would have to sell their assets to pay the tax, leaving them with little or nothing.

STILL MORE TAXES

Equally as bad, the stay-at-home relatives of rich expatriate Americans who remain behind as U.S. citizens could find themselves owing tax if they receive large gifts of money or property from their expat relatives.

The Act also imposes an additional new tax of potentially far-reaching scope: gifts and bequests to U.S. persons from covered individuals (beyond the annual gift tax exclusion of $12,000 per person) are subject to a U.S. "transfer tax" imposed on the U.S. transferee at the highest federal transfer tax rates then in effect (currently 45%).

Talk about highway robbery! Not only is wealth taxed away from a generous expatriate who gives a gift, the recipient of the gift is punished with a 45% tax on that gift.

NON-GRANTOR TRUST DISTRIBUTIONS

But as they say on those late night TV commercials, "But wait, there's more!"

The Act requires that trustees of certain "non-grantor" trusts (i.e., trusts of which covered individuals or others are not treated as the owners for income tax purposes) must withhold 30% of each distribution to a covered individual if that distribution would have been included in the gross income of the individual as if he or she were still a U.S. taxpayer.

Defying international law, the Act says no double taxation avoidance treaty of any country with the United States may be invoked to reduce this withholding requirement. Moreover, if the trustee distributes appreciated property to a covered individual, the trust will be treated as if it sold the property to the individual at its fair market value. This treatment of distributions applies to all future distributions with no time limitation.

Retirement Plans Cut in Half

Not content with all this tax persecution, the greedy politicians went after expatriates' pensions as well.

The Act forces an expatriate to pay up to a 51% tax on distributions from retirement plans. The same goes for most other forms of deferred payments. If there's a silver lining, it's that the tax isn't due until you actually receive payments from the plan. Plans covered by this provision include qualified pensions, profit sharing and stock bonus plans, annuity plans, federal pensions, simplified employee pension plans and retirement accounts.

Very Select Group

It is fairly clear that for anyone who falls within the definition of a "covered individual" under the 2008 expat tax law, the chance of legal avoidance of American taxes by ending citizenship is going to be a very costly endeavor. Indeed, under this confiscatory law, the richer you are, the more you stand to lose by leaving the U.S. behind.

But for those who are not "covered" by this punitive law, but who do have good prospects of amassing future wealth, this new law may well offer you a no-tax bonanza — if you are willing to reorder your life, acquire second citizenship, move to an offshore tax haven and turn in your U.S. passport. And in this era of economic globalization and instant international communications, many enterprising entrepreneurs are able to do business anywhere they desire.

Let's say you paid less than $139,000 in taxes for the last five years, your net worth is less than $2 million and you have no problem certifying that you complied with all U.S. federal tax obligations for the preceding five years. This law says you can leave home free!

No doubt there are many ways to rearrange your finances and title your property to avoid values being assigned to your balance sheet, keeping that net worth under $2 million. Indeed financial obligations might reduce your net worth. And once you are gone from the U.S., and have become a new citizen of a tax haven such as Panama, Belize, Uruguay, Singapore or Hong Kong, there is nothing to prevent assets being transferred to you.

In that case, it appears that the new law allows you to end your citizenship and with that, also end your U.S. tax obligations. And the new law also ends the former 10-year claim of IRS tax jurisdiction over you and your income and assets. In fact, as a foreigner, you too can enjoy the tax breaks American tax law affords to non-U.S. investors in America.

Something to think about!

GREEN CARD HOLDERS GET STUCK

The 2008 Act not only affects U.S. citizens who expatriate, but also can financially penalize "green card" holders who return to their home country. If a foreigner living in the U.S. has a green card and has lived in the U.S. for eight out of the most recent 15 years, they are considered a long term permanent resident, or "permanent resident alien" (so count your years here — you may have to leave soon to avoid the tax).

Most of these individuals never intended to make the U.S. their permanent home. Now, if and when they leave, if they have reached the asset/income tax threshold set in the 2008 Act, they too will be taxed as a "covered person." These people are not American tax dodgers but rather well-to-do Canadians, Britons, Indians, and other foreign residents concluding long-term assignments in the U.S.

When these foreign bankers, software engineers, chemists, and others leave the U.S. to retire or transfer to a new post abroad, the Act will tax them on the unrealized capital gains of their total global assets. That includes supposedly tax-deferred U.S. retirement accounts, as well as assets like a cottage in Quebec, a share of a relative's business in Bangalore, or a great-grandmother's pearls kept in a London flat.

Here's one example: consider someone who paid $10,000 for a vacation home in France in 1980, came to the U.S. in 1990 when it was worth $100,000, and left the U.S. in 2008 when it was worth $1 million. That person would be subject to a capital gains tax of $135,000 on that one asset.

Only "permanent residents" also known as "green card holders" will be stung. As a result, wealthy persons considering moving to the United States may increasingly select long-term visas rather than formal residence status, potentially depriving the country of wealthy immigrants. Some developed countries have so-called "exit taxes" but critics say that over time the Act will tarnish the image of the U.S. as a friendly place for foreign talent and capital.

Devastating for Foreign Workers

The U.S. National Association of Manufacturers described the proposal to tax expatriates as "potentially devastating" for American industry's many long-term foreign workers. NAM argued that the rules should target U.S. citizens who expatriate to avoid taxes, not workers who return to their home countries for personal reasons and must, by U.S. law, eventually surrender their green cards. Previously, long-term residents who surrendered their green cards could avoid taxes on their unrealized gains by spending fewer than 30 days of any year in the United States for 10 years. Even then, only U.S., not worldwide, gains were subject to tax.

Experts predict that American companies may respond by sponsoring fewer green cards or filling openings with workers on less attractive long-term visas, drawing a smaller and potentially less talented pool of workers to the U.S.

Green card holders now living abroad may consider immediately giving them up under a provision of the Act that allows retroactive dating for nonresidents. But green card holders now living in the United States have no way out, lawyers say.

Unwelcome Foreigners

One other point: there is still one more vindictive punishment for any "covered individual" who dares to ends U.S. citizenship. Once they are no longer U.S. citizens, they will be "foreigners" in the eyes of American law. Generally, foreigners can apply for any of the many entry visas the U.S. issues. For example, foreign tourists entering the

U.S. for visits usually are granted a 90-day visa that is renewable once for a total of 180 days. If a foreigner stays in the U.S. more than 180 days in one year, they run the risk of becoming a "U.S. person" liable for U.S. taxes.

However under the exit tax law, the IRS says: "...expatriated individuals will be subject to U.S. tax on their worldwide income for any of the 10 years following expatriation in which they are present in the U.S. for more than 30 days, or 60 days in the case of individuals working in the U.S. for an unrelated employer."

The politicians on the Far Left finally got their wish and enacted an exit tax on expatriates — much to the harm of America and its standing in the eyes of the world.

But don't let all this about exit taxes scare you. If you don't to come under the Act for net worth or other reasons, it means you can end your American tax liability by ending your citizenship and permanently detach yourself from the clutches of the IRS. It's something to think about.

How It's Done

Long before you formally surrender your U.S. citizenship, you should have reordered your financial affairs in such a way as to remove from possible government control and taxation most, if not all, of your assets.

Here are recommended steps to take:

- Arrange affairs so that most or all income is derived from non-U.S. sources;

- Title property ownership so that any assets that remain in the United States are exempt from U.S. estate and gift taxes.

- Move abroad and make a new home in a no-tax foreign nation so you are no longer a "resident" for U.S. income taxes;

- Obtain new alternative citizenship and passport;

- Formally surrender U.S. citizenship and change legal "domicile" to avoid U.S. estate taxes.

> Here's the process and time table you might follow: decision to expatriate leading to consultation with expert advisors (1-2 years); leading to liquidation of U.S. assets (1-2 years); leading to selection of appropriate jurisdictions for alternative citizenship and residency (1-2 years); leading to move to selected residency haven, leading to alternative citizenship (0-10 years); leading to surrender of U.S. citizenship.

One of the most important decisions is the choice of your new second nationality.

Millions of Americans already hold a second nationality; millions more qualify almost instantly for dual citizenship by reason of birth, ancestry, or marriage. At this point you may wish to review the information that I described above in "Strategy 2 — Dual Citizenship" at the beginning of this chapter.

Long before an individual relinquishes his or her U.S. citizenship, they should reorganize their financial affairs in such a way as to remove from possible government control and taxation most, if not all, of their assets.

Here are the steps that must be taken:

- Arrange financial and other affairs so that most or all income is derived from non-U.S. sources;

- Title property ownership so that any assets that remain in the United States are exempt from U.S. estate and gift taxes;

- Move abroad and make a new home in a no-tax foreign nation since that ends status as a "resident" for U.S. income taxes;

- Obtain new alternative citizenship and passport;

- Formally surrender U.S. citizenship and change legal "domicile" to avoid U.S. estate taxes.

PART 2 — PERSONAL FINANCIAL STRATEGIES

STRATEGY 1: AN OFFSHORE BANK ACCOUNT

Until relatively recently, only the wealthiest investors could benefit from having an offshore bank account. Only the richest of the rich could afford the fees and legal advice associated with going offshore. Now, after dramatic changes in international banking and communications, even a modest offshore account can be your quick, inexpensive entry into the world of foreign investment opportunities.

Put aside the erroneous popular notion that foreign bank accounts are designed for shady international drug kingpins and unscrupulous wheeler-dealers unwilling to pay taxes. For some people, offshore accounts will always evoke images of cloak and dagger spies from the U.S. Central Intelligence Agency or the U.K.'s MI-5, of shadowy clandestine operations and crooked officials in Third World nations.

Although these sinister images are entertaining, they hardly relate to our present practical purposes: to build offshore financial structures to increase your wealth legally and protect your assets. Forget the intrigue and embrace the fact that an offshore bank account is a highly effective and economic way to achieve your legitimate financial goals. There is nothing underhanded or sinister about protecting the wealth you have worked so hard to earn.

A foreign bank account can be employed as an integral tool in an aggressive, two-pronged offshore wealth strategy. One goal is to increase your asset value by cutting taxes and maximizing profits. The other is to build a strong defensive asset protection structure. As I will show you in these pages, the possible variations on these important themes are nearly endless.

Offshore banking is big business worldwide. Recent estimates calculate that US$3 trillion to US$5 trillion is stashed in nearly 40 offshore banking havens that impose no or low taxes, have less onerous regulations, guarantee privacy and cater to nonresidents. One-third of the entire world's private wealth is stashed in Switzerland alone!

The Benefits of Offshore Banking

Your offshore bank account is not just a place for safe-keeping cash. One of the great advantages of an offshore bank account is the ability to trade freely and invest in foreign-issued stocks, bonds, mutual funds and national currencies that are not available in your home country.

An offshore account is an excellent platform from which to diversify investments and take advantage of global tax savings. You can have instant access to the world's best investment opportunities, including currencies and precious metals, without concern about your home nation's legal restrictions that would otherwise apply if the bank was in your home country.

Offshore foreign stock, bond and mutual fund trading are not covered by laws such as the U.S. Securities and Exchange Act or its administrative arm, the SEC. You can purchase attractive insurance and annuity products not available in the U.S. and other nations. Tax savings may result from deferred investment earnings, capital gains, or appreciation, rather than receiving ordinary income that is not only taxed by the U.S as current income, but at a much higher tax rate.

An offshore bank account can mean opportunities to profit from currency fluctuations, the easy ability to purchase foreign real estate, and earnings from high interest rates available only in foreign countries. You can also trade precious metals and other tangible personal assets through most foreign accounts.

Another important benefit is the relatively strong asset protection foreign bank accounts can provide. The existence of your offshore account is not readily known to a possible claimant seeking to collect a judgment against your assets. The existence of the account must be revealed on your U.S. income tax return (IRS Form 1040), but that's not part of the public record. At times in a judicial proceeding, you may have a legal obligation to reveal an offshore account in a full statement of your assets and liabilities. But there are times when it makes good financial sense to discourage a potential litigant by letting him know just how difficult it will be to reach your offshore assets.

Because of defendant-friendly local laws in asset protection haven nations, foreign judgment holders often have a very difficult time enforcing a judgment obtained in their own country. To reach your assets, a successful creditor must start all over using the foreign judicial process to press a claim against your offshore assets. To do that, they must bear the expense of hiring foreign lawyers and paying for travel and witness transportation.

Besides promoting compromise, the delay in such a strung-out process allows ample time for a defendant to fight the action, or simply move cash or assets to an account in another country. Because of such offshore local laws, courts in these countries only rarely issue orders prohibiting such transfers (called "portability"), especially in civil cases.

Many of these nations have one- or two-year statutes of limitations accruing from the date an initial claim arises. Since a U.S. lawsuit takes years to get through the courts, this means an American court judgment could be void under the foreign nation's one-year cutoff date. In fact, the U.S. process often takes so long that time runs out in nations with five-year statutes of limitations.

Choosing and Opening Your Offshore Bank

Before you choose a bank, you must pick the right haven nation where you believe your banking needs will be met. I'll help you make that decision in these pages.

But first, ask yourself your true purposes for wanting an offshore bank account. Do you want expanded investment opportunities? Increased privacy? Protection from potential claims and creditors? All these worthy objectives can be accomplished offshore. Different strategies offer unique benefits and this book will show what may work best to meet your specific needs.

Your next step is to learn all about your offshore bank of choice and the services it provides. Check its reputation, financial condition and all associated costs.

In many countries, banking fees are rather expensive, far more than Americans are used to paying. Often, the net benefits of an offshore account are diminished by high fees. Run a mathematical model and find out what your net profit (or loss) might be. Few countries tax nonresident bank accounts per se, but some, like Switzerland, do collect withholding taxes on interest earnings.

If you want maximum privacy and strong protection from intrusive government officials, litigation and lawyers, avoid any offshore bank with established branches or subsidiaries located within your home country, especially if you live in the United States, its territories, possessions, or dependencies. American courts have been known to threaten instant shutdown or confiscation of U.S. branches or subsidiaries when their offshore parent bank fails to comply with a court's orders.

Never use your offshore account as a checking account for payment of home country bills. Bank fees for international check payments are extremely costly and worse, this creates recorded links that undermine your financial privacy.

On the other hand, if you're unconcerned about creditors or personal claims and you want ease and speed in setting up and managing an offshore account, head for the U.S. branch office of a foreign bank. You might also pick a major American bank like **Citibank** or **HSBC** with many offices and subsidiaries overseas. This latter course allows you to go offshore without ever leaving home. Just realize that this option offers little asset protection and no real privacy.

A more convenient and very private course of action is to obtain a **Barclays, Visa, MasterCard**, or other international credit card from your offshore bank. While offshore cards are more expensive than their U.S. equivalents, the offshore bank can deduct your monthly charges from your account balance. This means you earn money offshore, incur bills offshore, make deposits into and pay with your offshore account, all outside your home country. As with offshore checks, never use that offshore credit card in your home country. Do that and your financial privacy is reduced.

But under no circumstances should you attempt to hide reportable income that is taxable in your home nation in your offshore bank account. Nor should you use an offshore bank credit card as an unreported piggy bank to conceal income or personal expenses. That sort of illegal activity is tax evasion and it can land you in jail. The IRS has a vigorous continuing campaign against tax cheats who use offshore credit cards to hide income.

Source for Offshore Bank Information

U.S. laws force banks and financial institutions licensed to do business in the U.S. to disclose information about transactions in other branches, even if the branches are in another country. Many nations have similar laws. Failure to disclose can mean the bank and its officers may be held in contempt of court, fined and/or its managers imprisoned. Indeed, U.S. courts have imposed sanctions on the American branch of a foreign bank, even when refusal is based upon a foreign court order or law that forbids production of the requested data.

To find an offshore bank without domestic branches in your country, visit your local library and ask for the Thomson/Polk World Bank Directory (International Edition). This standard reference has a complete listing of banks in over 212 countries, including the U.S., with updated sections issued twice a year. It also analyzes a bank's financial size and strength, tells you how and whom to contact. One of its five volumes is a 300-page reference that includes industry ranking tables for banks with worldwide and U.S. holding companies, credit ratings, international banking holidays, Central Banks, currency exchanges, attorneys experienced in banking law, regulatory agency contact information and trade association contact information.

It also lists funds processing information including ABA routing numbers and Fed telegraph names for U.S. banks, Canadian transit numbers for Canadian banks and country routing or sort codes for international banks. The "Worldwide Correspondents Guide" section contains correspondent information for over 12,500 banks worldwide and includes city locations, phone numbers and routing numbers.

OPENING YOUR ACCOUNT

Except for the geography involved, opening an offshore bank account differs little from starting a domestic, home country account. Just like your local banker, offshore bankers want to see you in person when your relationship begins. For reputable offshore banks, a new account applicant must produce positive identification, a passport and/or birth certificate, a certified balance sheet and business and personal references that are checked carefully. Copies of your residential utility bills may be requested to prove your current place of residence. Most nations now have anti-money laundering statutes similar to the U.S. or U.K., so new customers must appear in person to open accounts.

The "know-your-customer" rules are now normal policy in international banking. Bank officials always want more business, but they don't want it from drug merchants, terrorists or crooked politicians. Only if your financial activity is likely to involve relatively small amounts of money will you be able to open the account by mail. Many offshore banks decline to provide even this small exception.

This one-on-one contact should be reciprocal. When you establish your account, immediately get to know your contact in the bank personally. That person should speak your language, understand your business and be totally reliable. Always have a "back-up" contact at the bank who knows who you are, in case your usual representative becomes unavailable for any reason.

Increasingly, offshore banks are demanding that U.S. and other foreign depositors sign a letter giving the bank permission to release account details to foreign investigators, thereby waiving the depositor's rights under bank secrecy laws. Without such permission, the bank may decline to open an account.

An offshore bank may also ask that an American complete and sign an IRS Form W-9, Request for Taxpayer Identification Number and Certification. This form is used by a U.S. person (including a resident alien) to give their correct Taxpayer Identification Number (TIN) to the person requesting it, and when applicable, to certify the TIN given is correct. The trend among offshore banks is to request the signed W-9, and if refused, the bank will not open a new account or may terminate an existing account. Many offshore banks reluctantly have come to this policy position under great pressure from the U.S. government. There is little that a private individual can do about it, accept to comply.

OUT IN THE OPEN

Here's a tip that may help you avoid unwanted scrutiny while accomplishing your offshore financial goals in relative peace.

Let's be honest: many offshore jurisdictions known for no-tax, privacy and anti-creditor banking laws are also prime suspects for certain unsavory financial activities. When your name appears on a bank account in places like **The Bahamas** or the **Cayman Islands**, it immediately raises red flags for suspicious U.S. government agents. (But then, so does the name of any tax haven.)

If privacy is your paramount goal, you should not use your own name when opening an offshore account. Instead, use the name of a trust, family foundation, limited liability company or corporate substitute under your direct or indirect control. If need be, set up your own trust or foundation in the nation where you chose to locate your offshore banking or in another tax haven nation. Even if you use this route, banks will ask you to certify who the "beneficial owners" of the legal entity really is, even though this may not be a matter of public record.

Still another way to obtain banking privacy is to "get lost in a crowd." Why not establish your offshore account in a major banking nation where privacy is better protected than in the U.S.? A good choice might be the **United Kingdom** or **Switzerland**. Such nations have highly respected private banks. IRS officials are less suspicious of accounts held in these established institutions. But even in these nations, caution is required.

You might choose a country where you have family ties, or one with an active international financial role, such as **Hong Kong, Singapore, Ireland** or **Austria**. In London, Vienna or Dublin, your bank dealings will not be deemed especially noteworthy, since thousands of Americans hold accounts in these places. If you create your own "privacy haven" out in the open, instead of going to a small bank in some exotic, far-flung locale, your money, and your privacy, usually will be much more secure.

Let us make clear that banking secrecy does exist in many reputable haven jurisdictions. Tax havens such as **Panama, Nevis, Belize, Andorra, Singapore** and **Monaco** officially impose banking privacy by law, waiving this protection only in criminal situations and usually only under court order. Unlike the U.S., where bank employees have been turned into surrogate government spies, many offshore nations impose fines and prison sentences on bank employees who violate the privacy of account holders.

But you should put one notion to rest right now —
there is no such thing as a totally "secret" bank account
anywhere in the world. Even in nations with the strongest
bank privacy laws, such as Austria, a bank account holder's true name is on record somewhere in that institution's
files. Even if the account is in a corporate name, or the
name of a trust or other legal entity, there's always a paper
(or computer) trail to be traced, especially if government
agents want to know about alleged criminals and their
finances.

A number of offshore banking jurisdictions now
have tax information exchange treaties (TIEAs) with the
United States and other nations. These agreements allow
the offshore jurisdiction to share tax information with the
U.S. or other governments upon a showing of probable
cause that a tax violation may have occurred in the case of
an account holder who is from the requesting country.

In 2009, a major change in privacy policies of offshore
banks occurred under the threat of "blacklisting" from
major nations. Almost all tax havens accepted the addition of "tax evasion" as a valid basis for foreign tax agency
inquiries concerning their citizens with accounts in an
offshore center. The new standard is that set by the Organization for Economic Cooperation and Development
(OECD), based on Article 26 of the "OECD Model Tax
Convention."

Under this OECD procedure, foreign tax authorities
wishing to take advantage of tax information exchange
agreements need to supply hard evidence of their suspicions (names, facts, alleged tax crimes) to the requested
government. If they have no "smoking gun," they won't
be able to get information. At this writing this new policy

is only in the implementation stage, so if you are interested, you should check latest developments.

Strategy 2: The Offshore Asset Protection Trust (APT)

One of the very best methods for asset protection is an asset protection trust (APT) located in an offshore haven jurisdiction.

A trust is a formal legal arrangement voluntarily created and funded by a person (the *grantor*) that directs another person (the *trustee*) to take legal title and control of the grantor's donated property, to be used and managed for the benefit of one or more other persons the grantor designates (the *beneficiaries*). The beneficiary of a trust receives income or distributions of assets from the trust and has an enforceable equitable title to the benefits, but does not control trust assets or manage trust operation. An offshore asset protection trust may also include another party to trust operation, the *protector*, a person vested with certain powers to monitor the performance of the trustee.

The creation of a trust arrangement is a planned, calculated, intentional act. It can serve a specific purpose or as part of a general estate plan. The trust grantor signs a written *declaration* describing his or her intentions, stating specific details of trust operation, income distribution and the extent and limits of trustee powers.

A well-drafted trust document will reflect the grantor's precise intentions. Drafting a trust declaration as part of an overall estate plan requires expert advice based on a thorough examination of all existing arrangements that affect the grantor's estate. To create a proper estate plan, the status of all other legal documents or devices, such as a will, or jointly owned assets, must be reviewed and coordinated with the trust. Conflicts must be resolved consistent with all applicable trust and tax laws. However, a targeted trust may be drafted only to accomplish limited or even single goals, such as asset protection.

Most offshore asset protection trusts are drafted as *discretionary trusts*, a form that allows greater planning flexibility. This means the trustee is given the power to decide how much will be distributed to beneficiaries and, in some cases, who qualifies as a beneficiary. The trust declaration may vest a trustee with the right to make payments for purposes, at times and in amounts, the trustee decides. A trustee often is given the authority to recognize beneficiaries within named classes of persons ("my children and their heirs"), or the trust may contain a right known as a power of appointment allowing the trustee to choose beneficiaries from a class of eligible persons.

WHAT A TRUST CAN DO

A trust may be created for any purpose that is not illegal or void as against public policy.

A trust can hold title to and invest in real estate, cash, stocks, bonds, negotiable instruments and personal property. Trusts can provide care for minor children or the elderly; or pay medical, educational or other expenses. A trust can provide financial support in an emergency, for retirement, during marriage or divorce, or even carry out premarital agreements.

To the uninformed, the trust process may seem complex and difficult, but, in fact, a trust is one of the most flexible yet efficient legal mechanisms recognized by law. Compared to the alternatives, it can provide superior asset protection and can assure that your bounty will be distributed exactly as you see fit.

THE APT

In recent decades, asset protection using the trust format as a vehicle has gained wide popularity amongst people of wealth who are "in the know."

The foreign asset protection trust (or APT) is a targeted form of trust created by a grantor resident in one nation under the statutes of another nation where the trust operations are based. Because the trust is governed by the laws of the nation in which it is registered or administered, it serves as a shield for the grantor's business and personal assets, deflecting would-be creditors, litigation and potential financial liabilities, perhaps even an ex-spouse bent on revenge.

Here are a few reasons why an offshore APT can be so effective:

- **An Added Layer of Protection:** The courts of asset haven nations often will not recognize automatically the validity of U.S. or other nations' domestic court orders in many cases. A foreign judgment creditor seeking collection must re-litigate the original claim in the local court after hiring local lawyers. He may be required to post a bond and to pay legal expenses for all parties if he loses. The sheer legal complexity and cost of such an international collection effort is likely to stop all but the most determined adversaries.

- **Minimal Needs:** An offshore APT need not be complex. Creation can be little more than the signing of formal documents and opening a trust account managed by your local trustee in a bank in the foreign country of your choice. Respected offshore multi-national and local banks routinely provide experienced trust officers and staff to handle trust matters. Most international banks have U.S. dollar-denominated accounts, often with better interest rates than U.S. financial institutions offer.

- **Greater Protection:** Under the laws of asset haven nations, assets placed in an offshore asset protection trust have far more protection than permitted under domestic U.S. trust law. The law in such countries is specifically drafted to provide an asset protection "safe harbor" that is unavailable in the U.S. and many other nations. With an offshore APT, foreign-held trust assets are not subject to the jurisdiction of your local or home country judicial system.

- **Fast Acting:** The statute of limitations imposed on initiating a foreign creditor's suit varies. In many jurisdictions, the statute begins to run from the date the APT was established. Some haven nations, such as the Cook Islands, have a limit of one year for initiation of claims. As a practical matter, it may take a creditor longer than that just to discover the existence of a foreign APT to which most of your assets have long since been transferred.

- **Better Investments:** An offshore APT is an excellent platform from which to diversify investments and benefit from the global tax savings I describe in these pages. The APT permits taking advantage of the world's best investment opportunities, without concern about your home nation's legal restrictions on foreign investments. As I explained previously, offshore foreign stock, bond and mutual fund trading are not covered by laws such as the U.S. Securities and Exchange Act or its administrative arm, the SEC. An offshore APT can also purchase attractive insurance and annuity products not available in the U.S. and some other nations. Tax savings may result from deferred investment earnings or capital gains, rather than ordinary income that will not only be taxed currently but at a higher rate.

- **Confidentiality:** The APT can provide far greater privacy and confidentiality, minimization of home country inheritance taxes and the avoidance of the probate process in case of death. It provides increased flexibility in conducting affairs in case of personal disability allows easy transfer of asset titles and avoids domestic currency controls in your home nation. An APT is also a good substitute for, or supplement to, costly professional liability insurance or even a prenuptial agreement, offering strong protection for your heirs' inheritance.

- **Estate Planning:** An offshore APT can serve the same traditional estate planning goals achieved by U.S. domestic strategies. These include using bypass trust provisions to minimize estate taxes for a husband and wife, trusts that allow maximum use of gift tax exemptions through planned giving and trusts that provide for maintenance and tax-free income for a surviving spouse.

Asset Transfer

As a practical matter, regardless of the time of APT creation, any assets physically remaining within your home country and its courts' jurisdiction generally are not protected from domestic judgment creditors. Simply placing title to property in the name of a foreign trust is paper-thin protection at best unless the property is actually moved offshore. If tangible assets actually are transferred to the foreign jurisdiction, as when funds, stock shares or tangible property is moved to an offshore trust account or the trustee's safe deposit box, a home country creditor will have great difficulty in reaching them, provided he even discovers the existence of the trust.

As a mandatory precaution, the APT and its trustee should always employ an offshore bank that is not a branch or affiliate of any bank within your home country. This helps insulate the offshore bank officials (and APT accounts) from foreign pressure. It gives greater legitimate protection from home country pressures or just informational snooping, whether government or otherwise.

Even with this enhanced financial privacy, in a given situation there can be great tactical advantage in letting a harassing party know your assets are securely placed well beyond their reach. The cost and difficulty of pursuit may well discourage any action on their part.

Up-Front Costs

Traditionally, the cost of creating a highly complex asset protection trust in a foreign nation has exceeded US$15,000, plus several thousand dollars in annual maintenance fees. Unless the total assets to be shielded justify such costs, a foreign APT may not be practical. A few years ago, *Business Week* estimated that "as a rule of thumb you should have a net worth of around $500,000" or more in order to justify a foreign asset protection trust. The magazine cited expert's fees for establishing and administering such trusts running as high as US$50,000, with some demanding a percentage of the total value of assets to be transferred.

While high cost once may have been the rule, the APT costs have changed for the better. These days, offshore trusts are not just for the very rich. The Sovereign Society has investigated and recommends several domestic U.S. and offshore asset protection trust providers with lower costs. If you would like information about these trusts, visit our website at www.sovereignsociety.com, or send an E-mail to info@sovereignsociety.com. Ask for a copy of *The Offshore Trust Report.*

STRATEGY 3: US$91,400 A YEAR — U.S. TAX-FREE

If you decide personally to follow your cash, assets and investments offshore, there's a very useful provision of U.S. tax law about which you should know.

The so-called "foreign-earned-income exclusion" allows a U.S. citizen who lives and works outside the U.S. to exclude up to US$91,500 (the 2010 amount) of foreign-earned income from taxable gross income. With a working spouse, you both can get $183,000 annually, plus exclusion of some housing allowances if an employer pays those. These housing allowances have been significantly curtailed by a 2006 law change, so check the latest IRS rules if you are interested at http://www.irs.gov.

It is important to note this is not a tax deduction, credit, or deferral. It is an outright exclusion of the earnings from taxable gross income. There are no taxes due at all on this offshore earned amount. To qualify for these benefits you must:

- establish a "tax home" in a foreign country

- pass either the "foreign-residence test," or the "physical-presence test"

- actually have earned income offshore

- live in the U.S. for no more than one month per year, and

- file a U.S. income tax return for each year you live abroad

Your "tax home" is the location of your regular or principal place of business, not where you live. But the definition of "tax home" is broader when determining eligibility for the foreign-earned-income exclusion. Confusion over this point snags many Americans overseas who think they are earning tax-free income. If you work overseas *and maintain a U.S. residence*, your tax home is not outside the U.S. In other words, to qualify for the foreign-earned-income exclusion, *you must establish both your principal place of business and your residence outside the United States.*

There is a complicated test that can also determine if you get this tax exclusion. It involves counting the maximum number of days you are in or out of the country. The more subjective test, known as the "foreign-residence test," is probably easier for most taxpayers to pass. You must establish yourself as a bona fide resident of a foreign country or countries for an uninterrupted period that includes an entire taxable year and you must intend to stay there indefinitely. If you do not pass this test, you are considered a transient or sojourner and will not qualify as a foreign resident.

According to the tax law, your residence is found in your "state of mind." It is where you intend to be domiciled indefinitely. To determine your state of mind, the IRS looks at the degree of your attachment to the country in question. A number of factors, none of them decisive or significantly more important than the others, are examined. The bottom line is that you must establish yourself as a bona fide member of a foreign community.

STRATEGY 4: OFFSHORE VARIABLE ANNUITIES

Even though the U.S., the U.K. and the European Union continue to tighten the tax and financial reporting screws on wealth, there still remain private and profitable, yet strictly legal ways to protect and invest assets. One of these is the offshore variable annuity.

This is one of the easiest, least expensive methods to invest in offshore funds. Moreover, you obtain deferral of taxes until funds are actually withdrawn. Another advantage is that your annuity investments can be transferred from one fund manager to another with no immediate tax consequences. Plus, you achieve significant asset protection. According to *The Wall Street Journal*, "Offshore annuities are becoming an investment vehicle of choice for those who have oodles of money they want to shelter from taxes."

Offshore variable annuity investments typically start around US$250,000, commonly exceeding US$1 million or more. In contrast, the average domestic U.S. annuity buyer's initial investment is only US$25,000 or less. The primary objectives in purchasing insurance offshore are asset protection, greater wealth accumulation and access to international investment opportunities.

Because they are located offshore, away from restrictive U.S. laws, foreign insurance companies can be flexible in negotiating fees. But keep in mind that, unless eliminated by a tax treaty, a one-time 1% federal U.S. excise tax is levied on all life insurance and annuity contracts issued to U.S. persons by foreign insurers.

DEFERRED TAXES

Foreign or domestic, a variable annuity is a contract, usually denominated in U.S. dollars, between you and an insurance company that provides tax deferred savings. It can serve as a savings or retirement vehicle using investment structures similar to mutual funds, sometimes called "sub-accounts."

Here's how it works: you buy a variable annuity contract (policy) for an agreed upon sum, often referred to as a "single premium." These monies are invested by the insurance company in one or more investments that you approve, such as an offshore hedge fund.

The annuity contract requires periodic payments by the insurance company to you representing the increased value of investments on which the annuity is based. The money compounds, tax deferred, until you withdraw part or all of it, at which time it is taxed as regular income. This tax-deferred accumulation can continue until the contract maturity date, usually when you are 85 or older — usually a time when total income is lower. An annuity is not "life insurance," so you need not take a medical examination to determine "insurability."

In most cases when the annuity matures, it either must be surrendered or converted to a life annuity that pays out a specified sum, at least annually, for the rest of your life, or for some other agreed period of time. Because most investors buy variable annuities for their tax deferred savings features, withdrawing funds as needed, most variable annuities never convert to a life annuity.

STRONG ASSET PROTECTION

Variable insurance annuities offer significant asset protection, shielding the cash invested and the annuity income from creditors and other claimants. Practical asset protection exists since: 1) the policies are issued by offshore insurance companies with no affiliates in the United States; and 2) the policy's underlying assets are held entirely outside your home jurisdiction. Any domestic investments are made in the name of the insurance company, not your name.

Statutory asset protection exists in many jurisdictions for annuity contracts as well. In the Isle of Man (a jurisdiction that is home to 192 insurance companies), claims by creditors can only be made through the local courts.

When a variable annuity is issued, the investment assets must be placed in this account and used only to satisfy the variable annuity obligation. If the company has financial problems, these segregated assets cannot be reached by insurance company creditors or creditors of other policyholders. The Cayman Islands, the home of many leading offshore insurance companies, has a similar "segregated accounts" law.

In Switzerland, according to Swiss attorney Urs Schenkero, "A life insurance policy...is protected from the policy owner's creditors if the policy owner has irrevocably designated a third party as beneficiary or if the policy owner has irrevocably or revocably designated his spouse and/or his descendents beneficiaries."

The Swiss Insurance Act prevents a properly structured insurance contract from being included in a Swiss bankruptcy procedure. The law also protects the contract from foreign seizure orders or orders including them as part of foreign estate proceedings. Under Swiss law, if you are unable to pay your debts or file bankruptcy, all rights under the contract are assigned to the beneficiaries. Other offshore jurisdictions with a well-developed insurance sector provide statutory protection against creditor claims for insurance policies.

OFFSHORE VARIABLE ANNUITIES AND TAXES

Section 72 of the U.S. Internal Revenue Code treats both foreign and domestic variable annuities the same. But the IRS rules must be followed by an insurance company in order for accumulations to qualify for tax deferral. Before you buy, always obtain a copy of a reliable legal opinion an insurance company has obtained concerning U.S. tax treatment of annuities issued by that company. Check with your tax advisors if in doubt.

To the extent that the funds you withdraw from a variable annuity represent deferred income, they are taxed at ordinary U.S. income tax rates. A loan against a variable annuity from the issuing insurance company to the owner, or a third party loan secured by a pledge of the annuity, is a taxable distribution. Certain unsecured loans, however, may be tax-free. Also, borrowing against an annuity when it is purchased is not taxable since no deferred income has accumulated.

Thus, you can acquire a US$2 million annuity contract and borrow up to US$1 million of the purchase price, pledging the annuity to secure the loan, with no adverse tax consequences.

Tax deferral is no longer available to U.S. investors who purchase foreign "fixed" annuities. A "fixed" annuity is an annuity contract guaranteeing a fixed income for a specified period of years or for life. A variable annuity's income varies depending on the performance of the underlying investments. Foreign fixed annuity contracts issued before April 7, 1995 retain tax deferral, as do domestic fixed annuities.

STRATEGY 5: OFFSHORE LIFE INSURANCE

Despite all the talk of "tax reform" in the United States, when a death occurs without prior proper planning, the combination of income tax and estate tax can consume 50% or more of a U.S. person's estate.

Such ruinous consequences can be avoided with several planning techniques, but only life insurance provides these four key benefits: 1) tax free build up of cash value, including dividends, interest, capital gains; 2) tax-free borrowing against cash value; 3) tax free receipt of the death benefit; and 4) freedom from estate and generation skipping taxes.

These benefits are available in any life insurance policy designed to comply with U.S. tax laws. However, for larger estates, a U.S. tax compliant life insurance policy issued by a carrier outside the U.S. offers five additional benefits:

1. **Increased asset protection.** No protection for life insurance proceeds exists under federal laws. While many states have enacted laws that provide limited protection for life insurance policies, coverage varies from significant to non existent. In contrast, many offshore jurisdictions provide statutory asset protection for the death benefit and investments held by an insurance policy. And, as a practical matter, it is much more expensive for a creditor to bring a claim before a foreign court than a domestic court.

2. **Access to global investments.** Offshore insurance policies provide tax advantaged access to international asset managers and to offshore funds that are generally not accessible to U.S. investors.

3. **Increased privacy.** Domestic assets, including life insurance policies, can easily be discovered by private investigators with access to any of the hundreds of "asset tracking" services now existing in the U.S. In contrast, assets held offshore are off the domestic "radar screen" and cannot easily be identified in a routine asset search. The confidentiality statutes of some offshore jurisdictions are an additional barrier against frivolous claims and investigations.

4. **Not reportable as a "foreign bank account."** A life insurance policy purchased from a non U.S. carrier is not considered a "foreign bank, securities or other financial account." This means that there is no requirement to report the existence of the income derived from an offshore insurance policy to any U.S. government authority. However, depending on what country you purchase an offshore insurance policy from, it may be necessary to make a one-time excise tax payment to the IRS amounting to 1% of the policy premium.

5. **Currency diversification.** Life insurance policies are free to make investments in non U.S. dollar assets that may gain in the event of future declines in the value of the U.S. dollar.

Needless to say, the IRS is not pleased with a planning technique that simultaneously eliminates federal estate taxes, creates a situation where no U.S. person is subject to tax upon transfer of the assets to the beneficiaries and permits the policyholder to invest in highly lucrative offshore mutual funds without paying tax.

To this end, the IRS announced rules that would limit the tax benefits for investors in hedge funds that are setting up insurance companies in offshore jurisdictions, but that are not in fact operating as life insurance carriers. The IRS also is concerned with foreign insurance carriers that are investing in hedge funds and has promised to more aggressively enforce existing provisions in the U.S. Tax Code that prohibit life insurance investors from managing their own securities portfolio and that require adequate diversification within the policy.

However, these IRS policy changes have been "in the making" for several years. A properly planned and executed offshore insurance policy should not be affected. But, it is essential that you obtain expert tax advice when considering the purchase of an offshore insurance policy.

Life insurance remains one of few remaining opportunities for offshore estate tax planning combined with asset protection and tax deferral. And, without major changes in U.S. federal laws, these advantages will remain for the foreseeable future.

STRATEGY 6: OFFSHORE INVESTING

In spite of the global recession of 2008–2009, some of the most profitable investments to be made still can be found offshore. And throughout these pages I will give you contact information for investment managers and firms that can assist you in your quest for profits.

At this writing, there are approximately 1,500 emerging-market investment funds managing over US$200 billion in equities. Add to that figure the billions denominated in other financial instruments and the total is overwhelming.

In the early months of 2009, notwithstanding the worldwide recession, investment in emerging markets surged and money poured into the funds that invest in them in amounts exceeding $4 billion a week. By mid-2009, investors had put $55 billion of net new money into emerging market stock funds. To put that into perspective, the funds have attracted new money equal to about 2% of their assets each week. In contrast, diversified U.S. stock funds saw outflows equal to about 2.4% of their assets over the same period.

International and "emerging nation" mutual funds offer a simple way for American investors to profit from the growth of foreign companies. Such funds eliminate the inconvenience associated with direct ownership of foreign shares. American investors can also profit from *American Depository Receipts*, or ADRs. These are listed securities traded on U.S. stock exchanges. ADRs represent shares of a foreign stock and are issued by U.S. banks that take possession of the securities. The banks convert dividend payments into dollars and deduct any foreign withholding taxes. ADRs give investors a greater guarantee of safety, as participating foreign companies have to meet certain U.S. Securities and Exchange Commission (SEC) accounting and disclosure standards.

Over the past 20 years, capital markets outside the U.S. have grown rapidly in size and importance. In 1970, non-U.S. stocks accounted for 32% of the world's US$935 billion total market capitalization. By 2009, foreign stocks represented over 65% of the total value of world stock market capitalization of over US$15 trillion.

Until the 2008–2009 recession began, top U.S. stocks performed well over the years; but international stock markets historically have outperformed Wall Street as a whole. The rapid growth of capital markets around the world has also created abundant opportunities for fixed income investors. Worldwide bond market capitalization now exceeds worldwide equity capitalization. Non-U.S. bonds account for more than half of the world's bond market value. Non-American investors have realized the enormous profit potential of cross-border investment.

Avoiding Roadblocks to Prosperity

International economic integration continues despite U.S. laws designed to hinder such activity. As I noted earlier, one of the main obstacles remains restrictive U.S. securities legislation. Any "investment contract" for a security sold in the United States must be registered with the SEC and similar agencies in each of the states. This is a prohibitively expensive process. The U.S. also requires far more disclosure than most foreign countries and burdens the process with different accounting practices.

As I have said, international fund managers are practical people who keep an eye on the bottom line. Many correctly calculate that operating costs in the U.S. would wipe out any profit margin they could achieve. Ironically, several mutual funds and hedge funds with top performance records are run from the U.S. by U.S. residents, but do not accept investments from Americans. To avoid SEC red tape and registration costs, investment in these funds is available only to foreigners.

Fortunately, there are ways for U.S. citizens to get around these obstacles. Although you're a U.S. citizen, you can qualify under the law as an *accredited investor*. As such, you will have a freer hand to buy non-SEC registered foreign stocks and mutual funds directly. An accredited investor is defined by SEC rules as an individual who has a net worth of US$1 million or more, or an annual income of at least US$250,000. In other words, you must have a lot of money.

You can also buy foreign securities through a trust, family foundation or corporation you have created offshore. Properly structured foreign legal entities — and I do mean properly structured — are not considered "U.S. residents, persons or citizens." These entities therefore have the unrestricted right to buy non-SEC registered securities.

SEC "Regulation S" has actually made it easier to make such investments. It clearly defines the exemptions allowed by U.S. securities laws. These exemptions permit investment in non-SEC registered securities through a foreign trust and/or corporation. The most important restriction: the grantor who creates such entities must include income from these sources as personal income on annual tax returns.

Typically, the IRS has a web of rules and regulations that aim to wring maximum revenue from Americans who go offshore. These tax laws are extremely complex, so move cautiously and only with expert professional advice. At every step of the way, find out exactly what the U.S. tax consequences will be before you proceed.

PART 3 — OFFSHORE BUSINESS STRATEGIES

STRATEGY 1: AN INTERNATIONAL BUSINESS CORPORATION (IBC)

One possible vehicle for offshore tax savings is an international business corporation (IBC). An IBC is simply a corporation registered in an offshore tax haven under its laws. Since the IBC does business offshore but not in the nation where it is registered, it is exempt from most local corporate and other taxes. Usually, there is an initial incorporation fee and then an annual maintenance fee.

An IBC can be used outside of the nation of incorporation for a variety of activities including consulting, investing, trading, finance, holding assets, or real estate ownership. In some cases, an IBC may confer a trade advantage or it may also be used as an integral part of a trust structure.

One of the main advantages of an IBC is that it can be used to pay legitimate business expenses and it can also be used to plough back profits to be used for business. So long as these profits are used for business purposes, this avoids most immediate U.S. income tax liabilities. But even undistributed corporate income may be taxable to the IBC owner.

U.S. TAX LIABILITIES

U.S. court decisions strictly interpret obligations of a U.S. person actively involved in an offshore corporation. These cases attribute "constructive ownership" to the involved U.S. person as an individual, or find actual control exists based on a chain of entities linking the U.S. person taxpayer to the offshore corporation. The courts seek to identify the U.S. person with actual corporate control, as compared to stand-in paper nominees with only nominal control.

Decades ago, U.S. taxpayers, corporate or individual, could defer some taxes by establishing an offshore corporation. Back then, the foreign corporation was viewed under U.S. tax laws as a foreign entity and shareholders had to pay U.S. income taxes only on dividends. Now the IRS "looks through" the corporate arrangement and taxes U.S. owners annually on the offshore company's earnings as well. If corporate income is primarily "passive" income, such as income from securities or interest, the IRS imposes penalty charges on the corporate shareholders.

There are some exceptions. First, the "look through" rule only applies to controlled foreign corporations (CFCs) that have passive business activities. Thus, you can defer taxes on income from non-passive activities such as real estate management, international trade, manufacturing, banking, or insurance.

A second set of IRS rules that tax offshore corporate profits are those that apply to what is called "passive foreign investment companies" (PFICs). In order to avoid a PFIC classification and tax penalties, at least 30% of the corporate income must be "active" income from the categories described above, plus management fees charged by the company.

For U.S. persons who control shares in an offshore IBC, there are major limitations on U.S. tax benefits that would otherwise be available to a corporation formed in the United States. That is because the offshore corporation is probably listed on what is known as the IRS "per se" list of foreign corporations, which appears in IRS regulations, section 301.7701-2(b)(8)(i). The listed corporations are barred from numerous U.S. tax benefits.

This means that U.S. persons cannot file an IRS Form 8832 electing to treat the corporation as a "disregarded entity" or a foreign partnership, either of which is given much more favorable tax treatment. Under IRS rules, the per se corporation that engages in passive investments is considered a "controlled foreign corporation," which requires the filing of IRS Form 5471 describing its operations. U.S. persons also must file IRS Form 926 reporting transfers of cash or assets to the corporation. A U.S. person who controls a foreign financial account of any nature that has in it $10,000 or more at any time during a calendar year must report this to the IRS on Form TD F 90-22.1. There are serious fines and penalties for failure to file these IRS returns and criminal charges can also be imposed. As a general rule, U.S. persons can be guilty of the crime of "falsifying a federal income tax return" by failing to report offshore corporate holdings.

Any eventual capital gains an IRS-listed corporation may make are not taxed in the U.S. under the more favorable CGT rate of 15%, but rather as ordinary income for the corporate owners, which can be much higher. There is also the possibility of double taxation if the IBC makes investments in the U.S., in which case there is a 30% U.S. withholding tax on the investment income. Under U.S. tax rules, no annual losses can be taken on corporate investments, which must be deferred by the U.S. owners until the IBC is liquidated. However, compared to these IRS restrictions, there may be offsetting considerations, such as complete exemption from foreign taxes, which may be more important in your financial planning.

Therefore, it is extremely important that U.S. persons obtain an authoritative review of the tax implications before forming an offshore international business corporation for any purpose, including holding title to personal or business real estate. A list of qualified U.S. tax attorneys and accountants can be found in the Appendix.

Certain tax havens, such as Panama, Hong Kong and the British Virgin Islands make it attractive to incorporate. When selecting a place to incorporate, here's what you need to consider:

• legal and political attitudes of the jurisdiction toward commercial activities

- corporate laws that facilitate incorporation and continuing management

- the level and speed of service obtainable

- the cost, both initially and for annual maintenance

All IBC-friendly jurisdictions have at least two requirements: 1) maintaining an agent for the service of process; and 2) payment of an annual franchise fee or tax. One of the best tax haven nations for IBC incorporation that I recommend is Panama.

Strategy 2: Using Tax Treaties for Profit

There is at least one thing worse than paying taxes in your home country: paying taxes in two or more countries on the same income. In this case, "look before you leap" is very good advice. Careless offshore financial arrangements can result in redundant taxes that eat up most or all of the profits you've made.

Bilateral (two-country) tax treaties were developed to avoid these problems. Formally known as "double tax conventions," these agreements usually allow the source country to tax most of the income earned within its borders, while the other country agrees not to tax that income, usually by giving credit for foreign taxes paid against domestic taxes owed. Those are the basic principles, but the variations within each treaty are endless.

Current U.S. tax treaties were negotiated individually over the last half-century and usually remain in effect for set time periods (20 years or more), so re-negotiation is ongoing constantly. Most U.S. treaties are with industrialized countries or nations with major commercial and banking activities. Some European countries, especially the **United Kingdom** and the **Netherlands**, have their own network of tax treaties with an extensive list of nations, including many of their former colonial possessions.

There's little point in discussing the terms of each U.S. tax treaty in detail here, since they change periodically based on renegotiation or official reinterpretation. The information presented here is as current as I can make it. To be certain you are current obtain professional advice on the status and impact of any tax treaty before investing offshore. U.S. treaties are on the web at http://www.irs.gov/publications/p901/index.html.

Tax treaty strategies are less important to someone who simply wants to use an offshore bank and investment account as a personal financial tool. But they can be of tremendous value when doing commercial business overseas in one or more nations. Depending on your business and the way a given tax treaty is structured, taxes can be significantly lowered or avoided completely.

THE TAX TREATY LOOPHOLE

In theory, bilateral tax treaties are supposed to remove or reduce the burden of double taxation. That's the theory, but not always the practical result. These agreements are designed to avoid or at least minimize double taxation. However, they have another, less publicized function: to facilitate information exchange between countries that helps enforcement of domestic tax laws in instances where citizens have offshore financial activity. (More about this privacy issue in Chapter 3.)

After World War II, with the British Empire crumbling, the United States routinely agreed to extend the terms of the existing U.S.-U.K. tax treaty to newly independent nations in the British Commonwealth. As the interdependent global economy began to grow, especially in the 1970s, these new countries and creative international tax planners found tremendous profits to be made under the terms of older, existing treaties. Former British colonies became low- or no-tax havens for certain types of exempted income earned by foreign-resident persons, trusts and corporations. Liberal local tax laws combined with the tax treaties created a bonanza in tax-free transactions. Pick the right country, the right business and you could be "home free" with tax-free profits.

The good news for U.S. taxpayers considering going offshore is that no-tax or low-tax countries have a significant financial interest in keeping these liberal provisions available. In addition, many U.S.-based multinational corporations want these favorable offshore tax provisions continued in order to keep their capital costs in line with those of foreign competitors. At this writing, one of the major tax increase proposals of President Obama would abolish or seriously curtail these offshore tax advantages of U.S. corporations.

Anyone planning an offshore business should seek guidance from an attorney who knows international tax planning and tax treaties. Choosing the right country in which to incorporate your business could mean a dramatically reduced tax bill, so it's well worth checking out.

Strategy 3: Profitable "Stepping Stones"

Creative offshore tax planning often calls for business

operations in more than one country. That way, you can use the most advantageous combination of available tax treaties. International tax practitioners like to call this the "stepping stone" principal. The IRS derisively calls it "treaty shopping." Stepping stone transactions are most useful when passive interest or royalty income is involved, though some other commercial and service business structures can also be profitable.

The stones work like this: a German investor naturally wants to earn the highest interest rates available. His tax advisor suggests investing through a Dutch company, because that nation has an extensive, ready-made tax treaty network with all other developed countries. The German could form his own Dutch corporation, but tax authorities prefer that he use an independent, pre-existing business. In effect, the German will invest money in an existing Dutch company that will invest it elsewhere. The Dutch company will charge fees for its middleman role, payments known as "the spread."

The tax treaty network allows a Dutch company to invest money virtually anywhere it wants. Under treaty terms, the interest it receives is not subject to withholding taxes in the countries where the money is invested. For example, the U.S.-Netherlands treaty provides for no withholding of tax by the U.S. on interest paid from the United States to a Dutch company. The Netherlands company is not required to withhold taxes when that interest, in turn, is paid to the German investor. No taxes all around.

The existing U.S. tax treaty network and the multiple "stepping stone" possibilities it offers to foreign investors, means the United States is a tax haven for the world, but not for its own citizens. Many foreign businesses and investors using U.S. tax treaties as part of careful structuring make money by basing their operations in America and legally paying little or no U.S. taxes.

Not surprisingly, the IRS disapproves of this wholesale treaty shopping. In tax treaty renegotiations, the U.S. insists, not always successfully, on "anti-treaty shopping" provisions. The actual terms vary, but basically the IRS wants to re-write treaties to limit tax benefits to those who are bona fide residents of the other bilateral treaty nation. In our example, that would have ruled out the German investor.

The IRS hates such arrangements. To them it's tax evasion using phony affiliates of businesses operating within the U.S. Fortunately for astute taxpayers, if it's done right, this system is legal and it works. The one key requirement is strict adherence to proper form and no cutting corners.

The moral: there are ways to save taxes offshore, but do it right and be sure you know what you can and cannot do.

I repeat, tax treaties change constantly and with those changes come the end of some formerly available tax saving strategies. Internal domestic tax laws change, too. What's here today is gone tomorrow. But serious international business people must pay as much attention to tax treaty developments as they do to daily weather forecast or stock market reports. It can be that essential.

ONE LAST WORD ABOUT REPORTING

So you've gotten your assets offshore. Now what? Do you have to tell the U.S. government that you have opened an offshore account?

The law says, "Each United States person who has a financial interest in, or signature authority over bank, securities, or other financial accounts in a foreign country which exceeds US$10,000 in aggregate value, must report the relationship each calendar year by filing Treasury Department Form 90-22.1 before June 30 of the succeeding year."

If you're a U.S. citizen or permanent resident alien and hold US$10,000 or more in one or more foreign financial accounts, you must report the existence of these accounts each year on your federal income tax return, IRS Form 1040 (Schedule B). You must also file a separate information return (Form TD F 90-22.56) with the U.S. Treasury. "Willful" non-compliance may result in criminal prosecution.

Instructions for Treasury TD F 90-22.56 read, in part:

"**F. Bank, Financial Account.** The term 'bank account' means a savings, demand, checking, deposit, loan, or any other account maintained with a financial institution or other person engaged in the business of banking. It includes certificates of deposit. The term 'securities account' means an account maintained with a financial institution or other person who buys, sells, holds, or trades stock or other securities for the benefit of another. The term 'other financial account' means any other account maintained with a financial institution or other person who accepts deposits, exchanges or transmits funds, or acts as a broker or dealer for future transactions in any commodity on (or subject to the rules of) a commodity exchange or association."

The US$10,000 account limit includes the total value of cash, CDs and negotiable securities held personally in your name in any offshore bank accounts. It excludes foreign investments held separately from the bank account itself. (If you have any question about these rules, consult with a qualified professional to find out whether or not you need to file these forms.)

Since the US$10,000 reporting ceiling does not apply to separately owned foreign investments, these are logical alternatives to be considered. Under IRS definitions, reportable offshore accounts do not include brokerage accounts or arrangements in which a foreign bank acts as a securities custodian. So, if you find yourself in danger of breaching the US$10,000 ceiling, use the account cash to buy foreign bonds or stocks and take delivery of the title certificate by registered mail at your U.S. address.

Be careful of the hair-splitting distinctions under the IRS foreign account reporting rules. If you physically place your foreign bond or stock certificate in a safe deposit box abroad, that doesn't mean the certificate value counts toward a reportable offshore securities account.

Be aware: the same rule doesn't hold true with most foreign mutual funds. Such funds register evidence of share ownership electronically in the name of the owner's foreign securities account, usually without providing actual certificates of title. Many EU countries have eliminated the issuance of paper stock and bond certificates entirely, evidencing share ownership by an investor only in corporate book entry form. The value of these non-certificate registry shares counts towards the US$10,000 limit for U.S. account reporting purposes.

NEW FORM, NEW DEFINITIONS

Effective January 1, 2009, the U.S. Treasury mandated "the use of a revised form for the reporting of foreign financial accounts." This new FBAR clarifies those who must file and the required details in the report. The revised FBAR now must be filed by any U.S. person who has a financial interest in, or signature authority, or other authority, over one or more financial accounts in a foreign country, if the aggregate value of the accounts exceeds $10,000 at any time during the calendar year. The first revised FBAR to be filed will be on or before June 30, 2010, for the current calendar year January 1 through December 31, 2009. For copies of the FBAR form, see http://www.irs.gov/pub/irs-pdf/f90221.pdf.

FOREIGN CITIZENS NOW INCLUDED

The definition of *"U.S. person"* now includes a citizen or resident of the U.S., or any person located in the U.S. "in and doing business in the U.S." This definition expands coverage to require foreign citizens who are physically present and doing business in the U.S. to file the FBAR. Previously the definition of "U.S. person" included only citizens and residents of the U.S., domestic partnerships, domestic corporations and domestic estates or trusts. Previously, a foreign person physically present in the U.S. for less than 180 days, or not a U.S. resident by treaty definition, was exempt from FBAR requirements. At this writing tax lawyers are seeking more definitive IRS instructions on what constitutes activity by a foreign person that would require filing an FBAR.

TRUST REPORTING

Accounts controlled by a trustee of a trust now must be reported not only by a trust beneficiary with a greater than 50% beneficial interest in the trust, but also by any person who "established" the trust and any "trust protector" that is appointed. A "trust protector" is defined as a person responsible for monitoring the activities of the trustee who has the authority to influence trustee decisions or to replace or recommend the replacement of the trustee.

The definition of *"financial accounts"* is also expanded to include, among others, foreign mutual funds, foreign hedge funds, foreign annuities, debit card accounts and prepaid credit card accounts.

The Qualified Intermediary (QI) Rule

The U.S. Internal Revenue Service has forced foreign banks and financial institutions into the unwelcome role of IRS informants, a.k.a. *"qualified intermediaries"* (QI). In effect, an agency of the U.S. government, the IRS, imposed extraterritorial tax enforcement burdens on foreign banks in this instance. The banks were forced to meet IRS established anti-money laundering and "know your customer" standards in order to get the "QI" stamp of approval.

Since 2001, U.S. persons holding U.S.-based investments purchased through offshore banks had a choice of either having the bank report the holdings to the IRS, or having the bank withhold a 30% tax on all interest and dividends paid. To avoid either, the U.S. investor could avoid buying U.S.-based investments through an offshore bank or financial institution.

In 2009, the U.S. Internal Revenue Service announced its intention to clamp down even further with greater long-distance oversight of foreign banks that provide accounts or sell offshore services to American clients. The IRS goal was to thwart what it claimed to be rampant offshore tax evasion.

IRS rules (IRS Announcement #2008-98) were proposed that toughened up the existing IRS qualified intermediary program that previously had allowed participating foreign banks to maintain accounts on behalf of American clients without disclosing their names to the IRS. Until then the IRS had allowed the banks to promise to identify clients, withhold any taxes due on U.S. securities in their accounts, typically 30%, and send the tax money owed to the IRS.

Under the latest QI rules that will take effect in 2010, foreign banks in the QI program must actively investigate, determine and report to the IRS whether U.S. investors or legal entities they control are the holders of the foreign accounts the bank opens. (U.S. persons already are required by law to report offshore accounts on the annual IRS Form 1040.)

Under these new rules scheduled to take effect in 2010, the QI bank will have a duty to investigate, determine and report to the IRS all accounts of U.S. persons or the legal entities they control to the same extent as that required of domestic U.S. bankers and to alert the IRS to any potential fraud they detect, whether through their own internal controls, complaints from employees or investigations by regulators.

In 2001, when the QI agreements were first imposed offshore banks went along with the scheme because they did not want to be denied access to U.S. financial markets and the U.S. banking system. Close to 100% of the offshore banks signed up. Many American clients at the time chose to have U.S. taxes withheld. Others instructed their bank to not invest in any U.S. securities and some chose self-declaration. No doubt, as in the UBS case, some Americans defied U.S. reporting laws and simply did not report.

No Americans Wanted

In 2008, numerous offshore banks, wary of increasing IRS pressures, began refusing to accept any new American clients. The tougher QI rules only increased this unfortunate anti-American trend. (The Sovereign Society knows and works with many American-friendly offshore banks and can guide you to them.)

The new QI rules take effect in 2010 and require foreign banks to alert the IRS to any potential tax fraud, whether detected through the bank's own internal controls, complaints from employees or investigations by regulators. The IRS will also begin auditing small samples of individual offshore bank accounts in the QI program, without knowing the clients' names, to determine whether American investors actually have control over foreign entities with bank accounts.

More than 7,000 foreign banks participate in the QI program with the aim of helping the IRS keep track of American offshore investors. Under the old rules, foreign banks needed to report to the IRS American only clients' investments in U.S. securities.

According to the IRS, foreign banks in the QI program hold more than $35 billion abroad in accounts for U.S. individual investors, partnerships, trusts, family foundations and corporations, but withheld taxes of only 5% on that amount in 2003. The IRS argues entities receiving the offshore income claimed exemptions under foreign double taxation treaties with the United States, but if U.S. investors controlled those entities, some were not entitled to the tax exemptions.

The clear threat to offshore banks contained in the QI rules is the possibility that an uncooperative foreign bank would be denied access to the entire American banking system, meaning they and their clients could not to do business with the major banking system of the world.

These tightened QI rules were said to be the result of allegations in 2008 that the world's largest private bank, the Swiss UBS, assisted many thousands of their American account holders to evade U.S. taxes.

The IRS claims that since 2001 it has halted the participation in the QI program by about 100 foreign banks that were accused of violating QI rules. But in my observation, far fewer banks were embargoed and those tended to be banks located in backwater places such as Vanuatu and the Solomon Islands where Russian criminal elements had established a financial presence.

It also gives the IRS leverage over foreign nations when demanding the exchange of tax and financial information. While countries such as Switzerland, Liechtenstein and Panama have strict financial privacy laws, until 2009 they were able to escape the worst anti-privacy parts of the QI rules. But as I mention early in discussing Strategy 1 above, in 2009 a major change in privacy policies of offshore banks occurred under the threat of "blacklisting" from major nations. Almost all tax havens accepted the addition of "tax evasion" as a valid basis for foreign tax agency inquiries concerning their citizens with accounts in an offshore financial center. The new standard is that set by the Organization for Economic Cooperation and Development (OECD), based on Article 26 of the "OECD Model Tax Convention."

NON-REPORTABLE FOREIGN INVESTMENTS

These investments appear to be excluded from reporting when they are purchased without opening a "bank, securities, or other financial account" or using such an account to maintain custody of:

1. offshore real estate

2. most insurance policies and

3. directly purchased foreign securities.

However, even a mere book entry in a foreign corporation's records is considered an "other financial account" if the corporation transmits or disburses funds or otherwise functions as a bank on behalf of the securities owner.

REAL ESTATE INVESTMENTS

Direct ownership of real property in a foreign country, including a timeshare arrangement, is not a reportable foreign account as defined in Form TD F 90-22.1. However, real estate holdings are generally a matter of public record in the jurisdiction in which they are located and they cannot be liquidated easily. If you own the real estate through a holding company or trust, that entity may be required to file its own disclosure forms.

If you wish to purchase and hold real estate in a foreign

country without disclosing your ownership, this can be accomplished by placing title in an international business corporation (IBC) located in a nation such as Panama where beneficial ownership does not have to be disclosed. Your IBC does not have to be located in the same nation where the real estate is located.

SAFEKEEPING ARRANGEMENTS

Valuables or documents purchased outside the U.S. and placed *directly* into a non-U.S. safety deposit or private security vault do not appear to constitute a foreign account. To avoid having to personally visit the box each time you wish to add or remove valuables, you can give a local attorney or other trusted intermediary a limited "power of attorney" allowing them to perform this function.

Many foreign banks offer custodial arrangements, maintaining custody of cash, securities or precious metals for the owner. Some argue such an arrangement may be non-reportable because the bank is merely safekeeping the assets. However, such an arrangement usually exists in tandem with an actual bank account and assets may be conveyed between them upon the owner's instructions. This is unquestionably closer to a reportable account relationship than simply renting and using a safety deposit box or private vault.

Safekeeping is available through companies that offer private vaults, many of them non-financial institutions. As such, they are subject to fewer recordkeeping and disclosure requirements and some permit anonymous vault rentals. Most honor power of attorney arrangements.

Materials held in a safety deposit box or private vault are not ordinarily insured against theft or other loss. Supplemental insurance can be purchased, but the existence and location of the assets must be disclosed to the insurer.

FOREIGN INSURANCE CONTRACTS

Foreign insurance policies appear to be exempted from reporting as "foreign accounts." There is no mention of "insurance companies" in Treasury Regulations pertaining to the reporting requirements. An insurance policy is a contract with the insurer taking on specific responsibilities in exchange for a sum of money, not an account relationship. However, U.S. persons purchasing foreign insurance contracts must file IRS Form 720 and pay a 1% excise tax, unless this tax is waived under a tax treaty.

AVOIDING DOUBLE TAXATION

Governments everywhere love taxes. The government in the nation in which your offshore bank account is located has the power to impose its own withholding taxes on your assets and deposits and many of them do just that. For example, in Switzerland a 35% tax is imposed on interest income. In many nations, taxes are withheld by the financial institution where the account is located. That's why it's important to check the potential tax liabilities beforehand, then make certain to locate your account in a "no-tax" jurisdiction.

If you have a bank account in a country that has a "double taxation treaty" with your home country, you may qualify for a credit against your national income tax obligation in the amount of the foreign tax paid. However, claiming that credit means you must disclose the existence of your offshore bank account to the authorities. You may want to skip the foreign tax credit claim, since average credits allowed vary from country to country according to the terms of the treaty in force at the time. In most cases, the tax authorities are unlikely to allow a credit of more than a fraction of the foreign tax withheld.

A word of caution about bilateral tax treaties: these agreements sometimes give home governments access to all kinds of information about the accounts of foreign investors. Normally, the offshore nation governs how much and what kind of information it will disclose to foreign officials. Swiss law, for example, in principle does not recognize non-payment of foreign income taxes as a crime. Accordingly, in the absence of a Swiss court order, most Swiss banks refuse to open their books to foreign tax officials if an account holder is accused only of non-payment of their home country taxes. However, other nations will give out such information, so before you make a final choice, carefully investigate the bank privacy laws of the nation under consideration and its treaties with the U.S. or your home country.

If you are concerned about this privacy aspect of offshore banking, obtain a copy of the U.S. tax treaty with the nation you are considering for placement of your financial business. Treaties are published by the U.S. State Department in the *Treaties in Force* series, which is available in major libraries worldwide. U.S. treaties also are available on the Internet at: http://www.state.gov/s/l/treaties/c15824.htm.

In previous editions of this book, I listed contact information of offshore banks and financial institutions that I judged to be useful. Because of the constantly changing policies of offshore banks and the refusal of some to accept U.S. clients, for information on currently recommended offshore banks, please contact The Sovereign Society at the address given on the front page of this book. Sovereign Society members have special access to offshore banking arranged for them at banks we recommend in many nations, including Switzerland, Liechtenstein, Panama, Singapore, Hong Kong and other offshore financial centers.

One more word of caution: in several places in this chapter when describing the meaning and requirements of IRS reporting rules, I have used the phrase *"appear to be."* That's because IRS requirements change almost daily as the agency issues new rules and new interpretations and as courts rule on tax issues. You should always check with a qualified U.S. tax professional, an attorney or accountant, if you have any questions about IRS rules.

Throughout this book I also use the phrase *"at this writing,"* which means that the statements I make were accurate at the time they were written. With the status of so many issues changing almost daily, you can keep up to date on all offshore matters with information from The Sovereign Society web site at http://www.sovereignsociety. com and by subscribing to our free *Offshore A-Letter* and our several currency and investment newsletters.

CHAPTER THREE

What You Need to Know About Offshore Havens

SUMMARY: Here I explain tax havens and asset havens; their laws, procedures, how to use them and what methods give you maximum benefits. In addition, I predict the future of offshore havens and explain why they are under attack by Big Brother governments and their tax collectors.

A tax haven is a country or other jurisdiction (some are colonial possessions of other nations) that promotes and guarantees no taxes or low taxes for foreigners who choose to live or do business there.

An asset haven is a country or jurisdiction that has adopted special laws and established a judicial system that guarantees strong legal protection for assets placed there, plus a high degree of financial privacy.

The same jurisdiction can be both a tax and asset haven and usually they combine both functions. However, any given haven may qualify in just one or the other of these two categories.

In this chapter, I explain the differences and similarities of havens, how to use them and where they are located. Specific, detailed treatment of our choices of the best haven nations can be found in Chapter 4.

Understanding Tax Havens

It may be surprising to the over-taxed citizens of the world to learn that many nations can finance their governments while imposing only low taxes, almost no taxes, or by offering special tax concessions to foreigners who bring in business and investments.

Seven American states have no state income tax: Alaska, Florida, Nevada, South Dakota, Texas, Washington and Wyoming. Two others, New Hampshire and Tennessee, tax only dividend and interest income. Just as these states offer their citizens a chance to escape from other state's income taxes, foreign tax havens may be the solution for offshore-minded people seeking national tax relief. And you don't have to move your residence to these offshore havens in order to enjoy their benefits — only your cash and/or other assets.

But in spite of what you may have heard, know that for U.S. persons, haven nations offer only minimal tax savings. And always keep this basic tax fact in mind: the U.S. government taxes all worldwide income wherever it is earned by Americans and wherever the U.S. person may live or have residence(s).

This means U.S. citizens and resident aliens (both groups, remember, are known in tax law as "U.S. persons") must, by law, report all of their income and pay U.S. taxes accordingly. Unlike individual U.S. taxpayers, many American-owned businesses profit by establishing themselves as foreign corporations in tax havens, since a foreign company owned by Americans pays only limited U.S. taxes on certain types of investment income. If these corporate profits are kept offshore, reinvested or ploughed back into the business, personal income and some other taxes often can be deferred indefinitely. At this writing in 2009, President Barack Obama has proposed to abolish these offshore tax breaks for American business.

U.S. offshore business ownership is highly complex when it comes to taxes (more about that in Chapter 11). The very best professional tax advice is needed to ensure you are in compliance with the law if you have ownership in an offshore business — and to make sure you are eligible for every tax break for which you may qualify.

Tax obligations differ in various nations according to their laws, so before you go offshore, check the tax status of your intended country with advice from a competent professional you trust, usually one located in the intended country.

UNDERSTANDING ASSET HAVENS

What makes a place an "asset haven?"

Asset havens are countries or jurisdictions with established laws that:

1. offer legal entities that provide asset protection, such as trusts, family foundations, limited liability companies (LLCs) and international business corporations (IBCs);

2. have laws that strongly protect financial and personal privacy; and

3. provide and support a judicial system that consistently favors asset protection.

Most asset havens also are tax havens — meaning they do not impose income, capital gains, estate or other taxes on foreigners who choose to open bank accounts or form LLCs, IBCs or trusts registered in the country.

However, not all asset havens are tax-free for foreigners or their business operations, an important factor to be considered in each and every case.

DIFFERENT HAVENS, DIFFERENT USES

Remember, an established tax haven jurisdiction does not necessarily qualify as an asset haven.

Most nations with favorable tax laws do offer strong asset protection as an added incentive to attract foreign money and investments, but some do not. In these pages, I'll tell you which countries or jurisdictions offer the best deals and how you can use them to your benefit.

Not all tax havens are *nations*. Many are colonies or territorial possessions of other nations (e.g., Bermuda is a partial self-governing overseas territory of the United Kingdom). The Cayman Islands and the British Virgin Islands are in this same status.

Historically, many tax havens have spurred economic development by fashioning themselves into both tax and asset havens. Some of these countries have never imposed an income tax. Others are countries with special tax legislation or incentives favoring certain types of business over other types.

As I explain in detail in Chapter 11, the United States is one of the world's leading tax havens, giving special tax treatment to foreigners (but not Americans) who invest in U.S. real estate and securities and commodities markets. The United Kingdom also gives some tax breaks to foreigners, although in 2008 some residential tax breaks were limited by the Labor government that has piled up huge budget deficits. In fact, the U.S. and U.K. are both leading world tax havens, if one bases that calculation on the total foreign-owned, tax-exempt cash and assets located and managed therein.

Tax Havens Come in Different "Flavors"

A tax haven is any country whose laws, regulations, policies and treaty arrangements make it possible for a foreign national who does business there to reduce personal and/or corporate tax burdens.

This is done by voluntarily bringing yourself — or your trust, foundation, LLC or corporation — within the country's jurisdiction. This general definition covers all four major types of tax haven nations, each categorized by the degree and type of taxes imposed.

It's important to understand these tax haven differences. Not all foreign tax haven countries are created equal. You must fully understand the tax characteristics of each type before you make your plans or decisions.

No-Tax Havens

In "no-tax" havens, foreign citizens who do business there pay no taxes — no income, capital gains or wealth taxes.

A foreign citizen can quickly and easily incorporate and/ or form a trust or LLC and register to do business immediately. You can expect a few minor administrative taxes, like stamp duties on incorporation documents, charges on the value of corporate shares issued, annual registration fees, or other fees not levied directly as a tax on income. In addition, there will be the non-governmental costs of engaging a local agent and the filing of annual reports.

The government in a no-tax haven nation earns considerable revenue from the sheer volume of foreign corporations and trusts that are registered within its borders, even if these entities conduct most or all of their business elsewhere.

No-tax havens — all of which are located in or near the Caribbean basin — include Bermuda, The Bahamas, the Cayman Islands, St. Kitts & Nevis, the Turks & Caicos Islands, Belize and St. Vincent and the Grenadines.

As you will see later in Chapter 9, I have some reservations about all of the above havens because of changes in their offshore laws in recent years, particularly the weakening of financial privacy and bank secrecy laws.

FOREIGN-SOURCE INCOME HAVENS

The second group includes "foreign-source income" tax havens. These countries have a "territorial tax" system. *They tax only income earned within the country's boundaries.* Income earned from foreign sources is tax exempt, since it involves no in-country domestic business activities, apart from simple housekeeping chores. Often there is no income tax on profits from exports of local manufactured goods, although there may be a tax on domestic manufacturing itself.

These countries allow you or your corporation to conduct business both internally and externally, taxing only the income from in-country sources. These nations include Costa Rica, Ecuador, Guatemala, Honduras, Israel, The Philippines, Thailand and Sri Lanka. Since none of these nations qualify as full-fledged tax or asset havens, I won't discuss them further, but I encourage you to research them further if you find them of interest.

Others in this group are full-fledged tax havens. Some only tax domestic business activity and foreign business is tax-exempt. Others impose zero business taxes. These jurisdictions include Panama, the Channel Islands of Jersey and Guernsey, the Isle of Man and the United Arab Emirates.

TAX TREATY NATIONS

The third type of haven is called a "tax treaty nation." While these nations impose taxes on worldwide corporate and trust income, their governments have reciprocal double taxation avoidance agreements with other nations — especially with major trading partners such as the U.S., France, Canada, Germany, and the U.K. These mutual agreements significantly reduce the withholding tax imposed on foreign income earned by domestic corporations and give credit against domestic tax liability for taxes paid by a local business to a foreign government.

Although these nations are less attractive for asset protection, they are suitable for lower taxed international corporate activity. Their main drawback is that international tax treaties permit the free exchange of information between national taxing authorities, allowing less privacy.

Among leading tax treaty nations are Switzerland, Cyprus, The Netherlands, Belgium and Denmark. To review information on the use of tax treaties, see Chapter 2.

Special Use Tax Havens

The final category of havens features several countries that impose the kind of taxes Americans and citizens of the United Kingdom know and dislike — high taxes. However, these high taxes are tempered by a government policy of granting special tax holidays, concessions, or rebates to favored business enterprises they want to attract and promote, usually as a means to increase local employment.

These concessions typically include:

- corporate tax credits for local job creation;

- tax exemptions for manufacturing and processing of exports; and

- tax benefits for international business or holding companies, offshore banks, or other selected industries.

In the U.S., critics call this kind of domestic business tax break "corporate welfare," but many nations (including the United States) offer these kinds of business inducements to foreigners. Among nations that offer generous special tax concessions to foreign-owned businesses are Chile, Portugal and Barbados.

For example, Barbados grants tax exemptions to retired foreigners who settle there. Living conditions are pleasant, with high literacy rates and educational levels. Special laws favor headquarters of international companies and major banks with income tax exemptions. The government also offers generous tax breaks and subsidies for foreign-owned local companies that increase employment. Cyprus offers similar benefits to retirees.

In 2009, Chile was in a good position to bootstrap its own recovery from the global recession. Past policies kept

Chile's government from having to spend a single peso on bank bailouts. Having paid down foreign debt during the fat years when copper prices were high, in 2009, Chile was one of the world's few creditor nations, with a debt rating that was upgraded by Moody's Investors Service.

CONTACTS

Chile — Pro Chile New York, 866 United Nations Plaza, Suite 603, New York, New York 10017; Tel.: 212-207-3266; Fax: 212-207-3649; Website: http://www.chileinfo.com/, Contact web page: http://www.chileinfo.com/contacto.php.

National Chamber of Commerce of Chile, Santa Lucia 302, Piso 4, Santiago, Chile; Tel.: +562-639-6639 / -7694; Fax: +562-638-0234. Website: http://www.caccgp.com/.

Portugal — Official government Website is http://www.portugal.org/ or see http://www.portugal-info.net/.

Portuguese Foreign Trade Institute (ICEP), Avenida 5 de Outubro 101, 1016 Lisboa Codex, Portugal; Tel.: +351-1-793-0103; Fax: +351-1-793-5028.

Barbados — Barbados Government Information Service, Bay Street, St. Michael, Barbados, West Indies; Tel.: +246-426 2232; Fax: +246-436 1317; Website: http://www.bgis.gov.bb/.

TAX-FREE ZONES

Closely akin to special use tax havens are "tax-free zones" established within specified areas of some countries. Often these zones are used as trans-shipment points for finished goods, such as the Colón Free Trade Zone in Panama (http://www.colonfreezone.com/) or the Hong Kong free zone. (For more about Panama and Hong Kong, see Chapters 8 and 9.)

Other tax-free zones, however, are major bases for industry, business and finance, complete with well-developed infrastructure and favorable laws to attract business to the zone. A good example is the Jebel Ali Free Trade Zone in the United Arab Emirates. The Zone's website is at http://www.jafza.ae/en/.

OFFSHORE HAVENS UNDER ATTACK

To understand the position in which offshore havens find themselves today, a review of the last decade of offshore financial and political events is in order. This historic background will help to explain the present state of affairs and how these affect your rights and offshore financial activities.

Beginning in the early 1990s, there was coordinated criticism of tax havens from the governments of major nations and especially from their eager tax collectors, led by the U.S. Internal Revenue Service. The leading welfare states run major budget deficits and need ever-increasing revenues to finance their spendthrift ways. The 2009 global recession was the excuse for leftist politicians in many nations to launch trillion dollar bailouts/stimulus plans. This created an even greater need for tax revenues to finance their socialist plans.

The big-spending political left especially hates legal tax competition among nations, which they insist is "harmful." Indeed, it is harmful — to their big spending and high tax plans. They know tax havens attract to smart investors. These high tax bureaucrats want to curb, if not abolish, tax havens. As part of their anti-tax haven crusade, they demand an end to financial privacy offshore, especially in nations that have strict bank secrecy laws, such as Switzerland and Panama.

Governments of these major high tax, high deficit nations, especially the United States, Germany and France, along with a coterie of allied leftist groups, for the last two decades have aimed their political and economic guns directly at legitimate offshore tax, business and banking haven nations. And if these tax hungry bureaucrats have their way, national sovereignty and independence will suffer.

The main antagonists working against tax haven nations have included the left wing of the Democratic Party in the U.S., certainly including President Barack Obama, the United Kingdom's Labor government, in power since 1995, the European Union, the Organization for Community and Economic Development (OECD) and its Financial Action Task Force (FATF), as well as the United Nations. Each of these big spending, high taxing groups, for their own, and for common reasons, has joined in a coordinated attempt to crush offshore havens which they insist are nothing more than centers for tax evasion.

One leader of the financial services industry on the Channel Island of Jersey offered an opinion in mid-2009 (which I dispute), that the number of offshore financial centers could shrink by half by the year 2015, as the worldwide crackdown on tax havens expands.

He referred to the 38 jurisdictions listed in 2009 as "tax havens" by Organization of for Economic Cooperation and Development (OECD). These included the Channel Islands of Jersey and Guernsey, Bermuda, the Cayman Islands, Switzerland, Liechtenstein, and less well-known and much small jurisdictions such as the Caribbean islands of Aruba and Montserrat and Nauru in the Pacific.

Any reduction may come about because smaller offshore centers will be under increasing pressure to meet tougher regulatory and disclosure rules from international organizations and governments, such as I have described here, all demanding greater transparency.

Beginning in 2009, tax havens were pressured to sign tax information exchange agreements or face possible financial sanctions from major countries. For some unknown reason, the OECD seems to have set the signing of 12 tax information exchange treaties as a measure of whether or not an individual jurisdiction should or should not be blacklisted as failing to adhere to "international standards." This set off a ridiculous scramble among tax havens rushing to sign their allotted 12 TIEAs in order to stay off the feared blacklist.

The next stage of political development in international information sharing on tax matters likely will be demands for "automatic" tax information exchange between jurisdictions, which privacy advocates and tax havens strongly oppose.

Such procedures may be challenging for some smaller offshore centers to implement. At this writing, most offshore centers only disclose information on individual accounts when there is a specific request from another country that has signed a tax information exchange agreement (TIEA) with that tax haven. No doubt, smaller offshore centers will struggle to attract the required talent to defend themselves against regulatory pressures and to administer new rules.

At this writing, it remains to be seen how successful these radical forces arrayed against offshore havens may be. Politics and legislative changes eventually may lead to some added curbs on the use of tax and asset havens by citizens of certain nations, including the United States. In my opinion, in the long run, tax havens and offshore financial centers will continue to play an important part in world finance and the financial activities of many astute people worldwide. They will survive because they efficiently serve important needs in the global financial system.

EUROPEAN UNION DEMANDS

In Brussels, the continental headquarters of the EU bureaucrats, they fly the hypocritical banner of "tax harmonization" (meaning high taxes for all of Europe). These "taxocrats" demanded and, in 2006, got an EU-wide withholding tax on interest income earned outside their home countries by foreigners. They also wanted a mandatory reporting system that informs a nonresident person's home government of income paid to them in other EU nations. They call this "tax information exchange." The EU argument is that member nations lose billions every year because of tax evasion by their nationals who move unreported cash to other EU nations or to offshore havens.

For several years, the EU tried unsuccessfully to force tax information exchange and cross-border taxes on all its nations — and on non-EU member Switzerland as well, the world's leading financial haven. In 2006, the EU finally achieved a partial victory.

They got less than they demanded because, in a weakened deal, Austria, Belgium and Luxembourg were allowed to retain their strict financial privacy, but each of these countries collects a withholding tax on nonresidents' earnings. These three nations then remit 75% of the withheld taxes to the countries of origin of the taxed investors with a tax on earnings of 35%.

Crucially for the EU plan, Switzerland, a non-EU member, and Liechtenstein (both with significant numbers of EU depositors) went along with this deal, but they too agreed only to collect the tax. Standing by their bank and financial secrecy laws, they refused to reveal the names of EU citizens doing business within their borders. (The EU tax directive does not apply to Americans or other non-EU investors that bank or do business within the EU area.)

The so-called "EU savings tax" demands also foundered in the face of official opposition from the United States. The Bush administration formally opposed the EU tax initiative, refusing to cooperate with the EU information exchange demands. Under the Obama administration that may change.

The EU savings tax initiative plan itself has serious flaws, including the fact that neither the United States nor major Asian financial offshore centers, such as Singapore or Hong Kong, had agreed to participate. That meant that EU depositors and investors seeking to avoid the EU withholding taxes could (and did) transfer funds outside the EU, Switzerland, or Liechtenstein, thus escaping both the reporting requirements and the taxes.

This EU tax collecting deal rightly was called "hypocritical" by leading offshore centers, such as the Republic of Panama. It charged that the EU took a lenient stance on tax havens within its own area, while demanding full tax cooperation from non-EU states. Several non-European offshore jurisdictions informed the EU that, given the exemptions provided Austria, Luxembourg and Belgium, they were no longer legally obligated to abide by their previous promise to dismantle "harmful tax practices." In effect they said, "No level playing field, no agreement from us." So, international tax competition continued — to the benefit of the world economy and individuals.

At this writing, the EU is making every effort to expand coverage of the savings tax from only interest income to which it is now limited, to income of any kind paid to EU individuals or to legal entities which they may control.

THE UNITED KINGDOM'S COLONIES

The U.K. Labor government officially announced an anti-tax haven campaign beginning as far back as 1999. This was significant because the British colonies (called by London "overseas territories") and the Crown dependencies of the United Kingdom include jurisdictions that were, and still are, some of the world's leading tax and asset protection havens.

London forced law reforms on the 13 U.K. overseas territories, which include many well-known tax havens, such as the Channel Islands (Jersey, Guernsey), the Isle of Man, the Cayman Islands, Bermuda, the Turks and Caicos Islands, the British Virgin Islands and Anguilla. The U.K. warned that each had to meet new "international standards" against money laundering and adopt "transparency" in their financial systems, including cooperation with U.K. and foreign law enforcement authorities.

The Labor government claimed the power to act unilaterally to change laws within the colonies and threatened it would do so if necessary. London would use the arcane royal "Orders in Council" signed by the Queen, which in effect imposes the government's policies and rules on any overseas territory.

What British Labor really wanted was greatly reduced financial privacy, total bank and investment account surveillance and a general end to the financial freedom that allowed selected U.K. dependencies to prosper as tax and asset protection havens.

The U.K. foreign office bluntly pressured the Crown dependencies of Jersey, Guernsey and the Isle of Man into writing *foreign* tax evasion into their local laws as a criminal offense. Similarly, the U.K. government pushed Bermuda and the Cayman Islands into enacting "all cries" money laundering laws that included criminalizing alleged foreign tax evasion. As London ordered, these jurisdictions weakened their strict financial privacy laws under threat of being cut off from the U.K. financial and banking systems.

In 2009, facing a parliamentary election in 2010, and way behind the Conservatives in the polls, a politically nervous British prime minister, Gordon Brown, began attacking all tax havens, even going so far as to call for "an end to tax havens."

He falsely claimed to have spent a decade, including his time as Chancellor of the Exchequer, trying to reform the U.K.'s tax havens. It was sheer audacity for Brown to take credit for the independent decisions by leading U.K. offshore financial centers to modernize and increase cooperation in response to international requests for information based on alleged tax evasion.

Indeed, during Brown's Treasury tenure, he did advocate more openness and stricter regulation on the U.K. tax havens, but the reform work was done by the individual overseas territories and the three Crown dependencies — and these efforts were so successful that they created far better financial regulatory regimes than those in London or the United States — the true disaster centers where the colossal global financial mess that erupted in 2008 were allowed to fester.

As long as a British Labor government is in power you can expect it will continue efforts to curb tax and asset havens, including those under London's colonial domination. Indeed, financial politics are involved, since curbing the competition of the British offshore tax havens means more financial business for firms in the City of London, many of them big donors to Labor's political campaigns.

THE UNITED STATES

For many years, the U.S. Internal Revenue Service has officially viewed offshore financial activity by Americans as probable tax evasion.

This has been the IRS stance, notwithstanding the fact that such activity is fully legal under U.S. laws — so long as it is reported properly and taxes due are paid. The IRS claims that there are millions of alleged tax evaders and money launderers whom it presumes guilty of these alleged crimes, based mainly on various legal financial tools these accused taxpayers use. High on the IRS' annual "Dirty Dozen" target list are a certain segment of those who create and use offshore corporations, family foundations, trusts and bank accounts located in known tax havens — especially those havens where financial privacy laws are strict. If it's offshore, the IRS presumes guilt.

In October 2001, some U.S. politicians took advantage of the September 11, 2001 ("9/11") terrorist attacks to get their previously rejected anti-offshore proposals enacted into law. Their catch-all anti-terrorist legislation sailed through Congress with little debate just six weeks after the terror attacks. This law, known as the USA PATRIOT Act, all but ends Americans' personal and financial privacy.

USA PATRIOT Act

Congress passed the PATRIOT Act without even knowing what was in it. Less than six weeks after 9/11, the Republican-controlled Congress rammed through a 362-page law, sight unseen, with few members having the courage to oppose one of the worst attacks on American liberties ever enacted into law. In spite of massive opposition to the law, it was extended and broadened in scope in 2006, at President George Bush's urging with majority support from both political parties in the Congress.

The PATRIOT Act gives U.S. government financial police the power to confiscate funds and obtain financial information in secret. It even asserts U.S. police jurisdiction beyond the nation's borders by pressuring foreign banks that do business in America under threat of losing that access. (Refresh your memory about this by reviewing Chapter 2.) A few of these police powers have been tempered slightly in the courts and some others remain under legal challenge.

Since its enactment, numerous abuses of this law have come to light, including extensive unauthorized wiretap surveillance and massive illegal issuance of tens of thousands of improperly authorized "security letters" by the FBI seeking personal and financial information without the approval of a judge. Although as a candidate in 2008, President Obama attacked the PATRIOT Act and its abuses, after he took office, he was silent about the need for reforming the law and endorsed President Bush's surveillance policies.

THE UNITED NATIONS

The United Nations for years has been trying to impose an expansive redefinition of "tax avoidance" on the world at large, fortunately without much success. A UN report argued that the common theme in financial crimes is the "enabling machinery" that exists in haven nations. The UN sees these haven nations as "an enormous hole in the international legal and financial system" that must be plugged tightly.

The UN report blatantly demanded an end to what it calls the "proliferation" of offshore trusts and international business corporations, curbs on attorney-client privilege, the use of free trade zones and the operation of gambling casinos. For good measure, it demanded an enforceable international financial reporting system in which all nations would be forced to participate. The UN has even laid plans for a global tax system, which it wants to operate, with each nation to be forced to pay taxes to the UN.

These UN demands, which have little chance of success, have served as a Greek chorus in the background as other groups described here have led the anti-haven battle.

OECD Blacklists Haven Nations

The Organization for Economic Cooperation and Development (OECD) is a Paris-based research and propaganda group financed by major nations, including the U.S., Canada, the U.K., France and Germany, sometimes called the "G-20." It is what is known as a "non-governmental organization" (NGO) and has no official standing. But it is an influential research and propaganda operation for the G-20's tax and economic policies. That influence has been built over the last 10 years by a large volume of well-written OECD reports, conferences and press conferences, almost of all of this presented from the leftist political viewpoint. As their G-20 sponsors have ordered, much of the OECD output has been aimed at the eventual abolition of offshore tax havens.

The OECD began a propaganda campaign in 1998 with the publication of a report entitled, *Harmful Tax Competition: An Emerging Global Issue*. In it, the OECD, for the first of many times, condemned the tax practices of more than 30 tax haven jurisdictions. The report was a skillful global public relations ploy on behalf of the G-20 high-tax welfare nations trying to stifle the drain of cash fleeing to tax havens. The OECD always defines "harmful tax competition" as any nation that chooses to levy low or no taxes. The goal is to end the tax competition that draws billions in cash from smart people, especially those citizens suffering in the high tax G-20 nations.

A corollary of the OECD "harmful tax competition" theme has been the accusation that billions of dollars in needed revenue are lost to governments because of massive tax evasion by foreigners hiding their cash and assets behind tax haven bank secrecy laws.

The 1998 report suggested ways to combat this so-called "harmful tax competition" including levying a tax on all funds transferred into tax havens and sanctions that would block havens from the global electronic banking system. It demanded that tax collectors in OECD member nations be given access to financial records in haven jurisdictions, thus negating national statutory guarantees of bank secrecy in countries such as Switzerland and Panama.

In 2000, the OECD released its first "blacklist," one of several condemning alleged "harmful tax practices" in 35 nations. But with the 2000 election of President George Bush, the OECD lost the key backing of the United States. During the Clinton years, then U.S. Treasury Secretary Lawrence Summers (now back in the White House as chief economic advisor to President Obama), was one of the strongest advocates of crushing tax havens and imposing high taxes worldwide. One can safely assume his views have not changed.

The OECD asked tax havens for signed commitments pledging to weaken their tax and privacy laws, and as an inducement, explicitly stated the commitments were binding only if all 20 OECD nations agreed to abide by the same tax rules. This was advertized as the "level playing field" guarantee — all nations would agree to do so or none would be bound to end tax competition. This "level playing field" promise soon caused a major problem for the OECD since some of its leading member nations, including the U.S., U.K., Luxembourg, Belgium and Austria, were tax havens then (and remain so to this day).

In 2003, the OECD finally conceded that, by their own definition, many of its own member nations were tax havens; that jurisdictions on the OECD's phony 41 blacklisted havens had no obligation to change their tax laws, unless and until all countries agreed to the same "level playing field" — a highly unlikely event.

From the beginning, all of these OECD anti-tax haven campaigns were a publicity front to benefit tax collectors from the G-20 high-tax nations. With smoke and mirrors it threw around, but never proved, numbers — hundreds of millions of tax evaders, billions of lost taxes. The historic fact that reduced taxes are the best incentive to keep people at home and to expand the economy was ignored. It never occurred to the OECD that tax havens would be unnecessary if governments would cut spending and lower taxes.

American free market leaders, including The Sovereign Society, consistently mobilized in opposition to the OECD's proposed global network of tax police. The goal of that coalition was to convince the Bush administration that tax competition should be encouraged, not condemned. When the U.S. government decided not to support the OECD, it was obvious that the initiative would collapse — and it did.

All that changed in 2008 when majority political control of the executive branch in Washington shifted to an avowed opponent of international tax competition, Barack Obama. As a junior senator from Illinois, Obama was a co-sponsor of the Levin-Obama Anti-Tax Haven Act, first introduced in 2005. A new version of this bill is pending in Congress at this writing with the endorsement of President Obama. A May 2009 White House statement falsely alleged that, "…our tax system is rife with opportunities to evade and avoid taxes through offshore tax havens." The President called for a crack down "on the abuse of tax havens by individuals" and charged that

American jobs were being lost because of tax havens, a truly ridiculous bit of demagoguery.

OECD Finally Triumphs

Over the years, deceitful politicians have used any convenient and plausible sounding excuse in their anti-tax haven crusade to fool the public. A complacent and largely ignorant news media aided and abetted this deceit, repeating false charges and doing very little investigative reporting.

During this time these politicians' anti-tax haven themes have shifted to take advantage of current hot button issues. In the 1990s, the accusation was that offshore financial centers were secretly hiding billions in drug kingpin money gained from illicit drug sales around the world.

When investigations showed that most drug funds were laundered in the U.S. and the U.K., the politicians used anti-terrorism as an issue, charging that terrorist funds were concealed by tax haven banking secrecy laws. Once again, official investigations revealed that the cash that financed the 9/11 attacks in New York and Washington came through normal banking channels in the U.S. and Europe, and not in any tax haven.

Even so, the PATRIOT Act that was adopted by the U.S. Congress only six weeks after the 9-11 attacks contained numerous restrictions on Americans' right to conduct financial matters offshore, based on the false claim of offshore terror funds.

When the 2008-2009 recession descended on the world, the worst in 30 years, these same dishonest politicians were quick to blame tax havens. The recession clearly was the product of greed and idiocy on Wall Street, in the City of London and elsewhere, aided by politicians in many countries. But at an April 2009 meeting of the G-20, the blacklisting OECD finally came into its full glory. Meeting in London, G-20 leaders made tax havens their chosen bête noire.

Impotent to do much about the global recession for which their tax and spending policies were partially to blame, U.S. President Barack Obama, U.K. prime minister Gordon Brown, French president Nicolas Sarkosy and Germany's chancellor Angela Merkel, joined in attacking offshore jurisdictions for imaginary sins — imaginary because tax havens had little or nothing to do with causing a global recession that originated in the G-20 nations themselves. The assembled G-20 hypocrites pledged, "To take action against non-cooperative jurisdictions, including tax havens. We stand ready to deploy sanctions to protect our public finances and financial systems" — as if tax havens actually were a threat!

The G-20 also adopted yet another OECD list (this time the color was gray, not black) naming 34 supposedly "bad" tax havens, the sole criterion for "bad" being their refusal automatically to surrender tax information about foreigners with bank or financial accounts in their countries.

The G-20 list's authors carefully excluded themselves, the United States and the United Kingdom among them, two of the leading tax havens in the world. In the G-20 statement, these hypocrites crowed: "The era of banking secrecy is over."

Tax Havens Conditional Surrender

Oligarchy is a form of government in which all power is vested in a few persons or in a dominant class or clique. It is government by the few over the many.

The 2009 G-20 London meeting established a new, international oligarchy in which a few left-wing politicians and their allied activists, representing major tax collecting countries in the world, imposed their tax policies on smaller nations and jurisdictions.

For the first time, using the global recession as their excuse, the G-20 moved to impose international banking sanctions and controls that had the potential to cripple the economies of any haven nation that refused to submit. Yes, these G-20 threats violated national sovereignty and ran roughshod over the laws in these jurisdictions made little difference — but in global politics might makes right, as the strong always remind us.

To put this in perspective, consider how an American president (and 300+ million Americans) would respond if the United States similarly was threatened with an organized global boycott, blacklisted as a financial pariah, subjected to trade and banking sanctions, and foreigners who dared to do business with America were threatened with higher taxes and punishment. Yet, that is what the President of the United States and the other G-20 countries decreed to be the fate of tax havens.

Faced with these real threats, the OECD's blacklisted havens agreed to abide by Article 26 of the "OECD Model Tax Convention." This article recognizes "tax evasion" as a valid basis for foreign tax agency inquiries concerning their citizens with accounts in an offshore center. Under this OECD procedure, foreign tax authorities wishing to take advantage of tax information exchange agreements need to supply evidence of their suspicions (names, facts, alleged tax crimes) to the requested government. If there is sufficient probable cause to believe tax evasion has occurred, the requested government must supply the information.

These exchanges will be formalized in tax information exchange agreements between nations. These treaties are based on an OECD model treaty that repeatedly has been updated. Each successive model has given tax authorities greater powers to retrieve financial information from the other treaty signatory.

Under OECD Article 26, bank secrecy laws, dual criminality requirements, and domestic tax interest requirements could no longer be invoked to prevent information exchange. These far more expansive tax information sharing provisions have gradually made their way into the international network of tax treaties and could well be incorporated into the many TIEAs under negotiation at this writing.

If a country agrees to implement information exchange arrangements without any express limitations "consistent with OECD standards," the laws that might have prevented your financial information from being disclosed to your domestic tax authorities may no longer offer any privacy protection. If you are concerned, you should obtain the text of any TIEA that applies in the offshore jurisdiction where you have an interest.

Faced with sanctions, in 2009 countries that agreed to this OECD principle included Andorra, The Bahamas, Belize, Bermuda, British Virgin Islands, Cayman Islands,

Gibraltar, Grenada, Liechtenstein, Monaco, Panama, St. Kitts & Nevis, St Vincent & the Grenadines, the Turks & Caicos Islands, Costa Rica, the Philippines and Uruguay, among others.

What This Means for You

For those with existing offshore investments and banking arrangements, and those considering going offshore, until now the trend had favored expansion of traditional financial freedoms.

At this writing, those offshore freedoms remain in place for Americans, although President Obama and his congressional allies have legislative plans to curb offshore financial liberties significantly. Similar plans are pending in the United Kingdom, Germany and other major high tax nations.

The current situation in America and other nations makes it imperative that you keep abreast of offshore developments. You can do that with information from The Sovereign Society.

There are still many attractive legal opportunities for offshore asset protection, business, investing, banking, currency trading, even making a new home offshore. We'll tell you how.

At this writing:

• It is legal to have and use an offshore bank account.

• It is legal to invest offshore in stocks, bonds and other investment properties.

• It is legal to create and donate assets to an offshore asset protection trust or family foundation.

- It is legal to form and operate an international business corporation (IBC).

- It is legal to purchase offshore life insurance and annuities that allow deferred taxes.

- It is legal to invest in offshore mutual and hedge funds, precious metals and real estate.

- It is legal to acquire dual citizenship and a second passport.

- It is legal to voluntarily end U.S. citizenship and thus remove oneself from the U.S. tax system.

The truth is that, with the strangulation of financial and personal freedom in the United States and other nations, now is the time for offshore wealth preservation and prudent asset protection planning. That means the transfer of at least some cash and assets into the hands of offshore asset managers in jurisdictions that have established histories of sound investment and currency management. In these pages we will tell you who and where they are.

CHAPTER FOUR

The World's Best Offshore Havens

This chapter is called "The World's Best Offshore Havens" because here we nominate the four leading offshore financial centers in the world as we judge them. We explain how each of these havens can be best suited to your need. Where appropriate, we provide contacts.

In choosing the top offshore havens, "we" (my colleagues and I at The Sovereign Society) reviewed the laws, political stability, economic climate, tax situation and the overall financial "clout" in dozens of different jurisdictions.

Applying these and other important criteria, we selected four havens as the world leaders — **Switzerland, Panama, Liechtenstein** and **Hong Kong**.

We evaluated five factors for each jurisdiction and rated each on a scale of 1 to 5 after asking the following questions:

1. **Government/political stability:** How long has the current system of government been in place? Is the jurisdiction politically stable?

2. **Favorable laws, judicial system:** How long a tradition has the haven had? Does its legal and judicial system have a reputation for "fair play" with regard to foreign investors?

3. **Available legal entities:** Does the jurisdiction have a large enough variety of legal entities to satisfy the

average person seeking an estate planning or business solution?

4. **Financial privacy/banking secrecy:** Does the jurisdiction have financial privacy laws? How strictly are they applied? Are there exceptions to these privacy laws and, if so, how extensive are they?

5. **Taxes:** Does the haven impose taxes on foreign investors and business? How easily can any taxes be avoided legally? Are there tax treaties or tax information exchange agreements in effect?

SWITZERLAND —
THE WORLD'S BEST MONEY HAVEN

Switzerland is our choice as the best all-around asset and financial haven in the world. For centuries, it has acted as banker to the world and in that role has acquired a reputation for integrity and strict financial privacy. It is also a great place for the wealthy to reside.

Switzerland may be neutral in politics, but it's far from flavorless. The fusion of German, French and Italian influence has formed a robust national culture, and the country's alpine landscapes have enough zing to reinvigorate even the most jaded traveler. Goethe summed up Switzerland succinctly as a combination of "the colossal and the well-ordered." You can be sure that your trains and letters will be on time.

The tidy, just-so precision of Swiss towns is tempered by the lofty splendor of the landscapes that surround them. There's a lot more here than just trillions of dollars (and euros).

Switzerland today still stands as the world's best all-around offshore banking and asset protection haven, despite the many compromises in recent years the Swiss have been forced to make under international pressure, most recently in 2009. (It was then that the Swiss agreed to the exchange of tax information using the OECD standard covered in Chapter 3.)

Factor	Findings	Rating
Government/ political stability	The words 'Swiss' and 'stability' are synonymous	5
Favorable laws, judicial system	Highly protective of personal wealth	5
Available legal entities	All major legal entities may be formed or are recognized under the Swiss legal system	5
Taxes	35% on interest paid, which can be mitigated under bilateral tax treaties; income taxes negotiable for resident foreigners	3.5
Financial privacy/ banking secrecy	One of the world's oldest bank secrecy laws, but with new significant compromises	4
Final Rating		4.5

A REPUTATION TO UPHOLD

A global survey of private banks published by PricewaterhouseCoopers found that the major attraction for a bank's new customers is its reputation. Certainly, Switzerland's solid financial reputation is central to the claim that this Alpine nation serves as "banker to the world." Indeed, at this writing good judgment and reliability are banking traits more sought after than ever before.

For over 250 years, as European empires and nations rose and fell, Swiss topography and determination have combined to defend their mountainous redoubt. All the while, the Swiss people maintained a more or less neutral attitude and policies towards other nations.

In 1945, after the 20th century's second "war to end all wars," Swiss voters overwhelmingly rejected membership in the United Nations. It was not until 2002 that a slim majority backed UN membership. In 1992 and 2001 national polls, Swiss voters also rejected membership in the European Union, rightly fearing EU bureaucratic interference with Swiss privacy and banking laws. A few years ago, a national ballot soundly rejected a specific proposal to ease Swiss bank secrecy laws and more recent polls echoed that position.

After each of these national plebiscites and during world recessions, ever-greater amounts of foreign cash flowed into Swiss banks, confirming the widespread notion that Switzerland is the place to safeguard cash and other personal assets. It is estimated that Swiss banks currently manage at least one-third of all assets held offshore by the world's wealthy. As a safe haven for cash, Switzerland has become something of a modern cliché.

According to the Swiss Bankers Association, with 9.1% of global assets under management (AUM), Switzerland is among the world's leading trio of wealth management centers, alongside the U.S. and the U.K. It is not accidental that the governments of both competitors have been among Switzerland's chief critics, pushing for an end to the Swiss bank secrecy law.

Switzerland is also the world's leader in offshore private banking, with a market share of 27%. Global wealth climbed to US$109.5 trillion in 2007 from US$99.6 trillion in 2006. Private banking assets held offshore account for US$7.3 trillion. The amount of high net worth individuals' assets was US$40.7 trillion in 2007. At the end of 2007, the value of AUM in Switzerland (securities holdings in bank custody accounts) reached CHF 5.4 trillion (US$5 trillion), more than 10 times the Swiss GDP.

At the end of 2008, due to the global recession and the bear market, this figure decreased to CHF 4.1 trillion (US$3.8 trillion). In 2009, Swiss private banks managed assets held by foreign account holders of CHF 2.15 trillion (US$1.988 trillion) according to the Swiss Bankers Association. This was roughly half of the country's private bank asset base of CHF 5.2 trillion (US$4.8 trillion) that, in the past, has helped the Swiss economy to remain strong.

Swiss GDP dropped 2.7% in 2009, the worst contraction since 1975.With the banking and financial services industry accounting for about 12% of GDP, the Swiss economy was more vulnerable to the global credit crisis than some others were. Zurich-based UBS AG, the European bank with the largest losses from the financial turmoil, cut almost 20% of its workforce. However, in 2009, Switzerland's adjusted unemployment rate was about 3.5%, at a time when the U.S. rate was nearly 10%.

LESS PRIVACY REDEFINES THE FINANCIAL SYSTEM

In recent years, the nation's image as bankers to the world's rich has taken some hits. Disturbing to privacy seekers was the major Swiss banks' surrender under pressure to demands of the U.S. Federal Reserve System. The 1998 merger of Swiss Bank Corporation and Union Bank of Switzerland creating UBS AG was approved by the U.S. Federal Reserve, but only after the banking giant agreed to provide U.S. regulators all information "necessary to determine and enforce compliance with [U.S.] federal law."

No doubt, that meant U.S. tax laws, too. U.S. regulators had threatened to shut down the bank's extensive U.S. operations. (At the start of 2008, UBS had about 80,000 employees worldwide, about 30,000 of them in the United States). Rather than defend their U.S. client's privacy rights, the bank compromised. As a result, The Sovereign Society advised U.S. depositors considering Swiss banks to avoid UBS AG and any other Swiss bank with U.S.-based branches, affiliates or banking operations, other than a mere "representative office."

Little did we (or the U.S. government) know that over a period of years after the Fed's 1998 approval, UBS allegedly assisted an unknown number of American clients, perhaps thousands of them, to engage in illegal tax evasion. UBS admitted its private banking managers conspired from 2001 to 2006 to defraud the IRS and the bank paid US$780 million to settle a federal investigation into these activities. At this writing, a suit by the U.S. Department of Justice against UBS seeking the names of an alleged 55,000 Americans that had UBS accounts is pending.

FINANCIAL PRIVACY STILL LIVES

Despite the privacy setbacks, the Swiss financial system — warts and all — still has plenty going for it. Unless there is a strong suspicion of criminal wrongdoing, under Swiss law it is still a crime for bankers to violate the secrecy of their clients. Until 2009, unless ordered to by a court to do so, Swiss banks uniformly refused to give client records to foreign tax authorities. Under the OECD standard accepted in 2009, banks will now do so when ordered to by the government, but under limited conditions and only by applying the terms of tax information exchange treaties that Switzerland has renegotiated with other countries.

In mid-2009, pursuant to its agreement to follow OECD tax information sharing rules, Switzerland and the United States signed a new tax information sharing agreement (TIEA). Swiss officials insisted that individual tax details would only be exchanged with the U.S. "in individual cases where a specific, concrete and justified request has been made." They ruled out "fishing expeditions" by foreign tax collectors.

Having a Swiss bank account has always been a red flag for tax collectors in other countries, especially those in the high-tax EU countries. Plainclothes tax police from neighboring France stalked the streets of Geneva, recording French-registered auto license plates. They then called ahead to have the cars stopped and searched at the French border. France also systematically screens mail to and from Switzerland for magnetically striped checks. German tax collectors apply similar surveillance methods.

Although the constraints of distance force IRS agents to be somewhat less zealous than their French counterparts, U.S. nationals who visit Swiss banks regularly or receive business mail with Swiss postmarks may find themselves subjected to an IRS audit.

EU bureaucrats continually attacked Switzerland on a related tax issue. They claim low corporate tax rates in the Swiss cantons amount to a tax subsidy for the many foreign owned corporations that take advantage of this situation. One Swiss official got to the core of the issue by explaining that low tax rates are not a subsidy and Switzerland would not raises corporate taxes to satisfy the tax hungry EU.

But for the usual anti-privacy, anti-tax haven crowd who habitually bash any offshore financial activity, Switzerland has always been a special target. They hate the Swiss Bank Secrecy Law because they believe that the privacy rights of the individual must be subordinated to government and that all offshore accounts are used for tax evasion.

Beginning in 2005, the EU began an anti-Swiss campaign demanding that banking secrecy, written into Swiss law in 1934, be abolished. The French and German governments even went so far as to call for a financial boycott of Switzerland unless they surrendered on bank secrecy. The Swiss said "no" and they meant it. When they finally agreed to collect taxes under the "EU tax directive," it was without revealing the names of any foreign person with a Swiss bank account. The Swiss stand was supported by the refusal of the EU's own members, Austria, Belgium and Luxembourg, to weaken their own bank secrecy laws.

Truth be told, Switzerland has resisted, valiantly, pressures that other, less resolute nations, could never have withstood. Much of that owes to the nature and independence of the modern day descendants of the original Helvetian tribes — and their inherited financial DNA. But another, more important reason, is that Switzerland controls trillions of dollars, euros, Swiss francs — more than one-third of all the world's assets — and money does more than talk. Quietly and successfully, that kind of wealth can and does resist the likes of EU bureaucrats.

Rob Vrijhof, a leading Zurich investment manager who serves on The Sovereign Society's Council of Experts, points out that "many of the attacks on Swiss bank secrecy in the name of 'justice' are, in truth, attempts to eliminate cross border competition, to impose an international tax cartel, or to undermine Switzerland's recognized status as a world financial center that easily competes with the City in London and with Wall Street."

VERY SPECIAL SWISS FRANC

Switzerland's currency, the Swiss franc, generally has reflected the state of Swiss banking — strong, valuable and unaffected by inflation and stylish monetary fads. In 1970, a U.S. dollar would purchase 4.5 Swiss francs. Since 1971, the franc has appreciated nearly 330% against the U.S. dollar. U.S. owners of Swiss franc denominated assets usually have profited as a result. That profit came despite traditionally low Swiss interest rates and the bothersome 35% withholding tax on bank interest.

1934 BANK SECRECY LAW

The rise of Adolf Hitler and the Nazi takeover of Germany in the early 1930s prompted the famous 1934 Swiss Bank Secrecy Law that remains in force today. That law was an effort to stop Nazi agents from bribing bank employees for information about the accounts of German citizens and expatriates. The law protects foreign depositors from unwarranted intrusions into their bank privacy, although now the law has been tempered in many important ways.

Swiss banks are prohibited from responding to inquiries about an individual account, whether from attorneys, credit rating services, or foreign governments. The law punishes violations of bank secrecy with fines up to SFR50,000 (US$33,000) and six months in prison. In most cases, the Swiss government cannot obtain information about an account without a court order. To obtain an order, investigators must demonstrate the probable violation of law and reasons to believe the particular account at issue is involved in that violation. Although non-payment of foreign taxes is not a crime in Switzerland and "tax fraud" is, that can be a rather elastic phrase.

In 2009, under G-20 and OECD pressures, the Swiss agreed to exchange tax information on foreigners' accounts, but only on a limited basis and after a showing of probable cause that foreign tax evasion may have occurred. This concession required renegotiation of over 70 existing tax treaties.

In spite of its reputation for bank secrecy, in 1990, Switzerland was one of the first European countries to make money laundering a criminal offense. That law resulted in the demise of the famous Swiss compte anonyme, as the French-speaking Swiss termed it — universally known as a "numbered account." Previously, it was possible to open a nominee account in which the identity of the account holder could be concealed from almost everyone except the highest bank officials.

Since 1994, a central office in Bern has been devoted exclusively to fighting organized crime. Mandatory "know-your-customer" guidelines are used by Swiss banks to investigate potential clients. Banks are particularly attentive to prospective clients that try to open an account with more than SFR25,000 (US$17,000) in cash or its equivalent in foreign currency.

In 1998, an even stricter money laundering law transformed Swiss banking in a fundamental way. Previously, bankers had the option of reporting suspicious transactions to police authorities. Now, under pressure from world governments pursuing corruption, drug cartels and organized crime, Switzerland requires banks to report "suspicious transactions." The position is now reversed. Failure to report is a crime; bankers can now go to prison for keeping secret the names and records of suspected clients. Not so long ago, they faced imprisonment for failing to keep such secrets.

Even before 2009, in some cases Switzerland released information in circumstances not involving a crime under Swiss law. The Swiss government has proven willing to freeze assets before an individual is even charged with a crime if a foreign government can demonstrate "reasonable suspicion" that the accused engaged in criminal conduct. This is especially the case in high-profile drug or political corruption cases, such as those involving Swiss bank accounts of someone like the late dictator of the Philippines, Ferdinand Marcos.

But there are limits to how far the Swiss will go. In 2001, the Swiss parliament rejected a new, even stricter anti-laundering bill. Indeed, moving towards greater privacy, in 2004 the Swiss Parliament voted to include banking secrecy as part of the national constitution.

Until 2009, the Swiss successfully had resisted pressure to compromise banking secrecy when the issue was foreign tax evasion. Threatened with sanctions and an international boycott led by the U.S., U.K., France and

Germany, they agreed only to bend enough to exchange information concerning alleged foreign tax evasion, and then only after Swiss government review in individual cases.

WORLD-CLASS BANKING SYSTEM

Although Swiss banking privacy has been legendary, secrecy is not the most important reason for Switzerland's success. Of far greater significance are the country's political, financial and economic stability and strength. Most of the world's largest companies and hundreds of thousands of honest, law-abiding foreigners bank with the Swiss. Indeed, at the end of 2009, Swiss banks managed over approximately US$5 trillion! It is no coincidence that the official international intermediary banking institution, the Bank for International Settlements, is located in Switzerland at Basle.

Switzerland is home to several hundred banks ranging from small private and regional banks to the two giants, UBS AG and Crédit Suisse. These major Swiss banks have branch offices in most of the world's financial centers, from New York to Panama to Singapore.

Swiss banks combine traditional banking with international brokerage and financial management. To guard against inflation or devaluation, Swiss bank accounts can be denominated in the currency you choose — Swiss francs, U.S. dollars, or any other major currency. An account opened in one currency can be switched to another denomination when the time is right for short-term profits or long-term gains and safety.

You can invest in certificates of deposit, U.S. and other

national stocks, bonds, mutual funds and commodities; buy, store and sell gold, silver and other precious metals; and buy insurance and annuities. Swiss banks can act as your agent to buy and hold other types of assets. Of course, Swiss banks also issue international credit and ATM bank cards. Bank officers speak English as well as many other languages. Swiss banks are equipped for fax, wire, e-mail, or telex and instructions are carried out immediately. Or just phone your own personal banker who handles your account.

To some extent, "know your customer" rules have complicated the process of opening a bank account in Switzerland and proof of identity and references are required. But, the biggest downside is the high minimum deposit required by most Swiss banks.

While only a few years ago, many banks were content with initial deposits of only a few thousand dollars, Switzerland's popularity among foreign investors, along with the cost of administering "know your customer" laws, has led to sharp increases in deposit minimums, the lowest now being about US$250,000. Most private investment accounts require a minimum of US$1 million.

An alternative can be found in banks run by the various Swiss "cantons," as the largely self-governing provinces are called. These banks offer full services, have relatively low minimum deposits and each cantonal government insures the deposits. Swiss banks usually require that foreigners applying to open a new account do so in person.

Because of onerous U.S. government regulations and reporting requirements involving Americans, many Swiss banks now refuse to do business with U.S. persons. Undoubtedly, the rough treatment of UBS by the U.S.

government makes all Swiss bankers reluctant to accept U.S. clients.

We can assist you in making appropriate contacts with reliable Swiss or other offshore banks that have passed our due diligence tests. If you wish to open a Swiss account, contact The Sovereign Society at 98 S.E. Federal Highway, Suite 2, Delray Beach, FL 33483.

Tel.: 561-272-0413

Website: http://www.sovereignsociety.com

Email: info@sovereignsociety.com

STRICT CONTROL, HIGH QUALITY

Swiss banks have attained their unique position with financial expertise, honesty, global capabilities and the high percentage and quality of their reserves, much of it in gold and Swiss francs. The Swiss financial industry is tightly regulated, with banks strictly supervised by the Federal Banking Commission (FBC).

Swiss law imposes stiff liquidity and capital requirements on banks. The complicated official liquidity formula results in some private banks maintaining liquidity at or near 100%, unheard of in other national banking systems. The Swiss reputation also rests on the fact that banks traditionally hold substantial unreported, hidden reserves. Every month, Swiss banks with securities investments must write the value of their holdings to current market price or actual cost, whichever is lower. That assures no Swiss banks will have unrealized paper losses, as often happens in other countries.

Swiss banks are also subject to two regular audits. The first audit is to ensure compliance with Swiss corporate law. The second is the banking audit, conducted by one of 17 audit firms specially approved by the FBC. These exacting audits provide the primary guarantee for Swiss bank depositors. Supervision and regulation of Swiss banking surpasses that of any other nation. Plus, the banks have comprehensive insurance to cover deposits, transfers, theft, or abnormal losses. This means that your funds are insured in the event of a bank failure — but that hasn't happened in Switzerland in many decades.

THE FIDUCIARY INVESTMENT ACCOUNT

One popular Swiss account for foreign investors is the fiduciary account. A Swiss bank investment manager oversees the account, but all its investments are placed outside Switzerland, as the account holder directs. Funds that pass through the account are therefore not subject to Swiss taxes.

The fiduciary account comes in two forms: an investment account and a fiduciary loan account. With the investment account, the bank places the client's funds as loans to foreign banks in the form of fixed-term deposits. In the loan account, the customer designates the commercial borrower. Although the bank assumes no risk, it provides an important service by conducting a thorough investigation of the prospective borrower's credit credentials.

Many international companies use fiduciary loans to finance subsidiaries. There is an element of risk in making such loans, though. In the event of currency devaluation, or the bankruptcy of the borrower, the lender can lose.

DISCRETIONARY ACCOUNTS

With more than 250 years in the international portfolio management business, Swiss banks are among the world leaders in investment management. Experienced money managers constantly analyze world markets, choosing investments with the greatest potential and minimal risk. Swiss banks offer a broad selection of investment plans diversified by industry, country, international, or emerging markets. Outside financial managers can be employed to invest deposited funds and bank loans can be arranged for investment purposes.

These accounts are best managed by a private Swiss bank or by an independent Swiss portfolio manager. The Swiss invented what has come to be called "private banking." They honed private banking to a fine edge centuries before U.S. "cookie cutter" banks discovered the concept. With a private bank, you get personal contact and individual service. However, most private banks require an initial US$250,000 minimum investment and a personal introduction from a well-known source.

THE SWISS ALTERNATIVE: INSURANCE

Switzerland is also a world-renowned center for insurance and reinsurance. Many Swiss insurance companies offer a broad range of financial services that, in some cases, approach the flexibility of a bank account. Indeed, many Swiss residents use their insurance company as their only financial institution.

Swiss insurance policies offer other important advantages, including:

- They generally offer higher interest rates than bank accounts.

- They may be configured to offer significant asset protection, unlike a bank account.

- Insurance accounts aren't subject to the Swiss 35% with holding tax on earned bank interest.

In 1998, amendments to U.S. tax law ended the tax deferral previously allowed on fixed annuity contracts issued by foreign insurance companies. All such annuity income must now be reported as part of taxable annual income. However, income from properly structured foreign variable annuities and life insurance contracts generally remains tax deferred.

SWITZERLAND AND TAXES

Switzerland is not a low-tax country for Swiss residents or companies, although tax rates are lower than in the surrounding EU nations. But foreign investors can avoid many local taxes by choosing certain types of investments that escape taxes.

By law, Swiss banks collect a withholding tax of 35% on all interest and dividends paid by Swiss companies, banks, the government or other sources. Foreign investors to whom this tax applies may be eligible for refunds of all or part of the tax under the terms of Switzerland's network of more than 70 tax treaties with other nations.

In addition, there are many legal ways to avoid Swiss

taxes by investing in accounts especially structured for foreign investors. These include non-Swiss money market and bond funds, fiduciary precious metal accounts and other instruments. For instance, Switzerland imposes no taxes on dividends or interest from securities that originate outside Switzerland. For this reason, many Swiss banks offer investment funds with at least 80% of earnings in foreign investments or, even better, in money market funds located in Luxembourg or Ireland.

TAX TREATIES ABOUND

To reduce the possibility that Swiss citizens or companies might be subject to double taxation, the Swiss government has entered into a global network of about 70 tax treaties.

Tax treaties, however, have the unfortunate side effect of eroding financial secrecy. It is not possible to claim a tax credit under a tax treaty without also revealing the income that was taxed. In addition, tax treaties have a second underlying purpose: they exist not only to help individuals and companies investing or doing business internationally to avoid double taxation, but also to facilitate information exchange between tax authorities.

The 1997 U.S.-Swiss tax treaty, still in effect, is a case in point.

While non-payment of taxes is not a crime in Switzerland, Article 26 of this treaty permits the two governments to exchange information about alleged "tax fraud and the like." It also allows authorities to transfer information that may help in the "prevention of tax fraud and the like in relation to taxes." At this writing, the treaty is now being renegotiated to include tax evasion as a basis for information exchange. The new provisions will embody in some form the OECD standards on tax information exchange.

In the past, the U.S. pressed hard to bend Swiss bank secrecy in specific cases. But even under the recently adopted OECD standard, the Swiss view is that that bank secrecy should be waived only in individual cases of alleged tax evasion in which probable cause is shown. Even after accepting the OECD rule, the government announced that it would not allow unsubstantiated "fishing expeditions," such as the IRS was seeking in the 2008 UBS tax evasion case.

TAX-ADVANTAGED RESIDENCY IN SWITZERLAND

Although it is not generally known, for those who wish to retire in Switzerland, it is possible to negotiate a lump-sum annual income tax payment (known as a forfeit) with cantonal tax authorities. The more populous and popular cantons are likely to charge more, but one of the smallest, Appenzell, will settle for lesser amounts per year, regardless of your actual income. The difficulty comes in obtaining a Swiss residency permit, an extremely scarce commodity. But if you are wealthy and offer proof of sufficient future income, you may qualify.

The forfeit deal is currently (2009) available to 3,600 foreigners who pay an average 75,000 Swiss francs (US$60,050) each in tax, earning Switzerland 300 million Swiss francs (US$240.2 million) per year. The system allows foreign citizens living there to negotiate a fixed tax rate based on their Swiss property factors, excluding income earned outside Switzerland. Deals vary widely among the 26 cantons, but the basic formula is to calculate a minimum of five times the annual rent or the rental value of the expatriate's home and his living expenses. That amount is taxed at an average rate of 30%. (Worth noting — many nations entice foreigners as individual or corporate residents by exempting them from all or most taxes, including the United Kingdom, Monaco, Luxembourg, Austria and Ireland.)

The Swiss may be conservative in many ways, but they welcome foreigners. In 2000, Swiss voters rejected a proposal to impose a constitutional limit on the percentage of foreigners in their country. The proposal would have set a ceiling of 18% on the number of foreigners in this country of 7.6 million people. According to the Swiss Federal Statistical Office, 21.6% of the total population — and around 25% of the work force (some commute) — in Switzerland are foreigners.

People come from all over the world to live here. In fact, 86.5% of Switzerland's permanent foreign resident population is of European origin, two-thirds of whom are nationals of an EU country. The largest group of foreigners is from Italy (18.2%), followed by nationals of Germany (12.7%), Serbia and Montenegro (11.7%) and Portugal (11.4%). The proportion of non-European nationals has increased by seven percentage points since 1980 to reach 13.4% in 2009.

PRIVATE BANKS

There are several leading Swiss banks with which The Sovereign Society has arrangements to accommodate our members. Please contact our office for information at 98 S.E. Federal Highway, Suite 2, Delray Beach, FL 33483; Tel.: 561-272-0413; Fax: 561-272-5427; Website: http://www.sovereignsociety.com Email: info@sovereignsociety.com.

OFFICIAL

Embassy of Switzerland, 2900 Cathedral Avenue, N.W., Washington, D.C. 20008; Tel.: (202) 745-7900; Fax: (202) 387-2564; Website: http://www.swissemb.org.

Email: was.info@eda.admin.ch.

U.S. Embassy, Sulgeneckstrasse 19, 3007. Bern, Switzerland; Tel.: + (41) 31-357-7011 or emergency: +(41) 31-357-7777; Fax: +(41) 31-357-7280;

Email: bernacs@state.gov
Website: http://bern.usembassy.gov.

PANAMA: PRIVACY AND PROFITS OFFSHORE

We recommend Panama as one of the best tax havens, asset protection havens and residential havens in the world. Only hours by air from the United States, Panama offers a variety of lifestyles and geographic diversity with a century-long history of working closely with Americans. Panama's real estate boom has cooled, but the multi-billion dollar expansion of the Panama Canal can only increase economic growth. In many ways, Panama has it all.

Alone among current offshore tax havens, Panama combines maximum financial privacy, a long history of judicial enforcement of asset protection-friendly laws, a strong anti-money laundering law, plus tax exemptions for foreigners. Thanks to its unique historic and often contentious relationship with the United States, it also exercises a high degree of independence from outside pressures, including those from Washington.

Factor	Findings	Rating
Government/ political stability	Although Panamanian politics remains volatile, it has become a stable democracy	3.5
Favorable laws, judicial system	Panama's offshore laws date from the 1920s, but significant corruption exists	3.5
Available legal entities	All major legal entities may be formed or are recognized under the Panamanian legal system	5
Taxes	Foreign residents and investors exempt from taxes on all income earned outside Panama	5

Financial privacy/ banking secrecy	One of the best	5
Final Rating		4.4

PANAMA REVISITED

In 1999, I returned to Panama for the first time in 20 years. Since then, I have visited many more times.

Panama is a very different place than I remember in the 1970s when I served in the U.S. House of Representatives as the ranking Republican on the Panama Canal subcommittee. My visits then were made during U.S. legislative implementation of the Carter-Torrijos treaty negotiations, at a time when Panama was little more than an American colony.

Today, Panama is winding down what was a major multi-year construction and real estate boom that produced thousands of modern condominiums and over a hundred skyscrapers, first-class hotels and restaurants, plus excellent digital Internet and other international communications. Downtown Panama City, the balmy, tropical capital on the southern, Pacific end of the Canal, suggests Los Angeles or Miami, except arguably more locals speak English here than in some parts of South Florida.

Yes, Panama also has a long history of government corruption that continues to this day. This hasn't seemed to affect the regulated banking sector. Nonetheless, bribery, cronyism, nepotism and kickbacks in government dealings regularly make headlines here. But that's certainly true far too often in the United States as well.

IMAGE OF PANAMA

When most people think of "Panama," they think — canal!

But the country is less well-known for what it has become in the last three decades — second only to Miami, which is Latin America's major international banking and business center, with strong ties to Asia and Europe and a special relationship with the United States that, however contentious, continues apace.

The big change came at midnight, December 31, 1999, when 96 years of official United States presence in the Republic of Panama ended. Panama finally got what its nationalistic politicians had demanded for much of the last century — full Panamanian control over its famous inter-oceanic canal.

A NEW ERA

Indeed, in many respects — financial privacy, solid asset protection and freedom from outside political pressures — Panama has moved to the head of the class.

There are good and historic reasons for Panama's enviable tax haven standing, including:

1. a territorial tax system that taxes only earnings from within the country;

2. constantly modernized asset protection laws, dating from the 1920s;

3. an array of useful statutory legal entities (trusts, corporations, private foundations);

4. a host of qualified offshore professionals and bankers;

5. some of the strongest financial privacy laws anywhere; and

6. considering its past history, a remarkable degree of political stability in a viable democracy.

That stability was again confirmed in May 2009 with the election for a five-year term of supermarket tycoon Ricardo Martinelli as president of the Republic. Very few presidential candidates in any nation come back from a crushing defeat with only 5.3 % of the vote, to win a landslide victory five years later by more than 60%. But that was what he and his conservative coalition party did in a sweeping victory, bucking a trend of radical left-wing leadership in other parts of Central and South America.

The new president pledged to bring foreign investors into tourism projects, cruise ports and airports, and direct more government spending to public infrastructure, such as a subway in Panama City, the capital. He promised much needed fiscal discipline and a close relationship with the United States and pledged to simplify the country's tax code with a 10% to 20% flat tax.

However, Panama still struggles to emerge from its status as a Third World country, with too much of its population living in poverty. Still, it is in much better shape financially than its Central American neighbors to the north, or Colombia to the south. Although economic growth has slowed in recent years, Panama still receives more than US$2 billion annually in direct foreign investments. In spite of the global recession, in 2008 Panama received foreign direct investment worth $2.4 billion, an increase of 26% from 2007. That represents 10.4% of the country's $23.1 billion economy. During much of the decade before 2009, its GDP grew at an amazing rate of 8% or more. Since the 1990s, inflation barely has exceeded 1% per year. Annual inflation has averaged 1.4% for the past 30 years, much lower than in the United States.

Then, there is the enormous wealth represented by the canal, generating over US$1 billion in annual revenues. While much of this income must be plowed back into maintenance, profits from the canal represent Panama's largest single source of income. And in a move that eventually will increase the current flow of 14,000 annual ship transits, the Panama Canal is undergoing a complete modernization at an estimated cost of US$6 billion. The world famous waterway is getting wider locks that will accommodate the largest ships now afloat, such as oil supertankers. The work, due for completion in 2014, the centenary year of the canal's opening, is providing a major boost to Panama's already growing national economy.

There are also the thousands of acres of land from former U.S. military installations, prized real estate with an estimated value of US$4 billion. Admittedly, its distribution and privatization has been slow and marked by charges of corruption, but development of this property in the next few decades will undoubtedly bring significant benefits to Panama.

Privacy, Profits and No Taxes

In many ways, the Republic of Panama is ideally suited for the offshore investor who wants to enjoy the increasingly rare privilege of guaranteed financial privacy and no taxes, either corporate or personal. In the past, Panama pointedly refused to commit to exchanging information with tax authorities in other countries. Since the G-20 demands directed at tax havens in 2009, Panama restated its this official position — it will not agree to exchange tax information unless and until all other nations, especially other tax havens, implemented that same policy.

According to Canada's Fraser Institute, Panama is near the top of the list of the world's freest economies, ranked eighth with Australia, Ireland, the Netherlands and Luxembourg. Panama has adopted more than 40 laws protecting foreigners' financial and investment rights, including the Investments Stability Law (Law No. 54), that guarantees foreign and local investors equal rights. Panama's central location makes it a natural base for world business operations. Most importantly, Panama isn't directly under the thumb of the United States. And unlike the British overseas territories of Bermuda and the Cayman Islands, it isn't under the control of London.

Among the current 80-plus banks, the major players are the 58 multinational banks representing 30 countries that primarily conduct offshore business. In 2009, all Panamanian banks held an official US$75 billion in total assets, with liquidity impressively high at an average 30%. They had virtually no exposure to the kinds of investments that undermined U.S., U.K. and other national banking systems. Banking alone accounts for about 11% of Panama's GNP. Nearly every one of the world's major banks has a full-service branch office in Panama, with representation from Japan, Germany, Brazil and the United States.

Reasserting Financial Privacy

Panama is one of the world's oldest tax havens, with legislation establishing tax advantages for corporations dating back to the 1920s.

A central part of the long tax haven tradition has been statutory guarantees of financial privacy and confidentiality. Violators can suffer civil and criminal penalties for unauthorized disclosure. Unless ordered to do so by a court, there is no general requirement to reveal publicly beneficial trust or corporate owners to Panama authorities and no required audit reports or financial statements. As of 2009, bearer shares were still permitted but indications were that they would soon be banned.

Panama has no double taxation agreements and no tax information exchange agreements with other countries. For years, Washington repeatedly suggested signing a TIEA with the United States, but Panama politely ignored such demands. At this writing, these pressures are being renewed in the wake of the G-20 attacks on all tax havens.

Panama has adopted some significant reforms in its banking system to minimize corruption and ensure that banking secrecy can be lifted in criminal investigations. However, this occurred only after pressure from the international community. In June 2000, the Financial Action Task Force (explained earlier in Chapter 2) placed Panama on a blacklist of 15 countries alleged to be tolerant of money laundering.

In October 2000, Panama's Congress unanimously approved a strong anti-money laundering law in line with FATF recommendations. In June 2001, the nation was removed from the FATF blacklist. That law covers all crimes and brings all financial institutions under the supervision of a government banking agency.

In contrast, Panama has stoutly resisted the OECD's demands for the imposition of taxes on foreign investors. In a ringing speech in 2002, Panama's foreign minister denounced OECD "imperialism" and said flatly that his nation will not bow to outside pressures. Panama's defense of tax competition has created major opportunities for it. One opportunity came in 2005 when the EU member states imposed withholding taxes on income from savings. The EU withholding tax inevitably caused EU funds to flow to non-EU financial centers that don't impose such taxes and that don't routinely exchange financial information with tax authorities. Panama qualified on both counts.

THE YANKEE DOLLAR

While "dollarization" is debated as a novel concept elsewhere in Latin America, since 1904 the U.S. dollar has been Panama's official paper currency.

Panama has no central bank to print money. And as Juan Luis Moreno-Villalaz, economic advisor to Panama's Ministry of Economy and Finance, noted, "In Panama… there has never been a systemic banking crisis; indeed, in several instances international banks have acted as the system's lender of last resort. The Panamanian system provides relatively low interest rates on mortgages and commercial loans. Credit is ample, with 30-year mortgages readily available. These are unusual conditions for a developing country and are largely achieved because there is no exchange rate risk, a low risk of financial crises and ample flow of funds from abroad."

I often have been asked whether Panama's use of the dollar as their currency means a declining dollar worldwide will hurt Panama's economy. The answer is that the health of Panama's economy depends on the same internal factors as any other nation, unique GDP growth, employment and direct local and foreign investment, and not solely on its currency. This separate and distinct economic existence has been demonstrated over decades as Panama has enjoyed very low inflation, while U.S. inflation at times soared to double digit levels.

WELCOME BANKERS

Panama grew as an international financial center after the enactment of Decree No. 238 of July 1970, a liberal banking law that also abolished all currency controls. The law exempts offshore business in Panama from income tax and from taxes on interest earned in domestic savings accounts and offshore transactions.

In 1999, a comprehensive new banking law was enacted that accelerated Panama's growth as a leading world offshore finance center. That law uses the guidelines of the Basle Committee on Banking Supervision, the international oversight group that sets banking standards, requiring all banks with unrestricted domestic or international commercial banking licenses to maintain capital equivalent to at least 8% of total assets. (In fact, Panama banks have far exceeded that minimal percentage requirement.) Government investigative powers and tighter general controls were increased, bringing Panama in line with regulatory standards found in European and North American banking centers. Under this law, a prima facie case of illicit financial conduct can launch an investigation of possible criminal conduct. The law also permits foreign bank regulators to make inspection visits to any of their domestic banks with branches in Panama.

Panamanian banks are very reluctant to open new accounts for Americans and other foreigners, unless the applicant has a home or an active business in Panama. In most cases, foreigners need a personal introduction to a bank, and that can be obtained by arrangement with the contacts listed at the end of this section.

Panama's financial sector also includes an active, but fairly small, stock exchange, captive insurance and re-insurance companies and financial and leasing companies. Another major business and financial attraction at the Atlantic end of the canal is the booming Colón Free Zone (www.zonalibre.com), a major tax-free transshipment facility, the second-largest free trade zone in the world, after Hong Kong.

IBCs and Foundations

Panama has liberal laws favoring trusts, international business companies and holding companies. In 1995, it enacted Law No. 25, a private interest foundation statute modeled after the popular Stiftung family wealth protection and estate planning vehicle long used in Liechtenstein. (More about that in the section on Liechtenstein later in this chapter.)

The law allows the tax-free family foundation to be used for investment, tax sheltering, ownership of commercial business and private activity, with the founder retaining lifetime control. Foundation assets are not counted as part of the founder's estate for death tax purposes and Panama does not recognize the often restrictive inheritance laws of other nations. This can mean significant estate tax savings for U.S. persons who choose Panama's family foundation as their estate planning vehicle.

Some argue that the Panamanian private foundation law is only a clone of the Liechtenstein law. While it is true that the Panamanian law is newer, the costs of operating a foundation in Panama are lower than in Liechtenstein. For South American clients and others from civil law backgrounds who are unfamiliar with the concept of an Anglo-American trust, a Panamanian private foundation often represents an ideal estate planning solution, even if just for the estate tax savings it allows.

Panama's international business corporation (IBC) Law 32 of 1927, is modeled after the U.S. state of Delaware's corporation friendly statutes. There are about 350,000 IBCs registered in Panama, second only to Hong Kong's 400,000. A Panamanian IBC can maintain its own corporate bank account and credit cards for global management of investments, mutual funds, precious metals, real estate and trade. Tax-free corporate income can be spent for business purposes worldwide and using the Panama IBC allows avoidance of home country zoning, labor, manufacturing, warranty, environmental and other restrictions.

Americans should consult a U.S. tax expert before forming a Panama IBC, since there can be some severe and costly U.S. tax consequences when using offshore corporations.

Leading Retirement Haven

Despite its relatively advanced industrial and financial infrastructure compared to other Latin nations, Panama remains an affordable place in which to live. A live-in maid earns about US$120 per month; first-run movies cost US$2.50. Unlike much of Central America, Panama boasts a first-class health care system with low costs compared to the United States — a doctor's office visit costs about US$25.

Because of Panama's geographical diversity, there is considerable climatic variation. Panama City, the historical and financial center, has a year-round tropical climate. Yet, only a few hundred miles away near the Costa Rican border are sub-tropical forests, with cascading waterfalls, mountainsides covered with flowers and spring-like weather year-round. There are also many low-priced buys on condominiums and other real estate, particularly in Panama City and the surrounding areas, a byproduct, in part, of the U.S. government exodus.

There is a wide variety of programs in Panama for foreigners who wish to make it their home, the best known of these being the *pensinado* program. All resident visa applications must be made through a Panamanian attorney. There is no minimum or maximum age requirement, except that those less than 18 years old, the legal age of emancipation in Panama, will qualify as dependants of their parents. None of these visas automatically grants the right to work. Work permits must be applied for and obtained separately.

In recent decades, the Republic of Panama deliberately has positioned itself as a first-class retirement haven, with some of the most appealing programs of special benefits for foreign residents and retirees anywhere in the world. Panama also offers a variety of visas for investors, persons of high net worth, wealthy retirees, small business and agricultural business investors and entrepreneurs, and those who simply want to immigrate and become Panamanian citizens.

The government makes retirement in Panama easy and laws provide important tax advantages for foreigners who wish to become residents. The only significant requirements are good health and a verifiable monthly income of at least US$500. There are no local taxes on foreign income and you can import your household goods tax-free.

OFFICIAL

Embassy of Panama, 2862 McGill Terrace, N.W., Washington, D.C. 20009; Tel.: (202) 483-1407. Consulates are located in New York (212) 840-2450 or Philadelphia (215) 574-2994, Atlanta, Chicago, Houston, Los Angeles, Miami, New Orleans, or Tampa. Website: www.embassyofpanama.org/; Email: info@embassyofpanama.org.

U.S. Embassy, Edificio 783, Avenida Demetrio Basilio Lakas, Clayton, Panama City (tel: + 507-207-7000). Personal and official mail for the embassy and members of the mission may be sent to U.S. Embassy Panama, Unit 9100, DPO AA 34002. Email: Panamaweb@state.gov; Website: http://panama.usembassy.gov/.

LIECHTENSTEIN: WORLD'S OLDEST TAX HAVEN

The very private people here want things low key. Yet foreigners "in the know" realize this is a financial powerhouse among nations; a constitutional monarchy that has graced the map of Europe since 1719 and that, in the last 60 years, has transformed itself into a world-class tax and asset protection haven. They prefer to keep it secret, but it's here that the world's truly wealthy quietly do business. And for good reasons. Liechtenstein still boasts some of the world's strongest banking secrecy and financial privacy laws, the OECD notwithstanding. Plus, it offers world banking and investment direct access through its cooperative neighbor, Switzerland.

With asset protection laws dating from the 1920s, a host of excellent legal entities designed for wealth preservation and bank secrecy guaranteed by law, this tiny principality has it all — plus continuing controversy about who uses it and why. In the not so distant past, one had to be a philatelist to know the Principality of Liechtenstein even existed. In those days, the nation's major export was exquisitely produced postage stamps, highly prized by collectors. Until the 1960s, the tiny principality, wedged between Switzerland and Austria, subsisted on income from tourism, postage stamp sales and the export of false teeth.

But in the last 50 years, its lack of taxes and its high degree of financial privacy propelled Liechtenstein to top ranking among the world's wealthiest nations. This historic Rhine Valley principality grew into a major world tax and asset haven, posting per capita income levels (US$118,000) higher than Germany, France and the United Kingdom.

Tiny Liechtenstein (16 miles long and 3.5 miles wide, population 32,000) is nestled in the mountains between Switzerland and Austria and has existed in its present form since January 23, 1719, when the Holy Roman Emperor Charles VI granted it independent status.

Factor	Findings	Rating
Government/ political stability	A popular absolute monarch, whose dictates are subject only to national referenda	3.5
Favorable laws, judicial system	Well-established and respected rule of law	5
Available legal entities	All major legal entities may be formed or are recognized under the Liechtenstein legal system	5
Taxes	Strong, but weakened by recent legislation and agreements	4
Financial privacy/ banking secrecy	Foreign-owned entities are mostly tax exempt	4
Final Rating		4.3

ABSOLUTE MONARCHY

The government is a constitutional monarchy, with the Prince of Liechtenstein (currently Hans-Adam II) as head of state. Until 2003, His Highness' power only extended to sanctioning laws passed by the popularly elected unicameral legislature, the Diet. For the most part, the Diet made the laws, negotiated treaties, approved or vetoed taxes and supervised government affairs. Proposed legislation was frequently submitted directly to citizen referendum.

This system changed on March 16, 2003, when Hans-Adam II won an overwhelming majority in favor of overhauling the constitution to give him more powers than any other European monarch. Liechtenstein's ruling Prince now has the right to dismiss governments and approve judicial nominees. The Prince may also veto laws simply by refusing to sign them within a six-month period. Tempering this authority is the fact that the signature of 1,500 Liechtenstein citizens on a petition is sufficient to force a referendum on the abolition of the monarchy, or any other change in the law.

In 2004, Prince Hans-Adam II ceded day-to-day rule of the country to his son, Prince Alois, now 42, while he remains the official head of state. This was seen as first step towards the eventual full succession to power of Prince Alois.

LEADING FINANCIAL CENTER

Liechtenstein's economy is well diversified and it is, for its small size, one of the most heavily industrialized countries in Europe. Still, financial services provide some 40% of budget revenues, so anything that tarnishes its reputation is a major crisis. Its 16 locally owned banks, 60 law firms and 250 trust companies employ 16% of the workforce. Its licensed fiduciary companies and lawyers serve as nominees for, or manage, more than 80,000 legal entities, most of them owned and controlled by nonresidents of Liechtenstein.

Liechtenstein was one of the first nations in the world to adopt specific offshore asset protection laws, as far back as the 1920s. Liechtenstein's unique role in international circles is not so much as a banking center, but as a tax haven. The nation acts as a base of operations for foreign holding companies, private foundations, family foundations and a unique entity called the Anstalt (i.e., establishment). The banks and a host of specialized trust companies provide management services for thousands of such entities. Personal and company tax rates are low, generally under 12% for local residents. Any company domiciled in Liechtenstein is granted total exemption from income tax if it generates no income from local sources.

Until recently there was a near-total absence of any international treaties governing double taxation or exchange of information with the one exception of a double tax agreement with neighboring Austria, primarily to cover taxes on people who commute across the border for work. In 2009, Liechtenstein was one of the first acknowledged tax havens to agree to adopt OECD tax information exchange standards that covers alleged foreign income tax evasion. As part of that change in policy, the principality began negotiating tax information exchange treaties with other nations.

Liechtenstein is independent, but closely tied to Switzerland. The Swiss franc is the local currency and, in many respects, except for political independence, Liechtenstein's status is that of a de facto province integrated within Switzerland. Liechtenstein banks are integrated into Switzerland's banking system and capital markets. Many cross-border investments clear in or through Swiss banks. Foreign-owned holding companies are a major presence in Liechtenstein, with many maintaining their accounts in Swiss banks.

Good Reputation

For the most part, Liechtenstein has an impeccable reputation with government regulators stressing the professional qualifications and local accountability of its well-trained financial managers. Liechtenstein's reaction to outside demands for stronger anti-money laundering laws has been very much in keeping with its conservative history.

In 2001, Liechtenstein was removed from the Financial Action Task Force blacklist. In 2000, it adopted tough new anti-money laundering laws that covered "all crimes;" created a Financial Intelligence Unit (FIU); imposed much stricter "know-your-customer" and suspicious activity reporting laws; eased its historic, strict financial secrecy; and abolished the rights of trustees and lawyers not to disclose the identity of their clients to banks where funds are invested.

Liechtenstein's longstanding tax haven status was the source of criticism by the OECD, which placed the principality on its questionable, 41 nation "harmful tax practices" blacklist because of its low taxes.

Stolen Names

Until early 2008, Liechtenstein managed to stay on the good side of the self-appointed international busybodies who make it their duty to attack tax havens and, most especially, banking secrecy.

It was then revealed that the German government illegally had bribed a disgruntled former Liechtenstein bank employee, Heinrich Kieber, to gain confidential bank information he had stolen from LGT Bank in Liechtenstein.

Herr Kieber worked for the LGT Group at LGT Treuhand (Bank) AG, in Vaduz until 2002. A man of questionable background, he had an outstanding 1997 international arrest warrant for a fraudulent real estate deal. He left Liechtenstein in 2002, after stealing confidential data from his employer, LGT Bank, and making copies of over a thousand names of foreigners with LGT accounts.

The German secret police paid Kieber €5 million (US$7.9 million) for the stolen data. The data, containing about 1,400 "client relationships," 600 of them Germans, was a major haul for German tax collectors. Germany shared the information with the governments of Britain, France, Italy, Spain, Norway, Ireland, Netherlands, Sweden, Canada, the USA, Australia and New Zealand.

Liechtenstein's billionaire royal family manages and controls LGT Bank and LGT Group. The nation's financial services sector produces 30% of Liechtenstein's gross domestic product and 14.3% of all people employed work in the financial services sector.

Banking secrecy and the government's refusal to share financial information, except in criminal cases, had been one of Liechtenstein's leading selling points. LGT Bank and Liechtenstein authorities rightfully advanced the theory that high-tax governments were using the stolen DVD and misinformation to scare people away from the principality and its banks.

After this highly publicized incident, the high tax governments of the G-20, assisted by the OECD, began a coordinated yearlong "surrender now" phase in their decade long anti-tax haven campaign.

To say the least, the worldwide publicity about the stolen bank list and the pressure from neighboring Germany, the G-20 countries and the OECD, hurt the principality's financial bottom line. Liechtenstein's banking industry suffered a 60% drop in profits in 2009, in part due to the global economic downturn, but also because of questions about its future as a leading tax haven. Assets under management by the principality's 15 banks were down 22% to 156.65 billion francs (US$144.3 billion). Unlike most other countries, Switzerland included, Liechtenstein's banks did not ask for or require any government bailout support.

SECRECY STILL GUARANTEED BY LAW

Liechtenstein's secrecy statutes have historically been considered stronger even than those in Switzerland. The 2009 adoption of the OECD tax information exchange standard weakened this secrecy to the extent that for the first time foreign tax evasion was included. Nevertheless, Liechtenstein still boasts some of the strictest confidentiality laws in the world. Liechtenstein and the United States signed a tax information exchange treaty in December 2008 that entered into force on January 1, 2010 providing for direct cooperation between the two countries' tax and judicial authorities.

Banks now keep "know your customers" records of clients' identities, but records may not be made public except by judicial or official government decision. Financial secrecy also extends to trustees, lawyers, accountants and to anyone connected to the banking industry. All involved are subject to the disciplinary powers of Liechtenstein's Upper Court. A court order or an officially approved request from a foreign government is required to release an account holder's bank records. Creditors seeking bank records face a time consuming and costly process.

As discussed in Chapter 3, coordinated outside pressures and the threat of blacklisting and sanctions resulted in capitulation to the OECD tax information exchange standards of most leading offshore financial centers. In 2009, Liechtenstein was the first tax haven to announce it would comply with Article 26 of the OECD model tax information exchange treaty. As in Switzerland, this means banks will now provide information in matters of foreign tax evasion when ordered to do so by the government, but under limited conditions and only by applying the terms of tax information exchange treaties in individual cases.

BIG BUCKS BANKING

Liechtenstein's banks have no official minimum deposit requirements, but their stated goal is to lure high net-worth individuals as clients. Opening a discretionary portfolio management account generally requires a minimum of SFR1 million (US$934,000). Trusts and limited companies registered here must pay an annual government fee of either 0.1% of capital, or SFR1,000 (US$934), whichever is higher. Most banks also charge an annual management fee of 0.5% of total assets under their supervision.

If you're considering opening an offshore bank or investment account, Liechtenstein is worth a comparative look. The principality has all the benefits of the other nations: a strong economy, rock-solid (Swiss) currency, political stability and ease of access, plus a few added attractions of its own. The government guarantees all bank deposits against loss, regardless of the amount involved, even though there have been no recent bank failures.

Until recently, Liechtenstein also had no information exchange agreements with any nation. But in 2003, bowing to U.S. pressure, it signed a mutual legal assistance treaty (MLAT) with the United States. The agreement covers a broad range of mutually recognized crimes, but does not include foreign tax evasion.

There was concern within Liechtenstein that the MLAT would open the door to "fishing expeditions" by U.S. tax authorities. However, the treaty gave Liechtenstein the right to refuse to disclose information that would require a court order with which to comply, if a court order has not been obtained. Liechtenstein has defended its sovereignty by invoking this provision whenever the United States has made what it viewed as unreasonable demands under the treaty, so the impact on otherwise law-abiding investors and businesses has been minimal.

That and a certified history of excellent asset protection and banking, makes this tiny Rhine Valley redoubt one of our top choices for offshore financial activity and estate planning.

Rob Vrijhof, senior partner in a leading Swiss investment firm and a member of The Sovereign Society's Council of Experts, does considerable business in Liechtenstein on behalf of international investors. He says he has seen a noticeable cleaning up of suspect practices, together with a new willingness to accommodate legitimate banking and investment. He says, "I recommend Liechtenstein unreservedly, if you can afford it."

Foundation/Trust/Corporation Options

Liechtenstein law allows limited liability companies (LLCs), but does not provide for formation of international business corporations (IBCs). But over the years, the country's legislators have been highly inventive when it comes to unusual and useful legal entities fashioned to serve special financial needs.

Government regulation of the Anstalt (see below), foundations, companies and trusts is extremely strict. This is primarily accomplished through training and regulation of managers, not by prying into the internal affairs of the entity or its holdings. As a result, business management services available in Liechtenstein are excellent in quality, if somewhat slow in execution.

The Anstalt

Liechtenstein is perhaps best known for the *Anstalt*, sometimes described in English as an "establishment" (the German word's closest English equivalent). The *Anstalt* is a legal entity unique to Liechtenstein and something of a hybrid somewhere between the trust and the corporation with which Americans are familiar.

The *Anstalt* may or may not have member shares. Control usually rests solely with the founder, or with surviving members of his or her family. Both have the power to allocate the profits as they see fit. The law regulating *Anstalt* formation is extremely flexible, allowing nearly any kind of charter to be drafted. Depending on the desired result, *Anstalts* can take on any number of trust or corporation characteristics. You can tailor them to meet specific U.S. tax criteria, and then obtain IRS private letter rulings recognizing your Anstalt as either a trust or corporation.

The only very limited information about the people involved in an individual *Anstalt* or company appears on public records. The beneficial owners of a company do not appear by name in any register and their identity need not be disclosed to the Liechtenstein authorities. On the other hand, diligent inquisitors may discover members of the board of directors by searching the Commercial Register. At least one member of the board must reside in Liechtenstein. Unlike U.S. corporations, the shares of a Liechtenstein company do not have to disclose the names of shareholders.

THE FAMILY FOUNDATION

Liechtenstein's concept of foundation is unique. Although Americans associate a foundation with a non-profit, tax-exempt organization, in Liechtenstein a foundation is an autonomous fund consisting of assets endowed by the founder for a specific, non-commercial purpose. The purpose can be very broad in scope, including religious and charitable goals.

One of the more common uses is as a so-called "pure family foundation." These vehicles are dedicated to the financial management and personal welfare of one or more particular families as beneficiaries.

The foundation has no shareholders, partners, owners, or members — only beneficiaries. It can be either limited in time or perpetual. The foundation and a beneficiary's interest therein cannot be assigned, sold, or attached by personal creditors.

Only foundation assets are liable for its debts. If engaged in commercial activities, the foundation's activities must support noncommercial purposes, such as support of the family. Unless the foundation is active commercially, it can be created through an intermediary. The founder's name need not be made public. Foundations may be created by deed, under the terms of a will, or by a common agreement among family members.

A family foundation can sometimes be more useful than a trust, since it avoids many restrictive trust rules that limit control by the trust creator. If you are interested in exploring the creation of a foundation, I recommend you obtain top quality tax and legal advice, both in your home country and in Liechtenstein.

HYBRID TRUSTS

You can use a Liechtenstein trust to control a family fortune, with the trust assets represented as shares in holding companies that control each of the relevant businesses that may be owned by the family. This legal technique brings together various family holdings under one trust umbrella, which, in turn, serves as a legal conduit for wealth transfer to named heirs and beneficiaries.

Liechtenstein's trust laws are practical and interesting due to the country's unusual combination of civil law and common-law concepts. In 1926, the Liechtenstein Diet adopted a statutory reproduction of the English-American trust system. They even allow trust grantors to choose governing law from any common law country. This places the Liechtenstein judiciary in the unique position of applying trust law from England, Bermuda, or Delaware

(U.S.A.) when addressing a controversy regarding a particular trust instrument.

Even though it is a civil law nation, a trust located in Liechtenstein can be useful in lowering taxes, sheltering foreign income and safeguarding assets from American estate taxes. The law allows quick portability of trusts to another jurisdiction and accepts foreign trusts that wish to re-register as local entities. The trust instrument must be deposited with the Commercial Registry, but is not subject to public examination.

In 2009, revisions and updates of existing 70-year old statutes by Parliament produced a new Foundation Act and amendments to the Law on Persons and Companies that took effect April 1, 2009 (Liechtenstein Law Gazette No. 220/2008).

OFFICIAL

The United States has no embassy in Liechtenstein. The U.S. Ambassador to Switzerland is also accredited to Liechtenstein. U.S. Embassy, Sulgeneckstrasse 19, 3007. Bern, Switzerland; Tel.: + (41) 31-357-7011 or emergency: +(41) 31-357-7777; Fax: +(41) 31-357-7280; Email: bernacs@state.gov; Website: http://bern.usembassy.gov.

Liechtenstein Embassy, 1300 Eye St. NW, Washington, D.C. 20005, Tel.: (202) 216-0460. Website: http://www. liechtenstein.li/en/fl-aussenstelle-washington/fl-aussenstelle-washington-home.htm.

Hong Kong: Special Administrative Region of the People's Republic of China

Hong Kong remains one of the freest economies in the world, as well as a major offshore financial center with strong common law-based laws governing banking and finance, even though it is controlled, ultimately, by a Communist government in Beijing.

Beijing's rule began in 1997 and has imposed restrictions, but on balance, semi-democratic Hong Kong remains relatively free, a reflection of Beijing's need for this historic city-state as a financial powerhouse and gateway for business with the world.

Factor	Findings	Rating
Government/ political stability	Political freedom has diminished, but free market economics still rule	3.5
Favorable laws, judicial system	The rule of law is highly regarded, but courts are susceptible to pressure from Beijing	3.5
Available legal entities	All major legal entities may be formed or are recognized under the Hong Kong legal system	5
Taxes	Traditional financial secrecy strong, but no specific statutory guarantee	3.5
Financial privacy/ banking secrecy	Foreign investors using this as a base can avoid most taxes and corporate taxes are relatively low	4
Final Rating		3.9

GATEWAY TO CHINA

If you're doing business in China (or anywhere in Asia), you should consider Hong Kong as your base of operations. It's a great place to obtain financing, do your banking, create the corporate or trust entities you may need to succeed in a very tough market — especially in China.

The huge mass of 1.4 billion people in China are experiencing some of the most rapid, although highly uneven, economic growth in recent world history. For some of the population, living standards have improved dramatically and this has increased room for personal choice, yet political controls remain tight. In 2009, the per-capita GDP was only US$6,000.

Over the three years through the end of 2007, China's gross domestic product (GDP) growth has exceeded 9% annually. In 2008, as China commemorated the 30th anniversary of the Communist takeover and its historic economic reforms, the global economic downturn began to slow foreign demand for Chinese exports for the first time in many years. The government vowed to continue reforming the economy and emphasized the need to increase domestic consumption in order to make China less dependent on foreign exports for GDP growth in the future.

The recession that began in 2008 only slowed expansion; the 2008 GDP was valued at US$9 trillion. Beijing channeled four trillion yuan (US$586 billion) as stimulus into the mainland economy and Hong Kong has benefited as well. In 2009, a wave of money flowing into Hong Kong from mainland China and the rest of the world propelled property and stock prices even as the economy faltered with a shrinkage of 6.5% in 2009 and unemployment reached a three-year high.

Hong Kong's pre-recession expansion spurred massive domestic consumer demand for every imaginable commodity and service, from thousands of high-rise apartment and condominiums, to millions of automobiles — and all sorts of financial services. All this rapid growth turned the eager eyes of world business towards the obvious profits to be made in China.

But with only a rudimentary, struggling financial system consisting of banks, stock markets and financial exchanges controlled by the Communist government and the military, the domestic economy lacks the experience and controls Western nations take for granted. Indeed, many of the existing financial institutions in China are loaded with billions in non-performing, politically allocated loans, thousands of shaky investments, all of it permeated with corruption.

To add to this certainty, accept the fact that, at present, there is no true "rule of law" or reliable judicial system in China, in the sense the Western world understands such basic safeguards. This means doing business in China lacks the legal protection foreign investors take for granted everywhere else.

GATEWAY TO THE WORLD

This mainland financial situation has served to accentuate and expand the role that Hong Kong has played with great success since the Communist revolution took control of China in 1949 — that of China's financial window and conduit to the rest of world. Hong Kong's position as the most important international financial services center in Asia, specifically, the gateway through which capital is most likely to flow out from China, appears unassailable.

Hong Kong is situated ideally — legally part of, but also different and somewhat apart from China. In Hong Kong, you can find what struggling mainland China sorely lacks — the legal, financial and investment expertise and experience that can provide you with a sensible approach to investing and doing business in China.

And that's where the profits will be — if you are prudent and careful in your approach. If you want to deal in China, unless you have longstanding family or business ties there, you are best served working with a Hong Kong-based partner who has firsthand knowledge of the Chinese market.

Hong Kong is proof that "money talks." China has too much invested in Hong Kong to destroy it all in a fit of rigid political ideology. Today, 30% of Hong Kong bank deposits are Chinese. China accounts for 22% of all Hong Kong foreign trade (including cross-border trade), 20% of the insurance business and over 12% of all construction. More than 2,000 Chinese-controlled entities now do business in Hong Kong, many of them "red chip" stocks, the value of which have declined steeply in the last year. China has long employed Hong Kong as a convenient financial window to the world. It serves as their banker, investment broker and go-between in what is now a multi-billion annual trade flow. In the past 17 years, some US$200 billion of direct foreign investment has flooded into China — 60% of which came from, or through, Hong Kong.

In the 12 years since it passed from British to Chinese rule, Hong Kong has remained a bastion of civil liberties unknown in mainland China, under an arrangement known as "one country, two systems." The result has been the continuation of a freewheeling press, an independent judiciary and a well-oiled bureaucracy.

Despite their wrong-headed attitudes regarding Hong Kong democracy, the leaders of the People's Republic of China realize that they have an enormous stake in Hong Kong's economic health. They want Hong Kong to keep running at full steam, but on their own terms.

But many democracy advocates and civil libertarians in Hong Kong are increasingly anxious about whether laissez-faire Hong Kong can maintain its independence from Beijing's authoritarian grip and its distinct identity as an amalgam of Western and Chinese sensibilities. In 2008, Beijing postponed promised direct elections to 2017 for the chief executive and 2020 for the full legislature. Its critics say China is wielding a heavier hand in Hong Kong's affairs.

WORLD-CLASS FINANCIAL SOPHISTICATION

In a strange twist of world economic fate, the clampdown by the European Union and the OECD on tax havens in the West created a benefit for other tax havens such as Hong Kong. An added factor: wealthy account holders from the Middle East started shifting cash towards Asia and away from Europe and the United States in the wake of the September 11, 2001 terror attacks.

Asian banks, many of them based in Hong Kong, were sitting on more than US$2 trillion of reserves in early

2009. Funds have been continuously pouring money into emerging markets and Hong Kong has been a major beneficiary if this global trend. No leading Asian banks were caught in the bank near-collapses in 2009, so no bailouts were needed.

WORLD LEADER

By almost any measure, Hong Kong is one of the world's leading financial and economic powerhouses. In total cash and assets, it is the world's third wealthiest financial center, after New York and London.

Hong Kong, described as a "barren rock" more than 150 years ago, is a great world-class city. It has no natural resources, except one of the finest deep-water ports in the world. A hardworking, adaptable and well-educated workforce of about 3.5 million, coupled with entrepreneurial flair, is the bedrock of Hong Kong's productivity and creativity. There is a Chinese phrase that describes Hong Kong well, *Zhong Si He Bing*, literally meaning "combination of east and west."

Hong Kong is the world's 9th largest banking center, 6th largest foreign exchange center, 11th largest trading economy, busiest container port and is Asia's second biggest stock market. With low taxes and a trusted legal system, international banking and business flow in and out, sure of stability and a high degree of financial privacy.

Long known as a global free market business center, as a measure of its collective wealth, Hong Kong's seven million residents in 2008 enjoyed a per-capita GDP of US$43,800. That impressive GDP figure is higher than that enjoyed by the citizens of Germany, Japan, the United Kingdom, Canada and Australia.

Hong Kong is still regarded by foreign firms as a highly advantageous location from which to do business. Almost 80% of foreign firms based in Hong Kong surveyed said they felt that it was an advantageous location for them, due to advanced telecommunications networks, a free trade environment, low taxes and effective regulation. On an industry basis, according to the survey results, the financial services sector was the most positive overall.

A major attraction for offshore business has been Hong Kong's relatively low 17.5% business tax rate. The ceiling for taxes on personal income and unincorporated businesses is 16%. Hong Kong's status as one of the world's top trading centers for stocks, bonds, commodities, metals, futures, currencies and personal and business financial operations long has meant that such transactions could be conducted there with a high degree of sophistication. That's still true and, in 2009, the city's 154 licensed banks held in excess of US$400 billion in assets.

HONG KONG AS A BUSINESS BASE

In Hong Kong, there is no specific legal recognition of an international business corporation (IBC). Hong Kong has a territorial tax system that also applies to "territoriality of profits." If profits originate in or are derived from Hong Kong, then profits are subject to local tax. Otherwise, they are tax-free, regardless of whether the company is incorporated or registered there. Interestingly, IBCs and all other foreign corporations generally may open a Hong Kong bank account without prior registration under the local business statute. This can save charges for auditing and annual report filing and removes the annoyance of having to argue with the Inland Revenue Department about the territoriality of the business.

On the other hand, one must be careful not to transact any taxable local business, because doing that without local registration is against the law. In cases where local business does occur, tax authorities generally are lenient, usually requiring local registration and payment of unpaid tax. But in some cases, IBCs have been forced to register as a listed public company at considerable expense.

Hong Kong offshore companies require by law a local resident company secretary, who usually charges about US$500 per year for filing a few documents with the Company Registry. Annual auditing by a CPA starts from about US$500 for companies with few transactions and can easily reach 10 times as much for a mid-size operational offshore trading company.

Hong Kong Corporations

There are more companies — over 500,000 — registered in Hong Kong than anywhere else in the world. (Here, they are called "private limited companies" and are identified with a "Ltd.," not an "Inc.") It is also home to the largest community of multinational firms in Asia. This is due, first, to the territory's colonial roots, which have for the past 150 years made it the natural hub in Asia for British companies and, second, to its consistent and longstanding reputation for openness, simplicity of operation and institutional familiarity.

In Hong Kong, there is no specific legal recognition of an international business company (IBC) per se, as there are in some offshore financial havens. The law recognizes only the one corporate "Ltd." form. Companies must have a minimum of one director and two shareholders. Shareholders or directors do not have to be residents of Hong Kong and they can be individual persons or corporations. Company incorporation does require a registered office in Hong Kong and a Hong Kong resident individual or Hong Kong corporation to act as the secretary. Hong Kong companies must be audited each year.

Hong Kong offshore companies require by law a local resident company secretary, who usually charges about US$500 per year for filing a few documents with the Company Registry. Annual auditing by a CPA starts from about US$500 for companies with few transactions and can easily reach ten times as much for a mid-size operational offshore trading company. See the Contacts section for our recommended local service professionals.

FINANCIAL PRIVACY

Until recently, Hong Kong's banking laws did not permit bank regulators to give information about an individual customer's affairs to foreign government authorities, except in cases involving fraud. Hong Kong never had specific banking secrecy laws like many other asset and tax haven nations such as Switzerland, Panama and Luxembourg.

As a matter of local custom, Hong Kong banks always requested a judicial warrant before disclosing records to any foreign government. Access is much easier for the local government, but there are few double taxation agreements with countries other than the People's Republic of China. At this writing, that will soon change since tax information exchange agreements are now being negotiated with several nations, under pressure from the OECD and the G-20, of which China is a member.

At the April 2009 meeting of the G-20 in London, at which a major attack was launched on all tax havens, the Organization for Economic Cooperation and Development (OECD) excluded Hong Kong and Macao, its sister Chinese SAR, from a list of jurisdictions that have "not yet substantially implemented" internationally agreed tax standards. Under pressure from China's president, the OECD instead acknowledged that the two Special Administrative Regions of China "have committed to implement the internationally agreed OECD tax information exchange standard."

Hong Kong's chief executive, Donald Tsang, sought to distinguish his city-state from the world's other tax havens. "Indeed our tax rates are low but this does not mean we harbor irregularities in our system," he said. In 2009, his government adopted legislation liberalizing the exchange of tax information with foreign governments. Hong Kong and Macao's willingness to embrace greater transparency, after years of resistance, underscored their fear of being tarred as bei sui tin tong or "tax evasion heavens," as tax havens are known in Cantonese.

There is an MLAT with the United States. Anti-money laundering laws and "know-your-customer" rules have made the opening of bank accounts for IBCs more difficult, but no more so than in other countries these days. Account applicants must declare to the bank who the "true beneficial owner" of an IBC or a trust is, with supporting documentation. Proof must be shown for all corporate directors and shareholders of the registering entity and any other entities that share in the ownership.

WHICH DIRECTION?

If you do intend to make business investments in Asia, keep in mind lessons other foreigners have already learned the hard way. Pick your Asian business partners (and business investments) carefully, avoiding the inefficient Chinese state-owned enterprises. Stick with solid basics like marketing, distribution and service. Guard technology from theft. And remember, a series of small ventures gets less government attention and red tape than big showcase projects that often produce demands for graft. Many foreign business investors have been burned by crooked bookkeeping, few shareholder controls, sudden government rule changes and systemic corruption.

Only recently, as the China's economy became more westernized, did Beijing finally begun to address the need for laws guaranteeing the right for citizens and foreigners to own and transfer private property. So, in dealing with China, remember: "Caveat emptor!"

Most importantly, keep a sharp eye not on the government's hype, but on what's really happening in China. All this uncertainty means that offshore financial activities by foreign citizens can prosper, but without immediate assurance of success. Unless the "New China" is definitely your sphere of intended business activity, you may want to look

---

elsewhere for your Asian financial haven in places such as Singapore or Malaysia.

On the Web:

Hong Kong SAR government: http://www.gov.hk/en/residents/.

Hong Kong Trade Development Council: http://www.tdc.org.hk/.

OFFICIAL

Hong Kong Government Economic and Trade Office 1520 18th Street NW, Washington, DC 20036 Tel.: (202) 331-8947; Website: www.hongkong.org/; Email: hketo@hketowashington.gov.hk.

U.S. Consul General, 26 Garden Road, Hong Kong; Tel.: + (852) 2523-9011 or Consular: + (852) 2147-5790; Fax: + (852) 2845-1598; Website: http://hongkong.usconsulate.gov/; Email: acshk@state.gov.

CHAPTER FIVE

The United Kingdom

Summary: Until recently, the United Kingdom was one of the leading tax havens of the world — but only for foreigners who chose to live there. That's all changed now. The U.K. is home to some leading private banks and offers some of the best offshore investments available. Here I explain what the U.K.'s benefits and possibilities are for you as an offshore investor. And I give you some historical background that will help to understand that when it comes to banking and finance — for the foreseeable future — "There'll always be an England."

ONCE AN EMPIRE

Despite her descent from empire status in the 20th century, England still is home to some of the leading private financial institutions in the world.

I am not referring to the several "nationalized" U.K. banks that, at this writing, verged on financial ruin, saved only by trillions of pounds sterling in government bailouts at the taxpayers' considerable expense. In 2008-2009 an estimated £1.2 trillion (US$1.7 trillion) was spent bailing out the Royal Bank of Scotland, HBOS, Lloyds, and Northern Rock, all them controlled by the U.K. government as a result (along with their billions in toxic assets).

What I refer to is that, both in personal service and privacy, there are a few remaining small British banking houses that have not been swallowed up in mergers and bailouts. In personal service, they still exceed anything comparable U.S. banks have to offer. This sort of traditional private banking was practically a British invention.

Then too, the Bank of England, the nation's official central bank, has been a relative pillar of economic stability for as far back as memory serves, although the deep British recession in 2009 and deficit spending stretched the powers of "the old lady of Threadneedle Street" (its ancient London address since 1734) to the breaking point.

For Americans, banking in England is just one step from home. Since the founding of the Jamestown colony in 1607, America has been linked inextricably to England — politically and financially. The shared experience of the colonial period, the American Revolution, two World Wars, the Cold War and more recent military conflicts, formed bonds between America and its parent nation that remain strong to this day.

For much of this history, England was the dominant partner in the relationship. English language, culture, law and institutions, mixed with New World influences, helped to produce what has become a distinctly American ethos. And while the United States clearly surpassed Mother England in both military and financial power, England remains a steadfast ally with which the United States continues to maintain a much-vaunted "special relationship."

The English Economy

Even in its decline, the United Kingdom remains one of

the world's great trading and financial powers. The "City of London," (England's equivalent of Wall Street), is the world's second leading financial center, after New York City.

With its relatively small size and limited resources, the U.K. economy still ranks among the four largest in Western Europe. During 18 years of Tory rule, ending in 1997, successive Conservative Party governments reversed the socialist trend that began in 1945, replaced nationalization with privatization and curbed the welfare state. State-owned sectors such as telephones, railways, airlines, power, water and gas were sold back to private concerns. The power of unions that held the nation captive with frequent, crippling strikes was greatly reduced.

Although the Labor Party returned to power in 1997, they did so by co-opting a large part of the Tory platform and emphasizing a need for political party change. Since their 1997 takeover, there have been some alarming signs of a Labor return to its worst doctrinaire socialist tendencies, including massive deficit spending and corporate and individual taxes so high that individuals and companies are fleeing for lower tax havens in Ireland and Switzerland. By the time you read this, the Conservative Party may well have been returned to power.

Until the 2008-2009 world recession, the U.K. economy, following world trends, registered steady expansion. Exports and manufacturing output were the primary engines of growth. Unemployment was down and inflation kept tolerably low. All of those numbers reversed direction during the recession, the worst in over 30 years. In mid-2009, Britain's government debt equaled 55% of GDP, but Standard and Poor's estimated it would approach 100% of GDP by 2013.

The U.K. is not without resources. It has large coal, natural gas and North Sea oil reserves. Primary energy production accounts for 12% of GDP, one of the highest shares of any industrial nation. Services, particularly banking and insurance, account for the largest proportion of GDP by far. Manufacturing continues to decline in importance, now employing only 20% of the work force.

Once the U.K. recovers from the recession, a major economic policy question remains, "On what terms will it participate in the financial and economic integration of the European Union?" The English view monetary union and other sovereignty issues with extreme caution. They seem unlikely to participate fully in any plan that will unduly limit their control over taxes and other important internal financial matters. The U.K. has consistently held out against EU demands that member states surrender the ultimate control over their tax policies.

The Labor government repeatedly hinted at U.K.-EU full financial integration, including monetary union. However, the British are reluctant to abandon the long-respected pound sterling in favor of the euro. Some observers claim that it will be very difficult for the British to resist monetary union, since refusal might lead to a long-term major loss of business for the City of London. But, an eventual euro acceptance may depend on a promised national referendum, the outcome of which would probably be in the negative, based on national polls.

Overall, the United Kingdom enjoyed several years of controlled economic growth before the crash. For the most part, until the recession hit, the British remained loyal to the renewed economic traditions that formerly made them one of the most prosperous nations on earth.

One of these traditions is a high level of service and privacy in their banks, financial and investment institutions.

U.K. BANKS

One major advantage of banking in the United Kingdom is the language. It is no exaggeration to say that English now has become the de facto international language of banking — and almost every other global endeavor. Language facility is certainly a big plus when banking offshore, where local customs and rules can be confusing enough without having to cultivate multilingual capabilities. But these days everyone, everywhere in offshore banking and finance speaks English.

For those seeking an offshore bank account with a reasonable degree of privacy and freedom from U.S. withholding taxes, London may be the place.

In spite of growing government intervention and demands for financial information, as a foreigner, it is easy to get lost in the crowd of foreigners who bank in London. There is an advantage to banking in a major world financial capital where you are only one among many. The IRS doesn't raise its eyebrows nearly as high when you report a London bank account, as it does for an account in the Cayman Islands or The Bahamas.

While confidence as a bank account holder comes only after the closest scrutiny, as a client you can reap the considerable benefits of one of the oldest and, in many respects, one of the most efficient private banking systems in the world. In global financial circles, a check drawn on the right English bank commands far greater respect than paper or a wire from some exotic Caribbean island haven.

U.K. Bank Privacy

A major judicial decision, in 1922, declared four situations in which an English banker could legally compromise a client's banking secrecy:

1. by an order pursuant to law;

2. when a duty to the public exists;

3. in the interests of the bank; and

4. with a client's express or implied permission. Until a few years ago, these principles continued to guide the English banking system's privacy policies.

The general rule used to be that U.K. Custom and Revenue agents had no right to seek the identities of the true owners of shares of stock. In cases where a bank account holder was discovered not to be a British resident, agents used to end their ownership inquiry as a matter of policy.

Today, anti-money laundering laws, tax reporting requirements and U.S. government pressures have produced seriously diminished banking privacy in England. The U.K. government, in partnership with the U.S., has been in the forefront pushing anti-money laundering "all crimes" laws on British overseas territories, Crown dependencies and British Commonwealth nations. "All crimes" refers to the expansion of the application of money laundering laws from their original anti-drug targets, to any type of financial offense, including foreign tax evasion.

The Bank of England supervised all British banks until 1997 when the Labor government made sweeping changes. The Bank gained power in setting short-term interest rates, not unlike the U.S. Federal Reserve Board. On the other hand, the Bank's seldom-used supervisory power over the national banking system was handed over to a new, combined agency supervising all financial institutions, the Financial Services Agency (FSA). Since then, some have criticized the FSA as a muscle-bound giant with too many duties and not enough practical sense.

With the adoption of the Financial Services Act of 1986, every individual and institution rendering investment advice came under the jurisdictional umbrella of the Securities and Investment Board, which controls a variety of regulatory organizations. As a whole, SIB was charged with keeping a close watch over banking, insurance, commodity investment, stock exchanges and financial advisory sectors. The FSA took over most of these powers in 2002.

U.K. MONEY LAUNDERING LAWS

The 2002 Proceeds of Crime Act gives the U.K. police plenary powers to seek financial information related to money laundering, terrorism and many other alleged crimes. Further, it imposes a positive duty on bankers, solicitors (lawyers) and other professionals to report any financial "suspicious activities" to the police. Thus, financial privacy has diminished to a great degree for anyone who is the subject of police interest.

As in the U.S., Britain's anti-money laundering laws place the burden of detection on individual banks, their managers and even clerks and tellers. If a bank fails to establish and carry out detection procedures, it may be fined, and uncooperative officials face a two-year prison sentence. British bankers are forced to spy on their own customers, just as their American counterparts are under the U.S. Bank Secrecy Act and the PATRIOT Act.

U.S.-Style Forfeiture

The Labor government also adopted U.S.-style civil forfeiture laws. Beyond the criminal element, everyone should have serious concern about such broad police powers. This law gives HM Customs and Revenue and the National Criminal Investigation Service (NCIS) a virtually free hand to rifle through tax files at will. The official line is that tax inspections are only targeted at individuals suspected of crimes. However, this paves the way for police "fishing expeditions" looking for evidence to build civil forfeiture cases. An important House of Lords decision held that anyone investigated for suspected U.K. tax offenses at least must first be given a warning and explanation of their rights.

As in the U.S., U.K. government forfeiture policy calls for cash confiscation from individuals suspected of criminal activity, even if insufficient evidence exists to convict him or her in a court of law. In theory, if a suspect is judged to be "living beyond his visible means," the police can ask a court to freeze his or her assets immediately pending investigation.

Future of British Banking

Beyond the larger question of which banks may fail in the United Kingdom without continued government bailouts, financial privacy is an important issue.

In 2009, the Labor government was a leader in the global attack on tax havens mounted by the high tax countries of the G-20. The major thrust of this contrived campaign was to force all countries into a system of automatic exchange of tax information among and between governments. It would be hypocritical if the U.K. failed to apply the OECD standard for the exchange of such information. Since 1975, there has been a tax information exchange treaty in place between the U.K. and the U.S., which allows great latitude in its application.

While British courts may legally compromise your financial privacy in response to a foreign judicial subpoena, in the past they did so only occasionally — and then under diplomatic pressure. But now it is most likely that the British system will consider revealing your bank records if there is substantial probable cause shown by your home government.

The U.S. Treasury and the IRS maintain large staffs at the American Embassy in London's Grosvenor Square because British officials are supposedly less than cooperative. English officials are supposed to frown on foreign government agents who demand information "fishing expeditions" in U.K. bank records. All things considered, your money may be only marginally safer in England than in the U.S. — if the Feds come knocking.

Private Banking Invented Here

Many English "private banks" offer a measure of discretion that American institutions will not (or cannot) approach. But added privacy is not the only advantage of private banking in the U.K. English bankers work hard to provide excellent service in addition to financial security.

Americans love convenience and speed, usually at the expense of civility and dignity in everyday life. The British are more willing to provide personalized and traditional services. And while it's not easy to find such care, banking with small, private British banks provides a welcome reminder of gentler, more civilized times. Of course, such service does not come cheap.

There are some trade-offs involved to obtain this kind of personal service. First, without a formal introduction from a prominent British person or a respected American bank manager, you won't be able to open an account with Child & Co. or at Rothschild's, for instance.

In truth, these small, exclusive British private banks neither need nor want a large number of customers, so applicants are screened with particular care. To gain entry, it helps to have an existing relationship with a U.S. bank that's affiliated with an international private bank network (such as the oldest privately owned bank in America, Brown Brothers, Harriman or J.P. Morgan). Making the necessary connections might take some time and effort, but the rewards are worth it.

Tax Haven for Foreign Residents Ends

Nearly two million foreigners live in England and, until 2008, many were able to escape most of the terribly high income and other taxes that U.K. citizens are made to suffer.

What shielded foreigners from taxes was the so-called "non-dom" income tax exemption, a major tax break for wealthy foreigners who made their homes in the U.K. Under U.K. tax law (until a change in 2008) anyone living in Britain but not born there and who qualified could choose what is known as "non-domiciled" tax status. In essence that meant they claimed a foreign country as their "tax domicile." The non-dom law made London a tax haven for thousands, from Russian oil tycoons to international investment bankers. In 2008, the country had 68 pre-global recession billionaires, three times as many as in 2004. Only three of its 10 richest people were born in Britain.

This allowed thousands of wealthy foreigners who lived and worked in the U.K. to pay taxes on the relatively small amount of money they actually brought into the U.K. each year ("remittances") and on what they earned in the U.K. They paid no U.K. taxes on much larger offshore earnings. Importantly, these foreigners enriched the U.K. by spending billions on real estate, goods and services and investments. According to British Treasury figures, about 112,000 people claimed non-domiciled status in 2006-07.

The British Left repeatedly attacked this non-dom tax arrangement. When Labor gained power in 1994, then-Chancellor of the Exchequer, Gordon Brown, pledged to close the "non-dom loophole," but did nothing. Finally in 2008, Brown, by then prime minister, adopted tough tax proposals on high-earning non-domiciled residents that included an annual levy of £30,000 (US$62,000) on those who had lived in Britain for at least seven years. This non-dom tax provoked a storm of criticism from business leaders who claimed it would drive well-paid foreign workers out of Britain, which appears to have happened to some extent.

The government also closed the loophole that allowed non-doms to bring assets purchased with foreign earnings into Britain without paying tax on them. Goods worth more than £1,000 kept in the U.K. for more than nine months became liable to tax. U.K. tax law still does not require payment of income taxes by non-doms on much foreign-source income, or estate taxes on foreign assets. If you should become a resident and can qualify as legally "non-domiciled" in the U.K. check the current tax status and what benefits may still be available.

In 2009, shortly after the Labor government announced an increase in the top rate of income tax to 50% for those earning more than £150,000 (US$240,000) a year, some well-known figures in the City of London were reportedly planning to abandon Britain. Leaders of private equity. Hedge funds and financial firms spoke of plans to leave in direct protest at what many consider the Labor government's use of the financial services industry as a political punching bag. Some claimed this could endanger the City's standing as a leading world financial center, and warned of a brain drain of talent away from London.

BIG TAXES ON FORMER RESIDENTS

In the past, the U.K. might have been generous tax-wise to resident foreigners, but it definitely is not kind to its own citizens who go offshore (known as "expats"), many to avoid high U.K. taxes.

Until 1998, U.K. citizens who lived and worked outside the U.K. for more than a year were exempt from taxes on their earnings, if they were physically in the U.K no longer than 62 days each year. The Labor government abolished this "foreign earnings deduction" in what it called "fairness." Now any U.K. citizen who earns any amount of U.K. source income while in the U.K. must pay taxes on their entire year's earnings, regardless of where in the world the income was earned.

The results were predictable and swift. In particular, nonresident U.K. athletes and entertainers were forced to modify their travel schedules to avoid earning even a single shilling of U.K. source income.

Case in Point: The Rolling Stones canceled the U.K. leg of their 1998 world tour as a direct result of tax law. The world's leading rock band claimed it would have lost over £12 million (US$23.7 million) if it played four concerts scheduled in 1998 in the U.K. Labor government spokespersons were quick to respond to the announcement of the cancellation as being driven by greed. But when the Stones offered to play the concerts for charity in return for a tax exemption, the government turned down the offer. The bottom line: Great Britain is a great place to live, but a bad place to be tax domiciled. Just ask Mick Jagger.

Another word of caution: at this writing, the Labor government is running massive budget deficits and is desperate for more revenue. Increased taxes on foreign nationals who are U.K. residents is always a possibility, so be sure to obtain the latest tax law information before conducting financial activities there.

AVOIDING U.K. WITHHOLDING TAXES

British bankers do not deduct withholding taxes on interest paid to nonresident accounts. That's because the law imposes no taxes on a foreigner's account. When opening an account, a foreigner must state that he is a nonresident and show proof with a passport. What are by now traditional "know-your-customer" rules in most countries and in the U.K. impose broad information requirements on all persons opening new accounts.

Estate Tax Treatment for Foreign Residents

If you decide to make a long-term home in the U.K., very careful tax plans must be made to avoid the possibility of U.K. estate taxes being imposed. British law treats a foreigner who is resident in the U.K. during 17 out of the 20 years prior to death for estate tax purposes, as having been domiciled in the U.K.

These U.K. death taxes can be avoided with the creation of a trust or IBC. When a foreigner purchases shares in a U.K. company, capital transfer taxes (estate taxes) may be payable to Customs and Revenue when the purchaser dies. But purchasing U.K. shares in the name of an IBC completely avoids U.K. death taxes.

I'll say it again: check with your tax professional before you do anything.

U.K. Investment Trusts

In the United Kingdom, what Americans call a "mutual fund" is known as a "unit trust." Another U.K. investment entity is an "investment trust," a closed-end financial fund that sells shares to individuals and invests in securities issued by other companies.

Initial purchase of British investment trust shares must be made through a brokerage house or bank. The shares are publicly traded on the London Stock Exchange, frequently at a 10% to 12% discount to net asset value. When you sell or switch between funds, you may face an even bigger discount. In the interval, you can have more money working for you than you are investing.

The accounts of investment trusts also are subject to regulation by the U.K. Financial Service Administration. That means these funds are audited periodically by major international accounting firms, but even so, check the facts carefully before you buy.

The British and the Scots pioneered the development of investment trusts and the total number trading in London far exceeds closed-end funds trading in New York. Many specialize in investments in non-British markets, a painless indirect route into European equities for Americans operating offshore.

Unlike U.S. funds, a U.K. investment trust's total investments may exceed 100% of the value of invested shares. Borrowing to buy additional shares is allowed, increasing both leverage and risk. U.K. investment trusts do not pay tax on capital gains realized within the portfolio and most dividends are distributed to the trust shareholders. Management charges are low compared to those of unit trusts (mutual funds) in Britain.

For investment trusts, smaller is not necessarily better. It is difficult to withdraw money from smaller trusts that may require written withdrawal notices or impose "no withdrawal" time periods. A good source for up-to-date information is the *Financial Times* of London (www. ft.com), the respected journal that publishes weekly net asset value figures for all funds. Check before you invest.

U.K. Unit Trusts

The unit trust is the equivalent of an open-ended mutual fund in the U.S.

British banks will hold stocks, bonds and unit trust shares and collect dividends and interest for foreign clients, with no withholding taxes levied on investment accounts. There is even a reimbursement of the 40% tax on corporate dividends when you file for relief from the U.K. Customs and Revenue. This unusual tax credit is payable to U.K. company shareholders as reimbursement for corporate taxes already paid by the company in which they own shares of stock. Customs and Revenue routinely informs U.S. authorities about U.K. tax payments made by Americans.

Communicating with Shareholders

British banks usually communicate well with unit trust shareholders on behalf of companies. In the U.K., official rolls of corporate shareholders are maintained either by the corporation, the unit trusts, or the bank that holds shares for nominee share purchasers. These institutions routinely keep shareholders up-to-date on any important developments.

Generally, U.K. investment and unit trust managers are more accessible than their American counterparts. In the U.S., heavy institutional investor involvement in the mutual funds market leaves fund managers with little time for small investors. In the U.K., firms customarily deal with masses of small investors and are significantly more forthcoming with information and help.

Borrowing from British Banks

Some U.K. banks offer major credit cards (denominated in dollars, sterling or the euro) that draw payments from a client's bank account including MasterCard Gold and the Eurocard, available in all other European countries. (See http://www.mastercard.com/uk/.)

For more information on acquiring an offshore Visa credit card, contact Lloyds Bank, Antholin House, 71 Queen Street, London EC4N 1SL, UK; Tel.: +44-171-248-9822; Website: http://www.lloydstsb.com/credit_cards/advance_card.asp. (American customers may not be accepted.)

Profits from Interest Rate Differentials

Some British and continental banks allow overseas investors simultaneously to deposit assets in a high-yield currency then borrow the equivalent value or more in a low-yield currency, such as the dollar or the euro. The lending bank requires the borrower to deposit the loan with them. The remaining difference between the yield and the fee the bank charges for the loan is credited to your account, which opens another possibility for high interest returns. Of course, the risk is yours; the interest rate is higher on the second currency precisely because there is a devaluation risk.

Gamblers who cover the exchange risk by buying currency "futures" may lose the interest advantage as well. That's because the price of futures reflects interest rate differentials and because significant transaction fees are charged for small sums. To beat the odds, you must predict currency trends more successfully than even the market can.

A leading offshore bank that offers the "invest loan" leverage to international clients is **Jyske Bank**. U.S. persons are serviced by **Jyske Global Asset Manage-**

ment (JGAM), a Jyske Bank subsidiary that is a registered Investment Adviser (RIA). Contact Jyske Bank at http://www.jbpb.com; or Tel.: +45 8989 6232 and JGAM at http://www.jgam.com or Tel.: +45 8989 5901 (Thomas Fischer). Address for both Jyske Bank and JGAM, is Vesterbrogade 9, 1780 Copenhagen V, Denmark.

Another popular U.K. bank plan (also available in other tax haven nations) enables business customers in good standing to borrow against their own deposits, effectively lowering taxable earnings and enabling a build-up in foreign exchange assets even as the loans are repaid. As a foreigner unfamiliar with local bank plans, get a second opinion from an accountant or tax planner before you proceed with any plans offered.

CHAPTER SIX

The United Kingdom's Offshore Havens

Even though the U.K. government under the Labor Party has done much to curb tax havens worldwide, the historic fact is that some of the world's major tax haven jurisdictions have been England's Crown dependencies, including the Channel Islands and the Isle of Man. Here I describe these jurisdictions, the impact the British Labor Party's policies have had on them and the possibilities for investment and tax savings still available there, including life insurance and annuities as U.S. tax-deferred investment vehicles.

Not far off the southeast coast of the United Kingdom are a group of islands that offer even more sophisticated financial services than those found in the fabled City of London.

So unique are these financial centers that tens of thousands of investors and businesspersons worldwide use the services of investment houses, accountants, lawyers, insurance brokers and trust and corporation services located there.

To the south of the U.K., in the English Channel off the coast of France, are the **Channel Islands** of **Jersey**, **Guernsey**, **Sark** and **Alderney**. To the west, between the U.K. and Ireland, in the Irish Sea, is the **Isle of Man**. While each of these semi-independent islands is associated constitutionally with the U.K. (as Crown dependencies), until recently each remained free of most of the U.K.'s tax and other financial restrictions. That has now changed, as you'll read below. In the past, that broad financial freedom, coupled with determined self-promotion, made these islands important world business centers in miniature.

Until recently, the British government tolerated this offshore finance industry, because on balance, it brought more expatriate and foreign wealth into the U.K. than was lost from the tax avoidance mechanisms the islands offered. When the Labor government took over in 1997, London's tolerance started to wane. Over the next decade, various restrictions were imposed. By 2009, the midst of the worst British recession in 30 years, Prime Minister Gordon Brown was demanding "the end of tax havens," demagogically blaming them for the economic downturn, which actually had its root causes in the City of London, Wall Street and elsewhere.

SECOND DISSOLUTION OF THE BRITISH EMPIRE

"I have not become the King's First Minister in order to preside over the liquidation of the British Empire." Winston Churchill's famous statement in November 1942, just as the tide of the Second World War was beginning to turn towards victory, pugnaciously affirmed that great British leader's loyalty to the global colonial institution he had served for most of his life.

Britain fought and sacrificed on a world scale to defeat Hitler and his allies — and won. Yet less than five years after Churchill's defiant speech, the British Empire effectively ended with India's independence in 1947 and the end of the British Mandate in Palestine in 1948.

In 2009, the Rt. Hon. Gordon Brown, Britian's prime minister, seemed bent on causing another major setting of the sun on what little remained of Britain's truncated empire. Under pressure from British labor unions and a nose-diving economy, Brown suddenly began attacking Her Majesty's overseas territories (OSTs). Most of these OSTs were, then and now, leading tax havens nurtured as such by London for the last half century (and by Brown himself in a decade as Chancellor of the Exchequer).

Under heavy fire for deficit spending and £1.2 trillion (US$1.7 trillion) in bailouts for the Royal Bank of Scotland, HBOS, Lloyds, and Northern Rock, Brown latched on to the idea that blaming offshore tax havens for alleged lost tax revenues was good politics. One British newspaper headlined: "Brown does a U-turn on tax havens."

On Brown's blacklist were most of the U.K. overseas territories, including the Cayman Islands, Bermuda, the British Virgin Islands and the Turks & Caicos islands. The Labor government also showed hostility to those Crown dependencies, Jersey, Guernsey and the Isle of Man — all major offshore financial hubs tied to the City of London.

So unique had these financial centers become that hundreds of thousands of investors and business persons worldwide use the services of their investment houses, banks, accountants, lawyers, insurance brokers, trust and corporation services.

Brown's move was a radical departure from the prime minister's historic position of protecting the pre-eminence of Britain's financial services industry, both in London and in the overseas territories. His move was a crude political attempt to counter criticism at home and pressure from high tax nations France and Germany that charged that the U.K. tax havens, like Switzerland, were obstacles to imposing a global "transparent financial system" — meaning an end to financial privacy everywhere.

OSTs Self-Clean Up

There was a special irony in Her Majesty's government suddenly attacking the British offshore tax havens that it had created with great care since the end of World War II. Over the last 15 years, the Blair/Brown Labor governments in London demanded and already had achieved substantial reforms in of all U.K. offshore financial centers, including statutory transparency, an important fact Brown never mentioned in 2009 when he suddenly turned on the offshore territories with his bogus attacks.

These offshore reforms are now written into local laws in these semi-independent islands. The reforms include:

1. much tighter financial regulatory reforms administered by supervisory agencies;

2. "all crimes" money laundering and foreign tax evasion statutes;

3. extensive banking client surveillance;

4. increased cooperation with foreign officials seeking tax and other information about persons and legal entities based on the islands;

5. a major weakening of previously strict financial privacy laws and,

6. imposition of the EU savings tax directive, which all of these offshore centers now enforce and collect.

As you read this, keep in mind the history I have recited and that these offshore financial centers (they no longer wish to be called "tax havens"), are in transition, so things change constantly. Before you act, make certain that you are informed of the current situation. For example in 2009, the U.K. Finance Act of 2008 took effect and gave HM Revenue and Customs broad new powers to start investigations quickly and request evidence such as bank account details in all U.K. offshore havens.

ASSET/TAX HAVEN STATUS IN DOUBT

As part of the worldwide campaign to curb the use of tax havens that I described in Chapter 3, the U.K. Labor government has done much to curtail the strict financial privacy formerly enjoyed by these islands. And because of their ambiguous constitutional status, the Channel Islands and the Isle of Man are particularly susceptible to pressure from London, even though they are not constitutionally fully part of the United Kingdom.

Of course, an honest taxpayer from any nation who is active financially offshore, and who knows and abides by his countries reporting rules, has little to fear from the reduced degree of privacy now available in the U.K. havens. But tax collectors often make mistakes and render wrong decisions, so you should know your privacy rights if you get involved by mistake, or otherwise.

Of concern to U.S. persons is the fact that the Isle of Man, Jersey and Guernsey each have signed Tax Information Exchange Agreements (TIEAs) with the United States. Oddly enough, it was not until the 2009 anti-tax haven furor that the Channel Islands signed TIEAs with London.

When the pressure from London began 15 years ago, the Labor government stated its willingness to precipitate a constitutional crisis by forcing these changes into law without the approval of the islands' governing bodies. London need not have worried. One by one, each island's politicians adopted the changes demanded with minimal protests.

To the average offshore investor, these changes don't mean much beyond a greatly reduced guarantee of financial privacy that was once nearly absolute. For those engaged in criminal activity, it means an increased probability of eventually being found out and prosecuted. The danger lies in a middle area of activity in which foreign tax collectors may try to conduct "fishing expeditions" looking for possible tax evasion simply because their citizens are active offshore financially. The TIEA with the United States could lend itself to just this sort of tax overreaching, although the island governments who administer the TIEA terms, deny that they allow IRS "fishing expeditions."

Because the islands are under a degree of control by the United Kingdom, they do not have the same freedom to act as would an independent tax haven nation, such as Panama. But, as discussed in Chapter 3, due to blacklisting pressure from the G-20 nations and the OECD, all U.K. offshore financial centers have agreed in principle to implement non-automatic tax information exchange upon request from a foreign government on an individual case basis after a showing of probable cause.

There are many outstanding, even unique, financial services that these islands offer that do not require as great a degree of privacy nor concern about government intervention. In considering the information that follows, keep in mind these important distinctions as you make decisions about placement of your assets and investments.

UNIQUE STATUS

These self-ruling British Crown dependencies have the power to set their own corporate and personal income tax rates. Through their constitutional association with the U.K., although they are not considered EU members, the islands enjoy some selected benefits of EU membership, such as the direct access to continental financial activities within the 27 EU countries.

When the EU savings tax directive was proposed, the Labor government agreed with the EU demand that it force all these islands' compliance. As a result, the Isle of Man, Jersey and Guernsey adopted a withholding tax rather than agree to complete tax information exchange. The islands remit 75% of the withheld taxes to the countries of origin of EU investors. The withholding tax is now 35%. The tax applies only to citizens of the EU nations and not to investment or interest earnings of U.S. persons. At this writing, the increasingly tax-hungry EU is trying to increase this tax and expand its coverage beyond taxing payment of only interest to taxing all earnings.

Financial Services of All Kinds

As a potential banking client or investor, you should know that the Channel Islands (Jersey and Guernsey) and the Isle of Man have a great deal to offer in the way of investments and useful legal entities.

The Channel Islands of Jersey and Guernsey offer full offshore banking, trust, investment, legal and accountancy services. Very few companies operate on the Channel Islands of Alderney and Sark. Jersey and Guernsey earn 50% to 60% of their GDP from the financial sector, with tourism at 30%. In recent years, there has been a marked consolidation of banks and banking staffs on the islands, a reflection of a world banking trends, plus some doubt as to the islands' future tax haven role. Nevertheless, total assets under management in each of these islands have continued to increase to record levels, a testament to their standing among global investors.

While the offshore finance industry has grown in the last two decades, the Isle of Man offshore business sector has also expended rapidly. The island possesses a smaller financial community than Jersey, with less strict start-up controls and more conservative operational attitudes.

Americans enjoy specific benefits when doing business through these islands, such as purchasing non-U.S. mutual funds that typically cannot sell shares in the United States because of SEC regulations. U.S. investors can invest in these funds by using an accommodation address on the islands, thus legally skirting the SEC rules that forbid offshore funds from sending materials or having direct contact with investors when physically located in America.

Ancient Origins, Modern Politics

For the most part, both Jersey and Guernsey base their legal systems on the ancient customs and laws of the French province of Normandy, their near neighbor at the eastern edge of the English Channel. The Channel Islands have also incorporated many common law features into their commercial code and activities, although with a French flavor. The Isle of Man's legal system follows English common law.

In theory, the British parliament lacks power to enact laws for these islands. Technically, they are not considered a part of the United Kingdom. Jersey and Guernsey were originally part of the French Duchy of Normandy, which famously conquered Great Britain at the Battle of Hastings in 1066. Her Majesty, Queen Elizabeth II, is the official head of state, not as Queen, but in her separate role and title as "Duchess of Normandy." The Channel Islands are the only part of the original Duchy of Normandy that still remains under Her Majesty's dominion.

The special status of the Channel Islands and the Isle of Man in relation to the United Kingdom means that while they are not actually part of the U.K., the U.K. is responsible for their foreign relations and military defense. In their internal domestic affairs, the islands govern themselves, although laws enacted by the legislative assemblies must be validated by "Royal Assent," until now a pro-forma procedure common to all British territories.

Taxes and Immigration

The islands' tax systems have been remarkably free of political manipulation for many years.

Successive legislatures have preserved the standard income tax rate at about 20% for more than half a century. In answer to OECD complaints about the two tax system formerly in place that exempted foreign owned business but not locals, corporate taxes have been reduced to zero for all businesses, with the exception of some banks and financial firms. There is no inheritance tax, gift tax, or other wealth taxes. The possibility of any increase in the income tax or the enactment of new taxes is remote because the islands want to continue to attract corporate business.

Nonresidents are subject to income tax only on locally earned income, but bank interest is exempt. A local trust is treated as a nonresident for tax purposes, provided none of the beneficiaries is an island resident.

Very few wealthy new immigrants are accepted annually by Jersey — only about seven a year. Jersey, the largest of the Channel Islands, is attractive for private residence or to establish an international business. There are no corporate taxes other than on some trust and banking operations. The Jersey government usually grants residence to persons who qualify to purchase property. Applicants for residence permits are required to prove a net worth of at least £20 million (US$32 million) and an income sufficient to produce an annual tax liability of at least £150,000 (US$240,000) at an income tax rate of 20% and to buy local real property worth at least £1 million (US$1.6 million). Guernsey is far less restrictive on newcomers who want to establish residence, but requires work permits for those who want to undertake any form of business. Establishing residency on the Isle of Man is simpler, mainly because it is comparatively spacious, with a land area more than seven times larger than Jersey and more than 10 times the size of Guernsey.

One of the lesser Channel Islands, Alderney, has a small number of financial service companies and places few restrictions on immigration by wealthy foreigners. Sark, an even smaller island, has few residents and tight property ownership restrictions, but no taxes.

JERSEY: TINY ISLAND, BIG BUSINESS

Jersey (pop. 92,000) has developed into one of the world's leading offshore finance jurisdictions in the last half century. It draws on its political and economic stability, product innovation and the quality of its regulation and legal system to support the successful development of its offshore finance industry. It has attracted many of the world's leading financial groups to its shores and its workers have the experience to cater to the diverse needs of global investors. Jersey has thriving banking, mutual funds and trust sectors. While it is a leading center for private clients who want a safe, well-regulated home for their assets, it has also diversified to become a preferred jurisdiction for worldwide corporate and institutional business as well.

Jersey's financial institutions are home to an astonishing amount of wealth and represent 50% of the island GDP. Per capita GDP in 2008 was US$57,000. The first merchant bank was established in 1963. By 2009, there were 49 banks representing many nations, although that number has been as high as 72. Banking assets in 2009 were £157 billion (US$250 billion). It is also home to an estimated £200 billion (US$320 billion) invested in 40 mutual funds. (It's impossible to quantify the value of trust assets exactly since they don't have to be reported to island authorities.) Individuals must be professionally qualified or have years of direct, hands-on experience to be licensed to set up and manage trust companies.

Jersey is innovative. It has developed financial alliances with the Gulf States and the United Arab Emirates. The finance industries in Jersey and the Gulf region see opportunities in jointly working to deliver financial services, including Muslim Shari'a law compliant products. There are firms in Jersey incorporating Islamic investment vehicles such as Sukuks, Islamic asset-backed investment certificates, certified as complying with the requirement of Shari'a principles.

THE ISLE OF MAN

Absent the French influence, the Isle of Man's history and legal system differ from those of the Channel Islands, but its advantages for offshore business users are similar.

Located in the Irish Sea just 30 miles from the U.K. mainland, the island is firmly established as an important international tax haven. Its independent parliament, the Tynwald, traces its origins back over a thousand years. The Tynwald is responsible for all domestic legislation, including taxation for its 76,000 citizens. The legal system is based on English common law, currency is the pound sterling and social and economic links with the U.K. are strong; the island defense and foreign affairs are conducted by the United Kingdom. The island is a member of the EU single market trade area and the value added tax (VAT) area, but is otherwise not part of the EU fiscal area.

The Isle of Man levies no capital gains tax, inheritance tax or estate duty, capital transfer tax, gifts tax or wealth tax. The income tax is the major tax at a maximum rate of 18%. The first £10,500 of personal income is taxed at 10%, rising to 18% on the balance up to £100,000 (US$160,000). Above that is tax exempt. Value added tax is the same as that in the United Kingdom (15%) at this writing, but 17% after January 1, 2010.

The Isle of Man offers an excellent communications network, modern business facilities and a highly skilled work force. The financial sector is the largest single contributor to GDP, employing more than 20% of the total work force of nearly 40,000. More than 40 licensed banks (including many international banks) offer comprehensive, discreet and confidential services that compare favorably with the banks in Switzerland or Liechtenstein. In addition to banking, high-caliber legal, accounting, insurance and other financial services are available on the island.

It is one of the few low-tax financial centers actively encouraging new residents. Work permits are easily available. Many thousands of international business corporations are registered here, attracted by the no tax policies. The government has gradually abolished almost all corporate income taxes. Currently, only financial institutions pay limited income taxes. There is no capital transfer tax, no surtax, no wealth tax, no death duty, no capital gains tax and no gift tax.

The government supports the island's financial sector, yet maintains strict control through a Financial Supervision Commission and Insurance Commission that licenses banks, investment advisors and insurance companies.

Investors are protected by strict supervision laws that govern activities by financial managers. Other laws protect investor rights, outlaw money laundering and seek to exclude undesirable elements. These tough controls assure financial integrity and have earned the Isle of Man a reputation for what *The Economist* called "stuffed shirt probity."

The Isle of Man's gross domestic product grew to almost USD$3 billion in 2008, the 24th consecutive year of growth. The ratings agency Standard & Poor's gave it its 'AAA' international credit rating, reflecting the island's strong economy and fiscal position, even in the face of the recession.

WHERE THE MONEY IS

Although banks on the Channel Islands and the Isle of Man are not directly supervised by the Bank of England, they apply its standards in practice. In some cases, reporting is even tougher than in the United Kingdom. Authorities take rule compliance very seriously. Investor and depositor protection is strong on the Isle of Man and comparable with the UK. Depositors are protected for 75% of the first £20,000 (US$40,000) per depositor, up to a maximum of £15,000 (US$30,000).

In spite of their ancient history, banking on the offshore islands is modern, sophisticated and user-friendly. Total deposits in the 47 banks in the Isle of Man banking system in 2009 exceeded £98 billion (US$156.5 billion). 35% of the island's income and 23% of the total workforce are employed in insurance, banking, and finance services. In 2007, among the 47 banks were 30 subsidiaries and branches of U.K. bank, five with Irish parent companies, three were from South Africa, and two each were from Spain, Switzerland, and the Isle of Man itself.

Fewer Brits use the islands for tax avoidance or retirement these days, because of determined anti-tax avoidance campaigns by HM Customs and Revenue tax collectors and the broader power they now have. Any financial services one can obtain in the City of London can be found here, with the Isle of Man and the Channel Islands giving a greater degree of personal service to clients.

Along with Jersey and Guernsey, the Isle of Man responded to its inclusion on the OECD's notorious "tax harmonization" blacklist by stating that it would not be pressured to the detriment of its offshore sector. In making a "commitment" to the OECD the Island would only agree to information sharing when and if its major offshore competitors do the same — the familiar demand for "a level playing field."

There are more than 200 licensed corporate and trust service providers on the Isle of Man. There are also nearly 40,000 companies and partnerships and about 40,000 trusts under the administration of these local service providers.

The investment industry has come expanded with substantial funds managed on the islands; in Jersey US$350 billion in assets were under management in 2008; in Guernsey, US$206 billion and Isle of Man US$82 billion.

There are a number of major stock brokerages, such as Jersey's **Le Masurier James & Chinn**, part of the **Banque Indosuez Group**, an international network offering the many benefits world scope can provide. Jersey also has other U.K. stock brokerages, such as **James Capel** and **Quilter Goodison** (purchased by Citibank in 2006). You can find banks like **Lazard Brothers** in Jersey, **N.M. Rothschild** in Guernsey and **Coutts & Company**, part of the National Westminster Bank Group, on both islands. There are also several independent brokerage houses that boast investment track records every bit as good as their bigger city brethren.

PRIVACY CONCERNS

All three islands at one time had similar policies against divulging any bank/client information unless compelled to do so by a local court order. If criminal acts such as illegal drug activity or money laundering were alleged, local courts would issue orders to release information only if a fraudulent transaction was shown. Prosecution by a foreign government, including the IRS, for alleged non-payment of taxes formerly was not sufficient grounds for a local court to order bank records or client information surrendered.

But all this has changed and financial privacy is far less now. Jersey now has a law that extends money-laundering offenses to cover "all crimes" including "fiscal offenses," just as the U.K. does. The law also allows confiscation of funds and assets alleged to be the product of crimes, as do U.S. forfeiture laws. While illegal drugs are the ostensible target of such laws, most observers believe the true object is to put an end to tax evasion, real or imagined.

An even greater destruction of financial privacy, at least for Americans using these islands as a financial venue, has been the signing of tax information exchange agreements (TIEAs) between the United States government and the Isle of Man, Jersey and Guernsey. This gives the IRS limited access to any records upon a showing of possible tax evasion or other alleged wrongdoing.

Problems can flow from having an offshore account in a bank that has direct ties to the United States or any other home country. You should carefully consider a Channel Islands or Isle of Man bank for your account, since most of the banks here are associated with major international financial institutions that have some U.S. or other national associations. Look for a smaller institution without direct connections to your home country. This distinction is important, especially in view of the spread of new forfeiture and "all crimes" laws in these jurisdictions and the existing TIEAs.

DEALING WITH AMERICAN INVESTORS

Access to investment and mutual funds on the Channel Islands and the Isle of Man are not limited to major corporations, insurance companies and wealthy investors. Middle class, small-share investors are also welcome, because volume makes profits. These funds typically allow free worldwide switching between funds that invest in the U.K., or in money market instruments denominated in sterling or foreign currencies.

Most unit trust (mutual fund) groups will not respond to inquiries from a United States address. That is because they are not registered with the SEC and won't sell directly to U.S. persons. A large number of portfolio managers do accept money from U.S. investors because they are not listed on the London Stock Exchange and don't require SEC registration. The way to avoid legally these restrictions is to invest through your own offshore-based trust, private foundation or international business corporation. But as I explained in Chapter 2, the U.S. Internal Revenue Service has forced foreign banks and financial institutions into the unwelcome role of IRS informants, a.k.a. "qualified intermediaries" (QI). Rules proposed at this writing will require offshore banks to determine who the beneficial owners of all legal entities are and to report that fact to the IRS. This requirement may hinder the ability to open an offshore account if the entity is U.S. controlled. If this concerns you, check with legal or accounting professionals on this issue.

British Expats Do Well

The Channel Islands are the preferred place for offshore money market funds sold to the British expatriate market. Because of a legal quirk, this once was the only place where a single corporate entity could offer money market funds in a variety of currencies, making it easier to offer free switching between currencies to customers investing only modest sums. A few other offshore havens now offer streamlined transactions, but the Channel Islands remain the center for multi-currency money market and bond funds.

The range of business being conducted on the Channel Islands and the Isle of Man is highly diverse. Mutual funds offer shares that literally span the globe. Major corporate employee pension and benefits programs are headquartered in the islands. This is especially true on Jersey, where one company, Mourant & Co., has carved a niche for itself in this area of business finance. Other corporate business involves debt, securitization plans, financial restructuring, stock and bond issues, captive insurance programs and leasing. Much of this activity is associated with the many trusts and corporations registered here under the laws of the three islands.

Equally diverse is the international range of private clients doing business in the islands, attracted by a long history of political stability, absence of exchange controls, reasonable privacy and good management.

LIFE INSURANCE AND ANNUITIES

The Isle of Man is known worldwide for its excellent insurance and annuity products. Many of these are popular with Americans, since under U.S. tax law, life insurance allows four key benefits:

1. Tax-free build-up of cash value, including dividends, interest and capital gains;

2. Tax-free borrowing against cash value;

3. Tax-free receipt of the death benefit; and

4. Freedom from estate and generation-skipping taxes. These benefits are available in any life insurance policy or annuity designed to comply with U.S. tax laws. The island also offers captive insurance plans and management of captives.

For a more detailed explanation of the many benefits of offshore life insurance and annuities, see the description I gave earlier in Chapter 2, under "Offshore Variable Annuities" and "Offshore Life Insurance."

SUMMARY

The Channel Islands and the Isle of Man are well established and regulated tax havens. In the last decade, each island has modernized financial services regulatory laws and each has agreed to tax information exchange procedures using the OECE standards I explained earlier in Chapter 3.

The islands operate under anti-tax avoidance pressure from the U.K. tax authorities, mainly directed at U.K. citizens doing business in the islands.

Nevertheless, these havens offer a long tradition and much experience in the creation and management of asset protection trusts, international business corporations and with offshore finance, banking and insurance. They offer some of the best professional investment experts and fund managers anywhere.

My advice is to be careful. Choose carefully and you can find some excellent offshore legal products, especially in mutual funds, annuities and life insurance as investment and tax deferral vehicles.

CHAPTER SEVEN

Special Havens in Europe

Europe has no monopoly on nations that qualify as tax or asset havens, but the development of civilization made Europe a financial center dating back to the Middle Ages. In Chapter 4, I described two European nations, Switzerland and Liechtenstein, as among the best financial havens in the world.

Here I describe some of the lesser-known European havens. Some are best for tax-free residency, others for banking, investment or international business corporations. In considering European venues for your cash and investments, keep in mind the continuing pressure from high tax countries within the European Union to end all financial privacy and to impose uniform high income and corporate taxes on all of its member states, a trend these havens resist.

Austrian Republic

Austria is not a haven in the sense of low taxes, but it is a "banking haven." That's because this nation has one of the strongest financial privacy laws in the world. That guarantee has constitutional protection that can be changed only by a national referendum of all voters. For a very few select of the foreign wealthy, Austria also offers low-tax residency for those who can qualify.

The Austrian Republic has long been a bastion of banking privacy strategically located on the eastern European border. From the end of World War II in 1945 to the collapse of Russian Communism in 1992 with the Soviet Union and the United States locked in armed confrontation, this convenient banking haven served as a willing Cold War financial and political go-between for both West and East.

Secrecy: It's the Law

When Austrian national banking laws were officially re-codified in 1979, the well-established tradition of bank secrecy was already two centuries old. During that time, Austrian bank secrecy and privacy produced two major types of so-called "anonymous accounts." These accounts usually required no account holder identification, no mailing address and no personal references. Just deposit funds and use the account as you pleased, all done anonymously. Both the Sparbuch bank account and the Wertpapierbuch securities account have been abolished, victims of the European Union's fixation with destroying financial privacy wherever possible.

Notwithstanding the demands of the EU, current Austrian bank secrecy laws forbid banks to "disclose secrets which have been entrusted to them solely due to business relationships with customers." The prohibition is waived only in criminal court proceedings involving fiscal crimes, with the exception of petty offenses. The prohibition does not apply "if the customer expressly and in writing consents to the disclosure of the secret."

As an additional layer of protection, Austrian law raises this guarantee of banking and financial privacy to a constitutional level, a special statute that can only be changed by a majority vote in a national referendum, a highly unlikely event. All major political parties support financial privacy as an established national policy of long standing.

As a member EU country, until 2009 Austria consistently and strongly opposed European Union demands for compulsory withholding taxes and financial information sharing. In 2009, in a change of policy under pressure from the G-20 countries and the EU, Austria agreed to apply Article 26 of the "OECD Model Tax Convention." This article recognizes "tax evasion" as a valid basis for foreign tax agency inquiries concerning their citizens with accounts in an offshore center. Under this OECD procedure, foreign tax authorities wishing to take advantage of tax information exchange agreements need to supply evidence of their suspicions (e.g., names, facts, alleged tax crimes) to the requested government. If there is sufficient probable cause to believe tax evasion has occurred, the requested government must supply the information.

Austria was one of three EU nations exempted from an EU-agreed tax information sharing plan (joining with Belgium and Luxembourg). All three nations, along with non-EU member Switzerland, declined to share tax information, but each collects the 35% EU withholding tax on interest paid to nationals of other EU member states. Foreign nationals of non-EU nations, including U.S. persons, are not subject to this EU withholding tax.

STOCKS AND BONDS

Until the world recession in 2008-09, the Austrian stock market had one of the world's best performance records in recent years. It benefited in part from the Eastern European expansion boom that began in the 1990s after the East-West Iron Curtain disintegrated and its formerly Communist-dominated Eastern European neighbors turned to free market polices.

Nonresidents are not subject to restrictions on securities purchased in Austria and they can be transferred abroad without restrictions or reporting. Nonresidents can purchase an unlimited amount of bonds and/or stocks on the condition that the money used for purchase is in either foreign currency or euros. When securities are sold, the cash proceeds can be freely converted and exported without restrictions.

TAXES

Austrian tax authorities found a way to profit from their attractive banking haven status — the government levies a 25% tax on the total bank interest earned. Foreigners can avoid the 25% tax on bond interest because no tax is withheld if a declared nonresident is the bank account holder. Interest paid on investments held in non-bearer form in Austrian banks, such as certificates of deposit, is also exempt from the withholding tax. Interest on convertible bonds, however, is subject to a withholding tax of 20% at the payment source.

Unfortunately, an American citizen bondholder is subject to capital gains tax in the U.S. on the full capital gain, despite the Austrian tax. A double taxation treaty between the U.S. and Austria eases this hardship; if you file a request with the IRS, the Austrian tax will be partly repaid, diminishing the net tax burden to 10%. The remaining 10% tax can offset part of the U.S. capital gains tax ordinarily imposed. The double taxation agreement does not apply to Austrian interest and dividends, which remain fully taxable in the U.S.

The Austrian government's decision to reduce the corporate tax rate from 34% to 25% in 2005 led to a 30% increase in new investment projects. In addition to cutting corporate taxes to one of the lowest levels in the EU, the reforms also reduced the tax burden on multinational firms using Austria as regional headquarters. Austria also offers significant tax concessions to holding companies, foundations and certain other investment incentives, all successfully designed to attract foreign capital.

Austria ranks among the 10 richest countries in the world on a per capita basis. Its capital gold reserves rank third in the western world. Its political and economic stability is reflected in its currency's performance prior to the adoption of the euro. The Austrian schilling appreciated against the U.S. dollar by 150% in its last 20 years before being replaced with the Euro.

LIVE IN AUSTRIA INCOME TAX-FREE

It is not widely known, but a wealthy foreigner who

can qualify to become a resident of Austria also may qualify for a unique tax break — 100% of annual income completely free of taxes! This preferential tax treatment, called a Zuzugsbegünstigung, is ready and waiting at the obliging Ministry of Finance.

A foreigner who is a new Austrian resident can qualify if the person meets all the following requirements:

- had no residence in Austria during 10 years prior to application

- doesn't engage in any business activity within Austria

- can prove sufficient income from outside sources

- agrees to spend a minimum of US$70,000 in Austria each year

- has a place to live and intends to stay in Austria for at least six months (183 days) each year

When all those conditions are met, a foreigner may be able to live tax-free in Austria. All income from foreign pension or retirement funds, dividends and interest from foreign investments and securities or any offshore businesses outside Austria are tax exempt.

In most cases, officials grant a tax break of at least 75% of potential tax liability — but a good local lawyer may be able to negotiate a 100% reduction. If you have foreign income taxable in your home country and there is no double taxation agreement between Austria and your country, the Ministry of Finance may grant you a zero tax base, or a special circumstances ruling, but only after you establish your residence in Austria.

Is Austrian residence status for sale to the very rich? To

be frank, yes. If you are a reputable and wealthy foreigner, there will be few obstacles to becoming a resident. Residency gives you the best of both worlds — life in an extremely desirable location, but without the high taxes Austrian citizens must pay.

Once in residence, you could apply for citizenship, but that would defeat the purpose. As an Austrian citizen, you'd be liable for full taxation. The only additional advantages would be having an Austrian passport and the right to purchase as much real property as you wish, which is otherwise very difficult for a foreigner merely residing in Austria.

On the Other Hand

Consider the foreigner who uses Austria as his second residence, but not as the "center of his vital interests" (a phrase from Austrian tax law). He goes skiing for three or four weeks each year in Austria. His legal domicile — the place where he lives most of the time and to which he eventually intends to return — is in another country. In his case, any Austrian source income is taxable in Austria, but all income not earned in Austria is taxable in the country where he lives. His exact tax status and obligations will be determined under the terms of a double taxation treaty that may exist between Austria and his country of domicile.

A Secure Future for Privacy

Even with its agreement to share tax information using the OECD standard, Austria's financial and banking privacy laws provide great security. As a result, it's wise to keep Austria near the top of your potential banking list, especially if your major area of business interest is in

Eastern Europe and Russia.

CONTACTS

Austrian Ministry of Finance, Hintere Zollamtsstrasse 2b, 1030 Vienna, Austria; Tel.: +43-1-5143-33; Website: http://english.bmf.gv.at/Ministry/_start.htm.

U.S. Embassy, Boltzmanngasse 16, 1091 Vienna, Austria; Tel.: + (43) 1-313-39 or after hours: + (43) 1-319-5523; Website: http://vienna.usembassy.gov/en/index.html; Email: embassy@usembassy.at.

Embassy of Austria, 3524 International Court, N.W., Washington, D.C. 20008; Tel.: (202) 895-6700; Website: http://www.austria.org/; Email: austroinfo@austria.org.

GRAND DUCHY OF LUXEMBOURG

Luxembourg is primarily a business and banking haven rather than a personal tax haven. It is also a haven for international holding companies and investment funds. Its strong financial privacy laws, which have a long history, were weakened somewhat in 2009 when it announced that it would adopt the OECD standard for tax information sharing.

RIGHT IN THE MIDDLE

Little Luxembourg (51 miles long by 34 miles wide) is a hereditary Grand Duchy. The House of Orange-Nassau and its branches have ruled here since 1815. The reign of the present ruler, Grand Duke Henri, began in 2000 and the Heir Apparent is Prince Guillaume, his son. Locals commonly speak French, German, English and their own peculiar version of German called Letzebürgesch. It's a dialect said to be incomprehensible even to those who have spoken "normal" German since birth.

Luxembourg City is a fortress, with a deep river valley surrounding the old city on three sides. From a castle built on its rocky promontory in 963, the strategic settlement grew, passed between Burgundian, French, Spanish, Austrian and Prussian hands. Each conqueror strengthened the natural site, until at one point the defenses included three fortified rings, 24 forts, a 14-mile network of underground tunnels and more than 400,000 square feet of chambers carved into the sandstone for soldiers, animals and supplies. Even though a peace treaty in 1867 decreed that this "Gibraltar of the North" be destroyed, you can still see plenty of intriguing remains: the old town and the fortress walls constitute a UN World Heritage site.

The pie-shaped country, with a population of 430,000, shares borders with Germany to the east, Belgium to the west and France to the south. A charter member of the EU, Luxembourg is also a part of the Benelux group along with Belgium and the Netherlands. Since 1922, Luxembourg has had a fully integrated monetary and economic union with its larger neighbor, Belgium. The local currency was the Belgium-Luxembourg franc, now replaced by the euro. Today, Luxembourg City is the home of the European Court of Justice, the secretariat of the European Parliament, the European Investment Bank and European Court of Auditors.

A MOUNTAINOUS OFFSHORE HAVEN

Although the nation's international banking activity dates back to the late 19th century, Luxembourg did not hit its stride as an offshore haven until the 1980s. It was then that the Eurobond markets located there really put Luxembourg on the global financial map. Luxembourg is comfortably in the world's top ten financial centers — 2009 government figures put it in 10th position — with a great accumulation of cash and a commanding presence in key areas such as holding companies, private banking, investment funds and reinsurance.

This growth process developed from forces over which Luxembourg had no control. Rather, growth came from foreign nationals seeking better profits and escape from their own governments' anti-free market policies, including:

- expanded foreign investment in European Common Market nations during the mid-1960s

- the U.S. imposition of an interest equalization tax in the 1980s that drove American corporations to borrow funds abroad rather than at home

- German domestic capital flow restrictions and mandatory lending ratios

- the 35% Swiss withholding tax on bank account and other interest

- currency exchange controls in France

- stiff bank account reporting rules in nearby Holland

To avoid these restrictive circumstances, astute western Europeans and Americans began searching for a safe place to invest their money. They also needed a convenient place to conduct business with maximum freedom and lower taxes. Right there in the middle of Europe, Luxembourg and its banks beckoned.

But keep in mind that Luxembourg is not a tax haven — it's an investment and banking center. The effective corporate tax rate is over 30%. Personal income taxes can range up to 38%. Holding companies, which have enjoyed a special status since 1929, escape most taxes. Microsoft, FedEx, AOL, iTunes and Skype are among companies with global or European headquarters in Luxembourg.

Pressure from All Sides

Luxembourg's conservative nature is revealed in a still popular 19th century local song lyric, *"Wir welle bleiwen wat wir sin."* This simply means, "We want to remain as we are" — a sentiment that easily could be the official national motto. This statement had special meaning while the European Union (especially neighboring Germany), pressured this tiny grand duchy for reforms of their banking and financial privacy laws for many years.

Unfamiliar to many Americans, Luxembourg is an established international financial and banking center. If you want a no-nonsense EU base for business operations and excellent private banking services, this is the place. Although this tiny country lacks the lure of the Swiss ski slopes or the white sands at Grand Cayman, it more than makes up for its lack of tourist attractions by offering tax-free operations and banking privacy.

BUSINESS BANKING A NATIONAL PASSION

About 60% of all Luxembourg bank activity is now denominated in euros. Another one-third is in U.S. dollars. Roughly 24,000 people, 11% of the workforce, are employed directly or indirectly in the Grand Duchy's nearly 160 banks and financial groups and nearly 30% of the GDP flows from financial business. German banks, in particular, operate here to escape domestic withholding taxes on interest and dividend loan limitations on corporate customers and they account for over 50% of all banking business. They also use the nation to deal in gold, as Luxembourg imposes no VAT. Luxembourg's authorities closely watch bank solvency and reserves. Bank accounts are insured against loss in an amount equivalent to about US$15,000 each.

Until 2009, the government did not believe it had a duty to ensure that a bank's foreign clients paid home country taxes. Tax evasion is not a crime here, although the government maintains tax treaties with many nations, including the U.S. and U.K. After the G-20 London meeting in 2009, Luxembourg joined other offshore financial centers in agreeing to apply the OECD standard allowing exchange of tax information in specific cases of alleged tax evasion by foreigners. The government also began negotiating a round of tax information exchange treaties with other nations, including France and Germany, two major past antagonists on the issue of bank secrecy. In mid-2009, it concluded a revised TIEA with the U.S. allowing information exchange in cases of alleged tax evasion.

Bank assets, liabilities and other operations must be reported to the Banking Commission. This enables the commission to maintain strict controls on the solidity and honesty of Luxembourg banks. Until the OECD 2009 agreement, the government provided information only when a crime was related to a bank account itself and the alleged offense was also a crime under local law.

World Connections

Luxembourg's financial picture depends on more than the solvency of its banks. The nation is a major transaction center and clearinghouse (Clearstream) for international currency and bond markets. This links its financial health to the state of the entire international banking system. The German and U.S. economies are especially important. Most banking clients in Luxembourg are multinational corporations, not individuals and their collective fortunes directly affect Luxembourg's financial stability.

The financial turmoil and the worst global recession in 60 years posed daunting challenges to Luxembourg's small open economy. The financial sector, hosting a large number of foreign-owned subsidiary banks, Europe's largest investment fund industry and second largest money market industry, was fully exposed to the turmoil. Besides financial service exports, the contraction in European demand also hurt the economy's traditional export sectors. As a result, Luxembourg faced its most severe recession since the steel crisis in the mid-1970s, but took credible steps to support and stimulate the economy and the financial sector.

Because of this tie to the prosperity of others, those seeking shockproof banking might do better with an account in Switzerland. This is particularly true if you possess sufficiently large deposit sums to command the personal attention of Swiss bankers. For those with less cash, but who still desire privacy every bit as good, as or better than the Switzerland, by all means, try Luxembourg.

VIRTUAL TAX FREEDOM FOR HOLDING COMPANIES

Since 1929, Luxembourg has been a tax-free haven for holding companies and investment funds. Both are tax exempt except for a relatively small fee at initial registration (1% of subscribed capital) and an annual taxe d'abonnement, computed at about 0.2% of actual share value for holding companies and 0.06% for investment funds.

Holding companies typically own foreign company shares or bonds. They can manage these interests, but cannot engage in local business beyond operational maintenance and staffing. Holding companies are exempt from taxes on dividends, interest and royalties, bond interest, profits from securities sales, or purchases and capital gains taxes. Luxembourg is home to approximately 2,000 holding companies (which include many major multinational holding and finance corporations) and the number is steadily growing. Holding companies are exempt from taxes on dividends, interest, royalties, profits from securities sales and purchase and capital gains taxes. The Grand Duchy's stock exchange is used extensively for issues of EU bonds, demonstrating Luxembourg's international importance. Numerous major banks operate there to handle this business. Luxembourg has also passed a series of new laws aimed at attracting mutual funds investment companies.

SICAV Investing

Luxembourg has its own mutual funds, known as Sociétés d'Investissement Collective à Capital Variable, or SICAVs. Each Luxembourg bank encourages clients to enroll in its SICAV, unless the investor has an unusually larger sum to invest. Banks earn fees of between 1.5% to 3% annually for managing client mutual fund investments, plus commissions on sales of bonds or stocks in the fund. The Luxembourg government also gets its slice from fees and taxes on the funds. There are more than 8,000 funds collectively with assets of more than one trillion euros.

Luxembourg is the center of ready-made offshore private banking. Your banker alternates as broker and mutual fund salesperson. He or she can help you select one or more SICAV funds to meet your investment objectives, then complete all the necessary paperwork. SICAVs accept relatively modest payments, starting at a US$25,000 minimum at most local banks.

OFFICIAL

Government of Luxembourg, Website: http://www. gouvernement.lu/.

Commission de Surveillance du Secteur Financier, L-2991 Luxembourg, 63 Avenue de la Liberté, Luxembourg; Tel.: +352-4292-9201; Website: http://www.cssf. lu/index.php.

Embassy of the Grand-Duchy of Luxembourg, 2200 Massachusetts Avenue, N.W., Washington, D.C. 20008; Tel.: (202) 265-4171; Fax: (202) 328-8270; Email Website: http://washington.mae.lu/en/Tip-A-Friend/(node_ id)/19042; Website: http://washington.mae.lu/en.

U.S. Embassy Luxembourg, Consular Section. 22 Boulevard Emmanuel Servais, L-2535 Luxembourg; Tel.: + (352) 46-0123 ext. 2213; Fax: + (352) 46-1939; Email: LuxembourgConsular@state.gov; Website: http://luxembourg.usembassy.gov/.

REPUBLIC OF ANDORRA

Andorra, nestled between Spain and France high up in the Pyrenees, is a residential tax haven for very wealthy foreigners who enjoy winter sports. It's difficult to become a citizen, but establishing residency is fairly easy. There are no income taxes or other taxes and banking privacy is very strict.

HIGH AND JAGGED

Andorra is a tiny, mountainous country with no taxes, no army and no poverty. Until 2010 when its only airport is expected to open, it has only been accessible from France or Spain by motor vehicles over mountainous roads in long journeys, depending on weather conditions.

The country's standard of living is high, the cost of living relatively low and the scenery delightful. According to legend, Charlemagne, Emperor of the Holy Roman Empire, gave Andorra its name. Gazing over the mountain region newly wrested from the Moors of Spain, he is said to have exclaimed, *"Wild valley of hell, I name you Endor!"* (The valley of Endor, at the foot of Mount Thabor in the Holy Land, was the campsite of the Israelites during the war against the Canaanites.)

With political and economic stability, no strikes, virtually no unemployment and the lowest crime rate in Europe, strict banking secrecy, remote Andorra could be your haven from the modern world's problems.

BARGAIN ISOLATION

Until the end of World War II, Andorra was a time capsule of traditional European mountain life. Napoleon, declining to invade the diminutive joint principality, said, "Andorra is too amazing. Let it remain as a museum piece." In the last three decades, the country has been transformed from a traditional pastoral and farming economy to one of commerce and year-round tourism. The population is increasing from 5,500 in 1945 — the same as in the 1880s — to around 84,000 today. Only about 14,000 are citizens, the rest foreigners. Most of the others have moved there for work opportunities or to escape onerous taxes in their home countries.

As Andorra's economy expands, its banking system has grown to meet the demand. Andorran banks are considered among the safest in the world. Some institutions do have outside shareholders, but the banks remain firmly Andorran in attitude.

Geography, Government

Andorra consists of 185 square miles, about one-fifth the size of the smallest American state, Rhode Island. Andorra's rugged terrain consists of gorges and narrow valleys surrounded by mountain peaks that rise higher than 9,500 feet above sea level. It is an independent nation-state and is governed by 28 elected members of the General Council. Until 1993, the President of France and the Bishop of Seo d'Urgel (Spain), as co-princes, were responsible for Andorra's foreign affairs and judicial system. These "co-princes" could veto decisions by the General Council. They controlled the judiciary and police, but did not intrude into Andorra's affairs, except in 1933, when French gendarmes were sent in to maintain order after the judiciary dissolved the General Council. For the next 60 years, demands for independence were a repeated political refrain.

In 1993, Andorrans voted to sever their feudal links with France and Spain. The country subsequently gained a seat in the United Nations as the third-smallest member-state. While citizenship is a daunting prospect — it can only be attained by marrying an Andorran and by staying in the principality for at least 25 years — the number of resident foreigners in Andorra demonstrates just how attractive the country is as a tax haven. Seventy percent of the people who live in Andorra are resident foreigners and these immigrants are demanding more political rights.

Andorra established formal links with the European Union in 1991. After two years of tough negotiations, Andorra signed its first ever international treaty by joining the EU customs union, the first non-member country to do so. Andorra now applies the common EU external tariff and trade policy. This allows free transit of its goods (except for farm products) within the EU market.

No Income Taxes, Duty Free

Andorra's simple, pastoral life of a half century ago is gone. Instead, it became the shopping mall of the Pyrenees because of its duty-free tax status. Although the duty-free status ended in 1993, the country still is exempt from the EU's value-added taxes, making it a sort of "Mall of Europe." An estimated 10 million visitors a year — mostly day-trippers — invade Andorra. They pour over the border and head for shops along the central valley road. On weekends, traffic jams are a prelude to the jostling, shopping, crowd-packed streets of Andorra la Vella, the capital.

Andorra's citizens and residents pay no taxes on personal income, capital gains, capital transfers, inheritance, or profits. There is no sales tax or VAT. Nominal local property taxes pay for municipal services — average annual rental property tax varies from around US$120 for an apartment to US$240 for a house of any size.

Little known outside of the skiing and financial communities, this small European tax haven saw some startling, double-digit rises in real property values in recent years, prior to the 2008-09 global recession. Buyers come from an active local market, second homebuyers looking for ski condos and international buyers who want to establish residence in a leading tax haven. A 2–3 bedroom condo here can sell for US$500,000, half the cost of similar digs in Monaco.

In 2009, for the first time in seven centuries, the government of Andorra opened up investment in resorts and other businesses to foreign investors. Along with lifting this curb on foreign investment, the government paid the usual lip service of now wanting to be seen as an "investment haven" and not a "tax haven."

RESIDENT OR "PERPETUAL TRAVELER"

A second residence in Andorra won't alter your domicile of origin for the purposes of home nation inheritance or estate taxes.

But if you're granted a passive residence in Andorra, you have the right to protection under the law, certain benefits from the health and social security systems, the right to a driver's license and the right to own and register resident-plate vehicles. Resident status does not confer the right to vote, nor does it allow local commercial activity, such as owning or running a business.

Anyone in Andorra who is not a resident is considered a tourist — but there's no legal limit on the period of stay. Tourists can even rent or purchase a property for personal use for as long as they wish. So it's easy to live in Andorra, "perpetual traveler" style, without an official residence permit.

If you're looking for residence status, there are two categories of permits — both of which are difficult to obtain — those that give the holder the right to work in Andorra and those that don't allow employment. Residence permits are issued for renewable four-year periods.

The annual quota for non-work permits in recent years has ranged from 200 to 500. The earlier you apply, the better your chance of success. Applicants must also show availability of sufficient economic means to permit residence in Andorra without having to work throughout the period of passive residence.

BANK SECRECY

Andorra has no exchange controls and bank secrecy is strict. The country allows numbered and coded accounts. Foreigners and foreign legal entities may open and operate bank accounts without the kind of restrictions now imposed even in Switzerland, provided the foreign party can justify the need for an Andorran bank account — establishing residence or buying a condominium in Andorra is sufficient reason.

Until 2009, bank secrecy laws precluded giving bank account information to foreign governments. Since then the Andorran government has applied the OECD standard for tax information exchange, providing information in individual cases where evidence of foreign tax evasion is alleged by a government with which Andorra has a tax treaty. Treaties were concluded with France in 2009 and were negotiated with Spain, Portugal and other nations.

Taking advantage of tax freedom and bank secrecy, Andorra is home to thousands of numbered bank accounts — most of which belong to prudent Spaniards. Annually, an estimated 10% of the billions of euros that escape Spanish regulation and taxes are thought to be funneled through Andorran accounts. Perhaps 1,500 tax exiles from the U.K. have residences here.

All seven local banks have a worldwide network of foreign correspondents. With no exchange controls, accounts can be held in up to twenty foreign currencies and traded in any quantity at the rate quoted in Zurich. Exchange rates for clients are some of the best in Europe.

A Local View: A longtime friend of mine who has lived in Andorra for many years tells me that "...the banks now require anyone opening an account here to appear in person. Lawyers can no longer open accounts for them. U.S. persons who reside here are not allowed to have any American securities in their local bank accounts. Since the adoption of strict American anti-money laundering and anti-terrorism laws, the banks here unanimously agreed to forbid any investments in, or holding of, U.S. securities. The banks are frank to say they don't want to waste excessive time and money in reporting to the IRS and the SEC. When the new U.S. laws took effect a few years ago the banks made Americans here sell all their U.S. investments or close their accounts." He also says, "Ownership of non-U.S. securities is freely allowed. Andorra does not allow foreign-owned corporations here, although there is a proposed law that might allow them in the future. Some locals see the advantages of allowing such offshore corporations, as in Liechtenstein or Switzerland, for example, but there is fierce resistance from others who fear they cannot compete if foreign financial firms set up shop here. Some of the local

THE ECONOMY

There are no accurate estimates of Andorra's gross national product (smart smugglers don't keep records), but tourism is the key factor. The country has developed summer and winter tourist resorts, with more than 250 restaurants and 1,000 shops. There are about 300 hotels, ranging from elegant to simple. Some have double rooms available for as low as US$50 per night. Tourism employs a growing portion of the labor force.

During the winter, skiers flock to Andorra's slopes. High peaks separate six deep valleys and though the Pyrenees lack the famous Alpine altitudes, they are breathtakingly steep and far less expensive to visit. The Andorran government encourages upscale tourism at its popular ski resorts, attractive because of comparatively low prices. Ski areas are state of the art and bountiful snowfall guarantees weekend visitors from throughout Europe. Hikers use the lifts in the summer.

Andorra's thriving tourist industry has hastened the country's economic transformation. Former shepherds — now wealthy investors — import cheap Spanish and Portuguese labor to support the building boom, which has transformed Andorra's central valley into a string of shops and condominiums. Don't get the idea, however, that all the land is developed. Only 8% of Andorra's land is both suitable and zoned for development. One can still find small villages in which to live. Many house less than 100 inhabitants and offer absolute peace and quiet.

Andorra's isolation will decrease further with the construction of its lone airport located in Seu d'Urgell, with first flights anticipated in 2010 or 2011. With a runway of 4,500 feet, it won't be long enough for some medium range aircraft. Most commercial airplanes will be smaller models with 60-80 seats. There will also be plenty of room for the private jets favored by the wealthy who now consider Andorra a viable and more accessible tax haven.

Today, locals say that the only poor Andorran is one who hasn't come down from the hills. For those who have made it, a Porsche, Ferrari, or BMW is the vehicle of choice. There are more cars than people in Andorra by far.

CONTACTS

Embassy of Principality of Andorra, 2 United Nations Plaza, 25th Floor, New York, NY 10017; Tel.: (212) 750-8064; Fax : (212) 750-6630; Email: andorra@un.int; Website: http://www.andorra.be/en/7.1.htm.

Embassy of Andorra, 51 bis Rue de Boulainvilliers, 75016 Paris, France; Tel.: 01 40 06 03 30; Website: http://www.amb-andorre.fr/; Email: ambaixada@andorra.ad; Tourism: http://www.yourandorra.com/.

Andorra Government: Website: www.andorra.ad/.

Andorra Property News: http://www.andorraproperty.info/.

Campione d'Italia —
Back Door to Switzerland

This little bit of northern Italy is completely surrounded by Switzerland and it's one of the least known residential tax havens in the world. But you have to buy a condo or home to be a resident. Foreigners who can afford to live here pay no taxes and foreign-owned businesses are also tax-free. It may be Italy, but everything here is Swiss — license plates, currency, postage and banking.

Switzerland may be the world's most famous offshore financial haven country, but there's another residential tax haven that's not only more exotic, but is itself an enclave geographically surrounded by Switzerland. And it's under Italian jurisdiction!

Commune di Campione, as the Italians call it, on the shores of beautiful Lake Lugano, is distinguished by its very uniqueness; a little plot of Italian soil, completely surrounded by Swiss territory. There are no border controls and complete freedom of travel. Home to about 3,000 people (including about a thousand foreigners), in the southern Swiss canton of Ticino, it is about 16 miles north of the Italian border and five miles by road from Lugano, Switzerland — a beautiful scenic drive around the lake, which I've personally enjoyed.

With no Campione border controls, there is complete freedom of transit. The village uses Swiss banks, currency, postal service, and telephone system. Even automobile license plates are Swiss. Strangely enough, because of ancient history and treaties, the enclave legally is considered part of the territory of Italy.

Campione is also a very pleasant place to live, located

in the heart of one of the best Swiss and nearby Italian tourist areas. The region boasts lakes, winter sports, and the cultural activities of Milan, Italy, are only one hour away by auto.

All that's needed to become an official resident is to rent or buy property here, although formal registration is required. However, living here is very expensive; you might have to pay US$750,000 for a very small townhouse. Foreigners may buy real estate without restrictions, unlike in Switzerland. But real estate prices are well above those in surrounding Ticino. Condominiums range from US$5,500 to $6,500 per square meter, and broker fees add a 3% commission. The real estate market is very small and prices are extremely high. The same apartment across the lake in Switzerland can easily cost half of what it costs in Campione.

This small market is served by a few local real estate agents, some of whom operate rather unprofessionally and some even without a license. A foreign buyer has to be very careful. If you are interested in establishing your residence in Campione and purchasing real estate there, you should be represented by a competent lawyer from the beginning. (See below for reliable professional contacts in the area we recommend.)

CORPORATIONS

Corporations registered in Campione have some advantages over Swiss companies. They use Swiss banking facilities and have a mailing address that appears to be Swiss, while escaping Switzerland's income and withholding taxes. Corporations are governed by Italian corporate law and can be formed with a minimum capitalization of about

US$1,000. Corporations can be owned and directed entirely by foreigners, a status Swiss law limits to some degree. Corporate registrations are usually handled by Italian lawyers in nearby Milan, and fees are modest. As part of Italy, EU business regulations do apply to Campione businesses, as do Italian corporate taxes, which can be high. Campione's generous tax breaks apply only to natural persons, but even for them it is not completely tax free.

The official currency is the Swiss franc, but the euro is accepted as well. All banking is done through Swiss banks, which gives its residents additional financial privacy. A famous casino generates substantial revenue, which is among the reasons local residents enjoy some special tax concessions. Campione is exempt from the Italian value added tax (VAT). However, the tax advantages only apply to private persons resident in Campione, and not to companies domiciled or managed from there. Unlike Switzerland or Italy, at this writing, Campione per se has no tax treaties with the United States, Canada and none with most other western countries, although that may change.

Residents of Campione do not pay the full Italian income tax. Based on a special provision in Italian law, the first SFR200,000 (US$185,000) of income is changed into euros, the official currency in Italy, at a special exchange rate. This produces a lower taxable income and consequently a lower tax rate is applied. However, this only applies on the first SFR200,000 of income. Besides this special concession, the usual Italian tax laws and tax rates apply. As in Italy, there are minimal inheritance and gift taxes, and income from interest of foreign bonds paid through an Italian bank is taxed at a special, reduced rate of only 12.5%. To say that the Italian authorities are less than zealous in collecting taxes here is an understatement.

Residence

To obtain a Campione residence permit, you must buy an apartment or a house. There is very rarely an opportunity to rent. Usual police clearance from the Italian authorities as well as approval by the local Campione authorities is also required. While residence permits are issued by Italian authorities, access to the territory of Campione is governed by Swiss visa regulations. This means that the passport you hold should allow you to enter Switzerland without a visa, otherwise you will have to apply for a Swiss visa beforehand. A passport is required for entry into Switzerland but a visa is not required for U.S. citizens for stays of up to 90 days.

Obtaining facts about Campione is much more difficult than for other tax havens because the enclave does not promote itself. There is no central office of information. Outsiders are not unwelcome, but no one readily volunteers news about this secret haven. A personal visit is mandatory for anyone seriously interested in making this their home.

Contacts

Local Government: Amministrazione Comunale, Comune di Campione d'Italia. Tel.: 031 27 24 63. Website: http://www.comune.campione-d-italia.co.it/.

Republic of Cyprus

This sunny island in the eastern Mediterranean Sea, politically divided between Greek and Turkish Cypriots, once was proud of its designation as a "tax haven." Since joining the EU in 2004, Cyprus has changed, raising corporate and individual taxes and sharing financial and tax information with other governments. But it still has attractive tax breaks for retired foreigners, especially if their income comes from offshore investments and royalties.

Colorful History

Cyprus, a developed island nation south of Turkey, is the third-largest island in the Mediterranean Sea (after Sicily and Sardinia). It once proudly billed itself as a "tax haven" but not any more. Its membership in the EU has caused it to alter many of its low tax and financial privacy laws.

With mild winters and dry summers (an average of 300 sunny days per year), Cyprus enjoys one of best climates in the Mediterranean. The population is about 800,000, with 80% of the people Christian Greek Cypriots, another 11% Turkish Cypriots and the remaining 9% foreign workers. Cyprus became an independent state in 1960, after 82 years of British rule. It has a system of democratic government based on human rights, political pluralism and respect for private property. Cyprus joined the EU in 2004 and is a member of the United Nations and the British Commonwealth. The island nation is split into two semiautonomous regions due to the long time conflict between Greek and Turkish Cypriots.

The island is politically divided into two distinct geographic areas. The government of the Republic of Cyprus is the internationally recognized authority, but it controls only the Greek Cypriot southern part of the island. The northern area operates under an autonomous Turkish Cypriot administration that governs about 37% of the land area. Another United Nations effort at reunification failed in 2004 when the Greek Cypriots rejected the plan.

With the fall of Communism in Soviet Russia in 1992, Cyprus became a financial (and literal) home away from home for Russian tycoons, bankers and businesspersons. Most of the country's 14,000 offshore companies are Russian-owned and there were more than 50,000 Russians living in the country as recently as 2004.

Cypriot banks manage close to US$30 billion worth of assets. The attraction: low taxes and, until recently, even lower government oversight of the financial sector. This made the island a hotspot for shady personal deals and "brass plate" firms; offshore entities that did no real work but raked in income earned abroad to avoid taxes. The country also has a "double-tax" treaty with Russia, which grants Cyprus-registered firms tax breaks on revenue earned in Russia.

ISLAND CHANGES

Once part of the Byzantine Empire, until recently Cyprus was a great place to make things disappear. This nation has long been a way station for international rogues and scoundrels, where officials have traditionally been willing to look the other way. Just 150 miles from Beirut, closer to the Middle East than to Europe, Cyprus has been a Mecca for cigarette smuggling, money laundering, arms trading and the like. The site of secret meetings between Israelis and Palestinians, it has also been a refuge for the Russian mafia transporting wealth of immense size and dubious provenance.

Cyprus is also a popular low-tax haven for public and trading companies, which can find significant advantages in the double taxation treaties network available to offshore companies. It is otherwise expensive and subject to significant disclosure requirements. After joining the EU in 2004, it rapidly increased financial information sharing with other governments. The tax environment also became decidedly less friendly. The former 4.25% flat tax on offshore firms that attracted so many Russians in the 1990s has risen to 10%. Financial oversight is still lax, but many Russians are fleeing the island out of fear that a crackdown is imminent.

The offshore regime in Cyprus also has changed as part of the island's accession to the EU and as a result of agreements with the Organization for Economic Cooperation and Development (OECD). The 10% corporate tax gives Cyprus the lowest rate in the EU, after Ireland (12.5%), with the exception of the Isle of Man, Jersey and Guernsey, which have a zero rate. A "residence" based system of taxation is now in place.

Even before the G-20 and OECD attacks on offshore financial centers, Cyprus changed its laws to allow the exchange of tax and finance information, and also signed many double tax treaties. The island also now boasts one of the world's toughest anti-money laundering laws. Cyprus plans to maintain its company and trust management regime, although the identity of the beneficiaries must be disclosed to the tax authorities when a company is registered or when a change of ownership takes place.

Retirement Tax Benefits

Cyprus usually does not offer citizenship to foreign nationals, but it may be a good place to settle as residents for some people. Residence is fairly straightforward if you can demonstrate an annual income of as little as US$7,500 for one, to US$19,000 for a family of four. Cyprus offers interesting tax benefits for a retired investor, author, musician or inventor — from the right nation. To obtain these tax benefits, one must become resident, but not domiciled in Cyprus. There are also certain residency programs for foreign nationals willing to make substantial investment in the island's economy.

Cyprus is an attractive destination for a retired investor or anyone who receives substantial royalty income. Foreigners who become residents are not allowed to carry on any local business unless granted permission, but they can conduct business from Cyprus anywhere in the world.

Cyprus may suit your needs if:

1. you are a retired investor who receives dividends or interest from countries with which Cyprus has favorable income tax treaties;

2. you are an author, musician or inventor who receives royalty income;

3. you already have a satisfactory citizenship and passport; or

4. you have a suitable legal domicile and have no problem retaining it.

Cyprus is a perennially popular location for international consultants and independent contractors and its burgeoning offshore sector accounts for the greatest percentage of expatriate workers. However, it is also a popular destination for active retirees (who are attracted not just by the lifestyle, but by the fact that the large number of double taxation treaties in place mean that retirement income from abroad will not usually be subject to withholding tax at source) and both of these groups are positively encouraged by the Cypriot government.

RESIDENCE & TAXATION

Although residence for the purposes of taxation in Cyprus is defined as the "presence in the country for more than 183 days," calculation of tax liabilities is complex, because the country has several different levels of taxation for the various categories of citizens living there.

However, as a basic guide, with the exception of foreign nationals working for offshore entities (for whom the rate of income tax is reduced by half), all groups are liable to pay the following taxes on income paid within Cyprus; income tax (at a progressive rate of up to 30%), capital gains tax (at a rate of 20%), estate duty (at between 20% and 45%) and real estate taxes.

LOW TAX FOR NON-DOMICILED RESIDENTS

A non-domiciled resident pays a flat tax of 5% on investment income received from abroad and remitted to Cyprus. The first US$4,000 of remitted investment income and all investment income that is not remitted to Cyprus is tax-free. Royalties are treated as investment income. Foreign earned income can be remitted to Cyprus in order to reduce foreign withholding taxes under one of Cyprus' many tax treaties. When that is done, any foreign withholding tax paid can be credited against any Cyprus tax owed. That may well wipe out the 5% Cyprus tax obligation.

Unfortunately, these benefits are not available under the terms of either the Cyprus-U.K. or Cyprus-U.S. tax treaties, but nationals covered by most other Cyprus tax treaties can benefit. Cyprus has tax treaties with the United Kingdom, Denmark, Sweden, Ireland, Norway, Greece, Germany, Hungary, Italy, France, Russia, Romania, the United States, Canada and Bulgaria.

To qualify for local residency, an applicant must provide evidence of good character, show independent financial means and document income. The Cypriot Immigration Control Board also imposes minimum amounts of income that must be received by residents during a tax year. Foreigners allowed residency may purchase property in Cyprus, but only after obtaining a permit. Approval to buy real property is usually a formality for a house or apartment in which you plan to live.

Cyprus has ended almost all currency exchange controls, but new foreign residents were usually exempted in any case. Cyprus imposes death taxes, but the estates of non-domiciled residents are liable for taxes only on assets located in Cyprus at the time of death.

CONTACTS

Embassy of the Republic of Cyprus, 2211 R Street, N.W., Washington, D.C. 20008; Tel.: (202) 462-5772; Website: http://www.cyprusembassy.net/.

U.S. Embassy, Metochiou & Ploutarchou Streets, 2407, Engomi, Nicosia, Cyprus; Tel.: + (357) 22-393-939; Fax:

+(357) 22-776-841; Website: http://nicosia.usembassy. gov/.

For information on residence applications, contact Chief Immigration Officer, Migration Department, Ministry of Interior Affairs, Nicosia 1457, Cyprus; Tel.: + (357) 2-302485; Website: http://www.mfa.gov.cy/mfa/mfa2006. nsf/index_en/index_en.

PRINCIPALITY OF MONACO

*Monaco is a tax haven for the exceedingly wealthy —
and great wealth is what it takes to afford living here.
It's home to many millionaires and billionaires from
around the world, many of them retired and enjoying
the good life.*

The 1.08 square miles of Monaco on the French
Riviera is home to over 33,000 people, but this unique
and ancient principality is not for everyone. If you want
to make this your permanent home, it helps to have more
than a modest amount of money and an assured income
for life. And it doesn't hurt to know the Prince and his
royal family.

Monaco, in general, is for individuals who have already
made their money — people who want to practice the
art of living while others mind the store for them; people
who want to spend time on the Riviera. If tax avoidance is
the only goal, there are cheaper places to do it.

Many residents are just upper class people who have
decided to retire in Monaco. They are drawn to the
pleasant atmosphere, Mediterranean climate and leisure.
Monaco has all the facilities that wealthy people consider
necessary: country clubs, health clubs, golf and tennis
clubs. Indeed, Monaco may have a small population and
area, but it has all the services and cultural activities of a
city the size of San Francisco.

Monaco's prices are expensive, but no worse than
London, Paris, or Geneva. These days, there are as many
Italian restaurants as there are French ones. Long before
the euro, money of any kind was the European common
currency in this principality.

Monaco is high profile. The world remembers Grace Kelly, the Hollywood film star, who married Prince Rainier in 1956. The international spotlight followed her until she died in a tragic car accident in 1982. During his long rule, Prince Rainier III worked hard to expand the economic and professional scope of the country. Few recent monarchs can claim credit for extending their dominions by one-fifth without conquest. But, by land filling the sea, the Prince managed to expand his tiny principality by 23% in his long reign beginning in 1949. This land expansion mirrored the late Prince Rainier's determination to make this a dynamic modern mini state.

Monaco is stable and any major changes are unlikely to come from inside. In 1997, the Principality celebrated its 700th anniversary of life under the rule of the Grimaldi family.

Three months after the death of his father, Prince Rainier III, on April 6, 2005, Prince Albert II formally acceded to the throne on July 12, 2005. The Grimaldi children had wild personal reputations and the details of their private lives constantly appeared in the gossip columns of the European press. As they have aged, things have calmed down, although Prince Albert has acknowledged paternity of a child born to an African airline hostess and another born to California woman.

Monaco has also been at the heart of a remarkable economic development based around trading, tourism and financial services in a tax friendly environment. Monaco manages to generate annually over US$8 billion worth of business. The state has an annual income of 593 million (US$800 million), carries no debts and possesses unpublished liquid reserves of at least US$1.8 billion.

The principality is no longer just a frivolous playground for the rich, although its government is funded primarily through casino gambling proceeds. Ever since Monaco's famed casino opened in 1856, the tourism industry has been booming. It currently accounts for close to 25% of the annual revenue. But Monaco is now a modern economy participating at a global level in a diverse range of sectors.

Some people may find Monaco's police presence a little severe. The principality has the lowest crime rate of any highly urbanized area in the world. This physical security is, of course, one of its great advantages.

Significant Tax Benefits for Residents

Undeniably, there are tax benefits to be gained from a move to Monaco. The authorities do not like the Principality to be known as the tax haven that, in fact, it is. It's a low-tax area rather than a no-tax area, but still a haven. Since 1869, there have been no income taxes for Monegasque nationals and resident foreigners — one of the main attractions for high net worth individuals. There are no direct, withholding or capital gains taxes for foreign nationals, except for the French, who because of a bilateral tax treaty with Paris, cannot escape the clutches of the French tax system. There are first-time residential registration taxes, but no ongoing real estate taxes.

Banking

The principality is a major banking center and has successfully sought to diversify into services and small, high-value-added, nonpolluting industries. The state has no income tax and low business taxes and thrives as a tax haven both for individuals who have established residence and for foreign companies that have set up businesses and offices.

There are corporate and banking advantages, too. Confidentiality is good as far as business records go and the same can be said for the banking services. The Bank of France is responsible for the Monegasque banking system and carries out regular inspections. The banking services in Monaco are not as comprehensive as they could be. There is a strong anti-money laundering law. The normal minimum for opening a bank account is €300,000, about US$400,000. Banking secrecy is strict, but the government exchanges information about French citizens with neighboring France and, in 2009, it announced its intention to abide by OECD standards governing exchange of tax information in cases of alleged foreign tax evasion.

RESIDENCY AND CITIZENSHIP

It is actually much easier to obtain a residency permit here than many might suppose. A clean record, solid bank references and a net worth of US$500,000 should do it. Fees for establishing residency are likely to cost in the US$10,000 to $20,000 range.

The principality has offered financial and fiscal concessions to foreign nationals for a long time. These have been restricted by the Conventions with France in 1963 and, more recently, by agreements with France after pressure from the EU. And here lies the major concern. Monaco isn't likely to initiate changes. But the rest of Europe, especially France, which has always exhibited a jealous dog-in-the-manger attitude towards the principality, might pressurize it into getting into line.

If you're on the move already, stability may not be an important issue. However, you might be looking for a base and would do well to consider Monaco. The lifestyle is attractive but is not everybody's cup of tea. If you are contemplating a move purely for financial or fiscal reasons, you might, depending on your specific requirements, do better elsewhere.

Once there, keep a low profile. Foreign nationals who are residents do not make any public criticisms of the country. Why? If the authorities consider you a troublemaker, they can issue a 24-hour notice of expulsion. There's no one to appeal to and you'll be out the door.

CONTACTS

Embassy of Monaco, 3400 International Dr., Suite 2K 100, Washington, D.C. 20008; Tel.: (202) 244-7656; Website: http://www.monaco-usa.org/; Email: embassy@ monaco-usa.org.

Diplomatic representation of the U.S. to Monaco is handled by the U.S. Embassy in Paris. The U.S. Embassy in France is located at 2 Avenue Gabriel, 75382 Paris Cedex 8, France; Tel.: +(33) 1-4312-2222; Website: http:// france.usembassy.gov/. The U.S. Consulate General at Marseille is located at 12 Place Varian Fry, 13086 Marseille, France; Tel.: +(33) 4-9154-9200; Website: http:// france.usembassy.gov/marseille/.

GIBRALTAR

The Rock, as it is known worldwide, is the United Kingdom's only continental European colonial possession, although it is forcefully claimed by Spain. Gibraltar has fashioned itself into a dual-purpose residential tax haven for high net worth individuals from around the world and as a professional base for tax free international business corporations and trusts.

ANCIENT COLONIAL STATUS

Gibraltar, a colonial possession of the United Kingdom, was ceded to England "forever" under the 1713 Treaty of Utrecht.

Neighboring Spain's 300 years of efforts to recover this British overseas territory, located on Spain's southern flank, have been rejected repeatedly by a large majority of the 28,000 citizens of Gibraltar, most recently by 99% in a 2002 referendum — and by the British government.

The colony's constitution grants local autonomy in many areas, but reserves strategic decisions to London. Its legal system is based on English common law. Gibraltar has been part of the European Union by its association through the U.K. since 1973. Constitutionally, Gibraltar is a Crown colony with internal self-government, the U.K. being responsible for defense, foreign affairs, financial stability and internal security. Gibraltar has its own House of Assembly with 15 elected members and two nominated members. There is a Council of Ministers, which consists of the Chief Minister and seven other Ministers.

ROCK-SOLID ECONOMY

The famous Rock is tiny — only 2.5 square miles — but boasts a comprehensive banking and financial services industry. Gibraltar has no exchange controls and offers first-rate communications and infrastructure. The colony's financial services industry is the mainstay of the local economy, providing 30–35% of GDP, with 5,000 jobs that depend on the offshore finance center.

Most of the 17 fully operational banks established in Gibraltar are branches of major U.K., Swiss or other European banks. Interestingly, Gibraltar has about 40 authorized banks entitled to accept deposits without establishing full branches in Gibraltar. At this writing, Gibraltar has 75 insurance companies, 43 trust companies and 551 licensed financial management companies managing over 3,745 registered trusts. There are about 41,000 registered corporations. The offshore and local banking sector holds assets of about G£10.7 billion (US$17.4 billion). Most Gibraltar banks offer special rates of interest to wealthier private depositors under the heading of private banking. Minimums are as low as US$10,000 in some cases, although some firms still maintain more traditional entry levels of US$100,000 or higher before offering special treatment to clients.

Gibraltar imposes no capital gains, wealth or estate taxes. The reopening of the border with Spain in 1985 enabled Gibraltar to expand its role as a major international finance center, against a background of political stability and administrative and legal systems derived from English common law and traditions. The absence of any exchange control restrictions together with exemptions and concessions from domestic taxes for certain categories of companies, high net worth and non-resident individuals and trusts administered for non-residents has created many opportunities for offshore investors and led to substantial growth in financial sector services.

Until 2009, Gibraltar was not party to any double taxation agreements, but it then agreed, as did all U.K. overseas territories, to apply Article 26 of the OECD tax information exchange model treaty. In mid-2009, it concluded a tax information exchange agreement with the U.S. allowing information exchange in cases of alleged tax evasion.

Gibraltar is also home to many "tax exiles" from many nations, wealthy individuals who enjoy the local tax-free regime for foreign residents. Under Gibraltar tax law, the category known as "high net worth individuals" (HNWI) receives the biggest concessions. With the payment of an application fee of US$750 and with two letters of reference, one from a banker, the HNWI receives a permanent certificate guaranteeing that they will only be taxed on the first US$70,000 of income. All additional income is tax-free. Of special note is the fact that there is no capital gains tax or estate taxes in Gibraltar.

Previously, when the OECD listed Gibraltar on its harmful tax competition "blacklist," the government countered with a cut in corporate tax rates across the board. Both the OECD and the European Union attacked Gibraltar's tax haven status and Spain joined the critical chorus for its own purposes. The EU had ruled that Gibraltar's offshore favorable tax status was incompatible with EU regulations that apply to the United Kingdom and its colonial dominions. Gibraltar appealed the EU ruling and in 2008 won a significant victory when the EU's highest court ruled that the Rock had "from a constitutional point of view, a political and administrative status separate from that of the central government of the United Kingdom." In effect, this affirmed the right of Gibraltar to set its own tax policies independent of the U.K., allowing its continuation as a tax haven.

THE FUTURE

Hanging over Gibraltar is its somewhat uncertain political future. The Labor government in London at one point signaled willingness to "share sovereignty" with Spain, an arrangement that Rock residents strongly oppose. More recently, the government in London said that any final agreement with Spain may be years, if not decades, away. London has pledged, if it can be believed, that no agreement with Spain will be made final unless the people of Gibraltar approve, which is highly unlikely.

CONTACTS

Government of Gibraltar: www.gibraltar.gov.gi/; or http://www.gibraltar.gov.uk/.

Financial Services Commission: P.O. Box 940, Suite 943, Europort, Gibraltar; Tel.: +350-200 40283; Email: info@fsc.gi Website: www.fsc.gi.

Gibraltar Tourists Board, Gibraltar; Tel.: + (350) 74950 / 74982; Website: http://www.gibraltar.gi/home/.

Gibraltar Information Bureau, 1156 15th Street, N.W., Washington, D.C. 20005; Tel.: (202) 452-1108; Fax: (202) 872-8543; Website: http://www.gibraltar.gov.uk/.

Affairs for Gibraltar, a British overseas territory, are handled through the U.S. Embassy in London. The U.S. Embassy is located at 24 Grosvenor Square, W1A 1AE London, United Kingdom; Tel.: + (44) 207-499-9000; Fax: + (44) 207-409-1637; Website: http://london.usembassy.gov/.

Gibraltar News: http://www.panorama.gi/.

REPUBLIC OF MALTA

*Malta offers special tax-free status for foreign retirees. It
courts international business and financial firms with
tax breaks and subsidies. But as a recent member of the
EU (2004), it has revising its tax laws and no longer
wants to be known as the tax haven that it is.*

South of the continent of Europe is Malta — a group
of islands in the center of the Mediterranean Sea, south
of the Italian island of Sicily and well positioned as a
cultural and political stepping stone between Europe and
North Africa. About 95% of the nearly 400,000 islanders
are natives, descendants of the ancient Carthaginians and
Phoenicians. Malta offers an excellent climate and quality
of life, modern health care and educational systems.

In 1530, the Holy Roman Emperor, Charles V, ceded
Malta to the governance of the Knights of Malta. They
built the fortifications in the harbor of Valetta, the capital,
so well that in 1565 a Turkish siege was repelled largely
due to the excellent defenses, which are still in existence
today. In 1798, Napoleon invaded Malta and expelled the
Knights. At the Congress of Vienna in 1815, Britain was
given possession of Malta. With the 1869 opening of the
Suez Canal, Malta became an important strategic British
base. During World War II, Malta was bombed heavily
by the German Luftwaffe since it was a valuable Allied
convoy port. In 1947, Malta was granted self-government
and in 1964, it became independent after being a British
colony for more than 200 years. Since 2005, Malta has
been a member of the European Union.

Almost entirely lacking energy or other natural resources and with a severe shortage of arable land, Malta is an

import-hungry country. The government has tried with some success to create a high-technology manufacturing sector and to establish processing and distribution facilities around its rapidly growing Freeport. There are extensive investment incentives and laws to increase the islands' role as a leader in international financial services. These provide a variety of tax and financial incentives to banks, insurance companies, fund management firms, trading companies, trusts and investment companies.

BUSINESS INCENTIVES

While it is not a tax haven for individuals as such, Malta's government actively courts foreign capital with attractive incentives aimed at investors and entrepreneurs. These include generous tax incentives, soft loans, training grants and customized facilities at subsidized costs. This pro-business policy seeks to build on Malta's many existing strengths: favorable trade relations with countries around the world; a strategic location on world shipping lanes; and a high quality, productive, English-speaking workforce.

ECONOMY

Traditionally agriculture was important, but Malta's economy has changed significantly. Major industries now include high-tech manufacturing, food and beverages, tourism and international financial services. The government actively seeks to attract foreign capital with generous tax breaks aimed at international investors. Malta is a good jurisdiction in which to establish low-tax international trading companies and treaty-protected international holding companies. Malta also has an important shipping register and is one of world's preferred jurisdictions for tax-free private yacht registrations.

In the last decade, Malta's economy has averaged an annual growth rate of more than 7%. The nation has maintained a surplus balance of payments, stable currency (now the euro) and inflation less than 1%. These factors reflect the overall strength and diversity of the economy.

Manufacturing, especially high-tech industries, now accounts for more than a quarter of Malta's GDP. About 26% of the labor force works in services, 22% in manufacturing, 37% in government and 2% in agriculture. Major industries now include textiles, machinery, food and beverages and high-tech products — especially electronics. Tourism is also a growing and increasingly important sector. Other key sectors that provide exceptional investment opportunities include trade, manufacturing, maintenance services and international financial services.

As noted, recent Maltese legislation provides a variety of tax and financial incentives to banks, insurance companies, fund management firms, trading companies, trusts and investment companies. This has increased the islands' role as a leader in international finance services. As an EU member since 2004, it has adjusted some of its tax breaks for foreign persons and businesses, so check for the latest facts if you are interested in Malta as a residence or business base.

RESIDENCE, NOT CITIZENSHIP

These sunny Mediterranean islands cater to expatriates looking for a second or retirement home. There are no property taxes and permanent residents pay a 15%

income tax on offshore income remitted into the country. Malta has three types of taxes: income, corporate and estate taxes — the latter applies only to property located on the island. Income tax rates for foreign residents range from 2% to 30%. A permanent resident is not taxed on capital gains paid from offshore, unless the person also is domiciled in Malta.

Foreign nationals are not eligible for Maltese citizenship, but they are welcomed as residents. Maltese residency is of three types:

1. Visitors staying less than three months are counted as nonresidents

2. Those remaining over three months are temporary residents.

3. Permanent residents are granted a permit entitling them to stay

Those in the latter category must own assets located outside Malta of at least US$360,000, or have a worldwide income of at least US$24,000 and demonstrate ability to remit to Malta a minimum annual income of US$14,400, plus US$2,400 for each dependent. A residence permit can be inherited by a surviving spouse, but not by other surviving descendants.

A permanent residence permit entitles its holder to reside permanently in Malta with the freedom to come and go. As an EU member and of the Schengen Area agreement residents of Malta can travel within that area without obtaining a visa. A permanent resident enjoys a privileged tax status, while at the same time benefiting from Malta's wide network of double taxation treaties. A further advantage of this status is that as long as the resident abides by the rules, they need not spend any particular time actually residing in Malta.

CONTACTS

Embassy of Malta, 2017 Connecticut Avenue, N.W., Washington, D.C. 20008; Tel.: (202) 462-3611. Email: Malta_Embassy@compuserve.com.

Embassy of the United States, Development House, 3rd Floor St. Anne St. Floriana Malta VLT 01. Mailing address: P.O. Box 535, Valletta, Malta, CMR 01; Tel.: + (356) 2561-4000; Fax: + (356) 2124-3229; Email: usembmalta@state.gov; Website: http://malta.usembassy.gov/.

Government of Malta: http://www.gov.mt/index.asp?1=2&l=2.

Malta Tourism Board: http://www.visitmalta.com/.

Central Bank of Malta: http://www.centralbankmalta.com/.

CHAPTER EIGHT

Asia, Mid-East & Africa

The growth in Asian national economies, as well as those in the Middle East and Africa have spawned new offshore financial centers (Dubai, Labuan, and Samoa) and also transformed existing low-tax jurisdictions (Hong Kong, Singapore). Here I describe the growing competition among some of these major offshore centers and the struggle on the part of newer centers to be accepted in the offshore world.

The Cook Islands — Far Out

*Way out in the South Pacific (in the middle of nowhere)
are the Cook Islands — home to a very modern set of
offshore financial laws that may be just what you need:
iron-clad asset protection trusts, IBCs, limited liability
partnerships and a very strict financial privacy law that
protects your personal business. But some people don't
like too much distance between themselves and their assets and — let's face it — for most people these islands
are very far out.*

Independent but Dependent

If you're researching the more esoteric part of the world
of offshore asset protection, you'll soon hear about the
Cook Islands. Since a quarter of a century ago when the
government first began adopting (and updating) a series of wealth and asset-friendly laws in 1981, the Cook
Islands — though small in population and remote from
the rest of the world — have come to play a definite role
in offshore financial circles.

A broad net of 15 coral islands in the central heart
of the South Pacific, the Cook Islands are spread over
850,000 square miles, southwest of Tahiti and due south
of Hawaii. The islands occupy an area the size of India,
with a declining population (12,000+), no bigger than
an American small town. Local time is 10 hours behind
GMT, with 9:00 am in Hong Kong being 3:00 pm the
previous day in the Cook Islands. This geographic location gives the Cook Islands a strategic advantage in dealing with both the Asian and American markets.

Indirectly, the islands are part of the British Commonwealth by virtue of their unique association with nearby New Zealand. From 1901 to 1965, the Cook Islands were a colony of New Zealand and NZ still subsidizes the CI government. The New Zealand subsidy has become a sore point in both nations. The islanders even enjoy dual New Zealand and Cook Islands citizenship. There is a written CI constitution with a Westminster-style parliament elected every four years by universal suffrage. The legal system is based on British common law and closely reflects that of New Zealand and other Commonwealth jurisdictions.

PLANNED OFFSHORE CENTER

The Cook Islands' offshore industry was the result of the government's official collaboration with the local financial services industry. Financial services now rank second only to tourism in the economy. Despite some 50,000 visitors a year to the capital island, Rarotonga, the Cook Islands have remained largely unspoiled. Cook Islanders have their own language and enjoy a vigorous and diverse culture, though most speak English. The New Zealand dollar is the local currency, but most offshore transactions are in U.S. dollars.

This is a microstate with macro aspirations, but the grasp may have exceeded the reach. Their checkered history of high finance has been marked by some scandals, sponsored by fast-talking American, U.K. and New Zealand expatriates. It's no secret that certain American asset protection attorneys have played a large role in advising the government on asset protection issues, actually drafting statutes for the island's parliament.

Constantly teetering on the brink of bankruptcy, the

CI government is chronically in debt, much of it a result of bad decisions. Two-thirds of the work force is on the government payroll, financing an old-fashioned spoils and patronage system that would make an American big-city political boss blush. In the 1980s and 1990s, the country lived beyond its means, maintaining a bloated public service and accumulating a large foreign debt. Subsequent reforms, including the sale of state assets, the strengthening of economic management, the encouragement of tourism, and a debt restructuring agreement, have rekindled investment and growth.

TAILORED WEALTH PROTECTION

But don't let the deficits and the distance put you off. There is much here to cheer the hearts of knowledgeable offshore financial enthusiasts.

Existing statutes meticulously provide for the care and feeding of IBCs, including offshore banks, insurance companies and trusts. All offshore business conducted on the Cook Islands must be channeled through one of the five registered trustee companies. A comprehensive range of trustee and corporate services is offered for offshore investors. The government officially guarantees no taxes will be imposed on offshore entities. Thousands of foreign trusts, corporations and partnerships are registered here, protected by an exceedingly strong financial privacy law, although that has been tempered by the adoption of OECD Article 26 standards for the exchange of tax information among governments. In 2009, the Cook Island's government welcomed the G-20 call for more transparency in tax information and adopted necessary amendments to its tax laws to conform to the new standard.

The Development Investment Act requires all foreign enterprises (those with more than one-third foreign ownership) to first obtain approval and register their planned activities with the Cook Islands Development Investment Board. There are various incentives and concessions for tariff protection; import duty and levy concessions; tax concessions by way of accelerated depreciation; allowance for counterpart training; and recruitment of Cook Islanders from overseas.

UPDATED LAWS

The Cook Islands has systematically adopted a series of new anti-money laundering, financial reporting and anti-financial-crime laws. These laws were sufficient to get them removed from the Financial Action Task Force blacklist, which was their stated objective.

The laws liberalize the extent to which local financial institutions are obligated to disclose information and override all other laws, making compliance with anti-money-laundering laws and standards paramount. However, the law instituted a procedure that provides due process before any information can be released, including a formal request to the Financial Intelligence Unit showing reasonable grounds to believe that money laundering or criminal activities have taken place. This ensures that any information disclosed is done through proper channels with legal justification. This procedure is also used for tax information exchange requests from foreign governments.

International companies incorporated here have a great deal of flexibility in corporate structure with provisions for ease of administration and maximum benefit in global commercial transactions. Incorporation can be completed within 24 hours.

In 1989, by an amendment to the International Trusts Act 1984, the Cook Islands introduced the asset protection trust (APT). This legislation was considered cutting edge at the time and has since been copied and adopted by other offshore centers. The Cook Islands also has laws allowing international banking and insurance business to be conducted tax free, also with strong privacy protections. Both government and trust companies here constantly develop new products to meet the complexities of the offshore world.

STRICT CONFIDENTIALITY

Strong financial and banking secrecy provisions apply in the offshore regime, requiring government officials as well as trustee company and bank employees to observe strict secrecy backed by criminal sanctions. The official registrar records of foreign companies and of international trusts are not open for general search, with defined exceptions under the Financial Transactions Reporting Act of 2004 and the Proceeds of Crimes Act of 2003.

In a major American legal case, the U.S. government tried to force the repatriation of funds under a Cook Island trust and lost, even though the Americans who created the trust for a time were jailed for contempt of court. Not even a federal court could crack the Cook Island trust laws. See the decision known as the "Anderson case" (*FTC vs. Affordable Media, LLC*, 179 F. 3rd 1228, U.S. Ct. of Appeals, 9th Cir. 1999).

In mid-2009, the OECD listed the Cook Islands as

one of the tax havens committed to the internationally agreed tax information exchange standard but one that had not yet substantially implemented it. The CI government says it is committed to the OECD Article 26 standard and will implement it.

CONCLUSION

Don't let those thousands of miles of distance scare you. Your offshore attorney is a lot closer to you and he or she should know how to use the Cook Islands and their asset protection laws to your benefit. See the names listed below.

CONTACTS

Ministry of Finance & Economic Management, PO Box 120, Rarotonga, Cook Islands Tel.: 682 22878.

Malaysia (Labuan)

Malaysia is a pleasant, hassle-free county in Southeast Asia. It's wealthy and has a pluralist culture based on a fusion of Malay, Chinese, Indian and indigenous cultures and customs. Malaysia's love of Western-style industrialization is seen in its big cities. Aside from the gleaming glass towers of the 21st Century, Malaysia has some of the best beaches, mountains and national parks in Asia. It is also home to an officially planned and promoted offshore financial center, called "Labuan" which seeks to become the world's Islamic financial center.

History

Malaysia exists under many different influences. It was ruled by the Portuguese, Dutch and British over five centuries. During the late 18th and 19th centuries, Great Britain established colonies and protectorates in Malaysia, which were militarily occupied by Japan from 1942 to 1945. In 1948, the British-ruled territories on the Malay Peninsula formed the Federation of Malaya and gained independence in 1957.

Malaysia was formed in 1963 when the former British colonies of Singapore and the East Malaysian states of Sabah and Sarawak on the northern coast of Borneo joined the Federation. Singapore became independent in 1965. During the 22-year term of Prime Minister Mahathir bin Mohamad (1981-2003), Malaysia was successful in diversifying its economy from dependence on exports of raw materials, to expansion in manufacturing, services and tourism. His leadership converted the nation's plantation-based economy into what has been called an "Asian Tiger."

The western half of Malaysia is bustling and commercial, with urban centers sprinkled throughout the tropical vegetation of the country. Much of this development in the west is driven by the energy of its Chinese business community. In the east, Malays constitute the majority and agriculture, fishing and cottage industries predominate. Life in the east is quiet and laid back where one experiences the traditional Malay culture.

Malaysia transformed itself from 1971 through 2000 from a producer of raw materials into an emerging multi-sector economy. Growth was almost exclusively driven by exports — particularly of electronics. As an oil and gas exporter, Malaysia profited when world energy prices are high. Healthy foreign exchange reserves, low inflation and a small external debt are all strengths that lend Malaysia financial stability. The economy remains dependent on continued growth in the U.S., China and Japan — all top export destinations and key sources of foreign investment.

PLANNED ISLAMIC FINANCIAL CENTER

Labuan, designated as a federal territory of Malaysia, is located off the northwest coast of the island of Borneo and faces the South China Sea. It comprises Pulau (a Malay word meaning "island"), Labuan and six smaller islands, with a population of 80,000. Bahasa Melayu (Malay) is the national language, but English is widely spoken, as well as Chinese dialects and Tamil. Islam is the official religion, but freedom of worship is guaranteed. Labuan, like the rest of Malaysia, has a parliamentary system of government based on the British common law.

Labuan's offshore center began in 1990, offering services that include banking, insurance, trust creation, international business corporations and investment fund management. Since 2000, growth has speeded up, especially after the opening of the Labuan Financial Exchange (LFX). The main advantage that Labuan enjoys is its role as a center for developing Islamic financial law.

Islamic financial practices follow Shari'a, Islamic law based on the Koran. The law specifically prohibits the receipt or payment of interest and any transaction that involves gambling or speculation, a category that includes futures contracts, interest rate hedging and other financial arrangements common in the West.

In lieu of the payment of interest, Islamic institutions pay investors a share of their profits. Making a profit is not prohibited, but Muslims believe that financial relationships should be equal rather than hierarchical. Thus, profit sharing is preferable to interest, which implies the unequal relation of debtor to creditor.

The amount of wealth estimated to be under professional management in the world Islamic financial sector is about US$200 billion to US$300 billion, a fairly small quantity in comparison with the global capital market, but still a significant and growing niche that Labuan seeks to serve.

CONTACTS

U.S. Embassy, 376 Jalan Tun Razak, 50400 Kuala Lumpur Tel. 60-3-2168-5000. Website: http://malaysia. usembassy.gov/; Email: embassyklpa@state.gov.

Malaysian Embassy, 3516 International Court NW, Washington, D.C. 20008; Tel.: (202) 572-9700.

Labuan International Financial Center (IOFC). Website: www.lofsa.gov.my/.

Republic of Mauritius

Mauritius is the most accessible island in the Indian Ocean, boasting a tropical paradise at a bargain price. Though geographically alongside South Africa, it's actually more influenced by its British and French ties and a predominantly Indian workforce. It is a favorite tax haven for wealthy Indians and a favorite target of India's tax collectors.

History

Mauritius is a volcanic island of lagoons and palm-fringed beaches in the Indian Ocean off the coast of Southern Africa and east of Madagascar. It has a reputation for stability and racial harmony among its mixed, 1.3 million population of Asians, Europeans and Africans. The island has maintained one of the developing world's most successful democracies and has enjoyed continued constitutional order.

Although known to Arab and Malay sailors as early as the 10th century, Mauritius was first explored by the Portuguese in 1505; it was subsequently held by the Dutch, French and British before independence was gained in 1968. A stable democracy with regular free elections and a positive human rights record, the country has attracted considerable foreign investment and has earned one of Africa's highest per capita incomes.

Since independence, Mauritius has developed from a low-income, agriculturally based economy to a middle-income, diversified economy with growing industrial, financial and tourist sectors. For most of the period, annual growth has been in the order of 5% to 6%. This remarkable achievement has been reflected in more equitable income distribution, increased life expectancy, lowered infant mortality and a much-improved infrastructure. Sugarcane is grown on about 90% of the cultivated land area and accounts for 25% of export earnings.

The government's development strategy centers on expanding and converting local financial institutions into offshore financial services and building a domestic information telecommunications industry. Mauritius has attracted more than 9,000 offshore entities (IBCs, trusts), many aimed at commerce in India and South Africa and investment in the banking sector now exceeds US$1 billion.

Moderate Tax Haven

The Mauritius offshore sector takes a cautious course. Until 1998, offshore laws allowed zero taxation across a range of offshore activities, including international business corporations (IBCs), banking, shipping, insurance and fund management, as well as in free trade zones. The legal system is a hybrid combination of both civil and common law practices.

Under a 2001 law, IBCs are known as "Global Business Licenses Categories 1 and 2." A GBL1 is used for international tax planning and structuring and is appropriate for investment funds or mutual funds seeking relief under double taxation agreements. A GBL2 is not considered as resident in Mauritius and is therefore exempt from local taxation, but it cannot access the benefits of the network of double tax agreements. It is primarily used for non-financial consultancy, trading, logistics, marketing or invoicing.

Mauritius has decided to be a "respectable" offshore financial center. Thus "tax free" is gone and there is now a tax rate of 15% in most areas, although corporate exemptions can reduce the tax considerably to as low as 3%. Mauritius has tax treaties with 27 countries that can be combined with offshore laws to produce profitable trade and investment, especially for the many thousands of wealthy Indian investors. Mauritius has been attacked by India because of its role as a tax haven for wealthy Indians. But a 2009 official Indian survey showed that Mauritius accounted for 43% of cumulative foreign direct investment (FDI) that flowed into India. Of the total US$81 billion FDI that came in from 2000 to 2009, almost half (US$35.18 billion) was routed through the Mauritius.

Mauritius has become a favorite of the Indian financial elite and a prime target of the Indian government seeking tax evasion. With a strong anti-money laundering law, it has managed to avoid both the OECD and FATF blacklists. Offshore laws are continually modernized and are kept up to date and competitive.

CONTACTS

Embassy of Mauritius, 4301 Connecticut Avenue, N.W., Washington, D.C. 20008; Tel.: (202) 244-1491; Email: MAURITIUS.EMBASSY@prodigy.net; Website: http://www.maurinet.com/embasydc.html.

U.S. Embassy, Rogers House, Fourth Floor, John F. Kennedy Avenue, P.O. Box 544, Port Louis, Mauritius; Tel.: +(230) 202-4400; Fax: +(230) 208-9534; Email: usembass@intnet.mu; Website: http://mauritius.usembassy.gov/.

Government of Mauritius: http://www.gov.mu/.

INDEPENDENT STATE OF SAMOA

If you're looking for a tax haven that has an inside track with the People's Republic of China, or if you need to form a trust or corporation yesterday, this small Pacific island nation that sits on the other side of the International Dateline may be your best bet.

The few professionals who really know tax havens realize the relative importance of Samoa, a group of islands in the heart of the South Pacific Ocean, about halfway between Hawaii and New Zealand.

New Zealand occupied this former German protectorate, then known as "Western Samoa," at the outbreak of World War I in 1914. It administered the islands as a UN mandate and then as a trust territory until 1962, when the islands became the first Polynesian nation to reestablish independence in the 20th century. This country with a little more than 183,000 people dropped the "Western" from its name in 1997.

Samoa became one of the first countries in the South Pacific to recognize the People's Republic of China in 1975. That led to the Samoa creating an Asian niche market for its offshore finance center targeting business in China and the Far East. Along with the Cook Islands, the strategic location of Samoa just east of the International Date Line in the South Pacific, allows an Asian investor the unusual ability to register a company yesterday. For those looking for legal entities to be used in the Asia in general or in China, Samoa is an interesting potential alternative to Hong Kong and Singapore.

The economy of Samoa traditionally depends on development aid and loans from other countries (China,

Japan, Australia and New Zealand), family remittances from more than 100,000 Samoans who live abroad, agriculture and fishing. The country is vulnerable to devastating cyclones. Agriculture employs two-thirds of the labor force and furnishes 90% of exports, featuring coconut cream, coconut oil and copra. The manufacturing sector mainly processes agricultural products. Tourism is an expanding sector, accounting for 25% of GDP; about 122,000 tourists visited the islands in 2008.

OFFSHORE FINANCIAL CENTER

The Samoan Government supports maximum deregulation of the financial sector, encourages investment and continues fiscal discipline. Foreign reserves are in a relatively healthy state, the external debt is stable and inflation is low. The government is a mix of parliamentary democracy and constitutional monarchy under a British common law legal system.

Because of massive amounts of aid from China, Samoa tends to be an offshore financial center especially for Chinese investors and caters to them.

There are five major laws enabling Samoa's role as an international finance center:

1. The International Companies Act of 1987 is the international business corporation law;

2. The International Banking Act of 2005 allows three types of bank licenses subject to the Basle international banking standards. All holders of international banking licenses must establish an office in Samoa,

have at least two directors who must be individuals and employ at least one person.

3. The International Trusts Act of 1987 governs the creation and registration of offshore asset protection trusts;

4. The Trustee Companies Act 1987 is the licensing law for trustee companies, which include corporate service providers, those who deal directly with clients. Government licensing of trustee companies policy ensures that only established professionals with international connections that are accepted.

5. The International Insurance Act of 1988 allows four categories of insurance licenses, general, long term, reinsurance and captive.

All entities established under the offshore laws, except for licensed trustee companies, are exempt from all local taxation, currency and exchange controls and stamp duties. Samoa is doing something right when it comes to its offshore role. Samoan banks' external assets grew from US$846,000,000 in 2006 to US$1,210,000,000 in 2007 and US$1,473,000,000 in 2008.

Fortunately for Samoa, out of concern for its offshore finance center it enacted the Money Laundering Prevention Act of 2000. Thus, the islands never appeared on the OECD and FATF blacklists. Samoa was among the first countries to commit to the OECD principles of transparency and tax exchange of information, but only if and when all other jurisdictions agree to level playing field. In 2009, they joined other offshore financial centers in restating that commitment.

CONTACTS

Samoa International Finance Authority, P.O.Box 3265 Apia, Samoa. Tel + 685 24071. Email: offshore@lesamoa. net; Website: http://www.sifa.ws/.

U.S. Embassy, 5th Floor ACB Bldg, Beach Rd, Apia. P.O. Box 3430, Apia. Tel.: + 685 21631. Email: AmEmbApia@state.gov; Website: http://samoa.usembassy.gov/.

Samoa maintains its diplomatic representation in the United States at 800 2nd Avenue, Suite 400D, New York, NY 10017; Tel.: 212-599-6196. Email: samoa@un.int.

REPUBLIC OF SEYCHELLES

The 115 islands of the Seychelles are indisputably a tropical paradise. However seductive the travel brochure images, they simply can't compete with the real-life dazzling beaches and crystal-clear waters. All this and a fledgling tax haven that wants to serve your offshore needs quickly, efficiently and at a lower cost.

The Seychelles (population 82,000) is an archipelago of 115 islands in the Indian Ocean off the east African coast about five degrees south of the Equator. It gained independence from the United Kingdom in 1976.

Most Seychellois are descendants of early French settlers and the African slaves brought to the islands in the 19th century by the British, who freed them from slave ships on the East African coast. Indians and Chinese (1.1%) account for other permanent inhabitants. About 4,000 expatriates live and work in Seychelles.

Seychelles culture is a mixture of French and African (Creole) influences. Creole is the native language of 94% of the people; however, English and French are commonly used. English remains the language of government and commerce.

PLANNED OFFSHORE FINANCIAL CENTER

Seychelles has comprehensive and modern international financial services laws adopted within the last decade. The legal system is based on a mixture of the English common law and French civil code. The company, banking, trust and other financial services laws are mainly based on English law and patterned after successful Caribbean offshore jurisdictions. Confidentiality is guaranteed by law and all civil proceedings concerning offshore entities may be held in closed session rather than in public.

In 1994, the government passed a series of laws that launched the offshore financial center. The Seychelles International Business Authority (SIBA) regulates the offshore industry and registers offshore companies. SIBA also supervises the Seychelles International Trade Zone (SITZ), a development to encourage direct foreign investment.

Over 25,000 IBCs have been registered in Seychelles, increasing 40% annually in recent years. This increased demand is attributed to lower, competitive pricing, fast and efficient processing and turnaround for incorporation, acceptability to international banks, tax-free foreign investments, a high degree of privacy and asset protection and ease of administration.

The commercial banking sector includes Barclays Bank PLC, Mauritius Commercial Bank, Bank of Baroda, Habib Bank and Seychelles International Mercantile Credit Banking Corporation (SIMBC) trading under the name "Nouvobanq." The first four are branches of foreign banks and the last is a joint venture between the Seychelles government and the Standard Chartered Bank African PLC. Commercial banks offer the full range of services.

CONTACTS

Seychelles International Business Authority, Industrial Trade Zone, P.O. Box 991, Mahe, Republic of Seychelles. Tel.: 248-380 800, Email: siba@seychelles.net, Website: http://www.siba.net/.

Permanent Mission of Seychelles to the UN, 800 Second Ave., Suite 400, New York, NY 10017, Tel.: (212) 972-1785; Email: seychelles@un.int; Website: http://www.un.int/wcm/content/site/seychelles. Seychelles has an ambassador resident in New York accredited to the United Nations, to the United States and Canada.

The U.S. Embassy in Mauritius also serves the Seychelles. U.S. Embassy, Rogers House, Fourth Floor, John F. Kennedy Avenue, P.O. Box 544, Port Louis, Mauritius; Tel.: +(230) 202-4400; Fax: +(230) 208-9534; Email: usembass@intnet.mu; Website: http://mauritius.usembassy.gov/.

REPUBLIC OF SINGAPORE

Singapore has become a major international financial center — but it's not exactly an offshore tax haven. It has traded its ancient Orient image for towers of concrete and glass and its rickshaws have been replaced by high-tech industry. Singapore appears shockingly modern, but this is an Asian city with Chinese, Malay and Indian traditions from feng shui to ancestor worship as part of daily life. These contrasts bring the city to life — but don't talk local politics.

HISTORY

The Republic of Singapore (population 4.7 million) has the distinction of being a small island, a state and a city — all in one. Located just a few steamy miles north of the Equator, it has Malaysia and Indonesia as close and sometimes uneasy neighbors. The climate is hot and very humid with rainfall of over two meters (about seven feet) annually.

Colonial Singapore gained its independence from Great Britain in 1965. Lee Kuan Yew became its autocratic leader and served until 1990, when his son, now in office, replaced him in his official capacities. The father remains the power behind his son's throne and his one-party state still does not tolerate dissent or opposition. There are no jury trials. Civil matters, such as alleged libel or slander, can escalate into criminal issues with serious consequences, especially for political opponents. Draconian laws keep crime (and freedom) to a minimum, but the enforced stability attracts massive foreign investment. Moreover, as I can attest, the streets are very clean, since spitting or littering can land you in jail. Clean streets are a tradeoff for individual political freedom.

Singapore has an open economy with strong service and manufacturing sectors as well as excellent international trading links. Rising labor costs and appreciation of the Singapore dollar against its neighbors' currencies threaten competitiveness. The government's strategy includes cutting costs, increasing productivity, improving infrastructure and encouraging higher value-added industries and an expanding offshore financial and banking sector. In applied technology, per capita output, investment and labor discipline, Singapore has key attributes of a developed country. Traditionally, manufacturing has been dominated by the electronics industry, which, along with commerce and a highly developed service industry and tourism, has been the backbone of Singapore's rise to one of the leading newly industrializing economies in the world.

The common language is English. Most Singaporeans are Asian, with commerce dominated by ethnic Chinese. Malays make up 15%, with Indians, Thais, Vietnamese, Laotians and a very small number of Europeans. Europeans hold most management positions and are generally well regarded. In Singapore, state regulation has created a paradise if you like high-rise buildings, crass materialism and minimal personal freedom.

Singapore is not a tax haven. It supports welfare state programs of free schools, low-fee universities, childcare, socialized medicine and subsidized housing. Tax rates are slightly below those of the U.S. Income over S$400,000 (US$264,000) is taxed at 33%. In 2008, the corporate tax rate will be reduced from 20% to 18%. In addition, there is an increase in the partial tax exemption income threshold from S$100,000 to S$300,000. The exempt income will be calculated as follows: 1) 75% tax exemption for the first S$100,000 of income and; 2) 50% tax exemption for the next S$290,000 of income.

New exporters can usually get a 15-year tax holiday. Real estate is taxed at 15% of the annual rental value. The maximum estate tax is 10% with an exemption of S$500,000 (US$330,000) to S$1 million (US$660,000), depending upon the nature of the assets. Import duties are very low, except on motor vehicles, which bear a 125% duty.

Real GDP growth averaged 7% between 2004 and 2007, but dropped to 1.2% in 2008 as a result of the global financial crisis. The economy contracted in 2008 but still grew at 1.2%. Manufacturing and financial services are growth sectors. Tourism has been as high as 9.7 million visitors, benefiting the retail, hotel and service sectors. Generally, Singapore is a shopper's paradise, especially for electronics of all kinds. Over the longer term, the government hopes to establish a new growth path that will be less vulnerable to global demand cycles, especially for information technology products — it has attracted major investments in pharmaceuticals and medical technology production — and will continue efforts to establish Singapore as Southeast Asia's financial and high-tech hub.

OFFSHORE FINANCIAL CENTER

Singapore has grown into a world offshore financial haven, certainly comparable to Hong Kong and way ahead of its neighbor, fledgling Labuan in nearby Malaysia. Singapore has cultivated a sophisticated private banking sector, offering discreet financial services aimed at luring wealthy clients. Along with Hong Kong, it sees itself as a second financial gateway to expanding China, the eventual colossus of the East.

I visited Singapore for a legal conference and personally saw how local trust laws have been updated on a par with leading offshore trust nations such as Bermuda or Panama. Singapore also had strengthened its banking secrecy laws patterned after the strict privacy laws in Switzerland. However, in 2009, under pressure from the G-20 major nations, as were all tax havens, the government announced that it would adhere to the OECD standards governing the exchange of tax information among nations. It said it would implement the OECD standard to assist only bona fide requests for tax information and not "information fishing" for no good reason. It also began signing more TIEAs. This was said to be in keeping with "...Singapore's role as a trusted center for finance and a responsible jurisdiction, with strong and consistent regulatory policies and a firm commitment to the rule of law."

The government actively recruits wealthy businesspersons as residents. For those active in offshore finance, the island city-state wants to establish itself as Asia's newest private banking hub by luring the superwealthy away from places such as Hong Kong and even Switzerland.

Singapore's strengthened bank secrecy laws are one enticement, but the government also is allowing foreigners, especially Europeans, who meet its wealth requirements, to buy land and become permanent residents. The goal is to attract private wealth from across Asia, as well as riches that Europeans and other Westerners are moving out of

Switzerland and European Union nations to avoid new tax and reporting laws there.

Many Swiss banks, such as Bank Julius Baer, are beefing up their operations in Singapore to capitalize on the new business opportunities. The number of private banks operating in Singapore has nearly doubled to 35 in the past six years, according to officials. Authorities estimate that money managed by private banks in Singapore has grown 20% each year since 2000 to more than US$300 billion in 2009. In 2009, there were 106 foreign commercial banks in Singapore, of which 24 are full service banks, 40 are wholesale banks dealing only in foreign currencies and 42 are offshore banks.

CONTACTS

Government of Singapore: http://www.gov.sg/.

Embassy of the Republic of Singapore, 3501 International Place NW, Washington, D.C. 20008; Tel.: (202) 537-3100; Website: http://www.mfa.gov.sg/washington/; Email: singemb_was@sgmfa.gov.sg.

The U.S. Embassy, 27 Napier Road, Singapore 258508; Tel.: + (65) 6476-9100, Website: http://singapore.usembassy.gov/.

United Arab Emirate of Dubai

Dubai is one of the world's newest international financial centers. It aims to rival New York, London and Hong Kong, and seeks to serve the vast, oil-rich region between Europe and Asia. Since it began its campaign for world recognition as a major tax haven, it has attracted leading Fortune 500 and regional firms, but the global financial recession has slowed things down considerably.

History

The United Arab Emirates (UAE) are located in the Middle East, bordering the Gulf of Oman and the Persian Gulf, between Oman and Saudi Arabia.

Strategically located Dubai, one of the seven emirates, has become the leading UAE commercial gateway to more than 1.5 billion consumers in Asia, Africa, Europe, India and the Middle East. Fueled by billions of dollars in oil wealth, construction was everywhere, but now it has slowed noticeably. The emirate has worked to build a reputation as the Middle East regional business center. The Dubai government says that a quarter of all Fortune 500 global firms now service the Middle East and North Africa from a Dubai base.

Until recently, most Americans or people outside the Middle East had never heard of Dubai. This city-state first intruded on the consciousness of Americans in 2006 when a Dubai-based corporation planned to buy a company that managed several of America's major seaports. To listen to chauvinistic U.S. politicians at that time one would have thought Arab terrorists were about to invade

America again. The UAE is not considered a tax haven in the conventional sense but it comes within the type of country G-20 governments oppose because of its no tax regime. When the giant U.S. corporation Halliburton relocated its offices to Dubai there was a political outcry — even though it was within their legal right to do so.

Proud Tax Haven

Yes, Dubai is a tax haven and proud of it.

Jebel Ali, the first free trade zone in the UAE led the way in 2003 as a planned offshore financial center and as a major port. That was followed by a free trade zone at Ras Al Khaimah (RAK), another sheikdom, which also launched an offshore financial facility. RAK created an International Companies Registry, which allows foreign investors to register offshore companies without the need to establish a physical presence. Jebel Ali and Dubai offshore centers have positioned themselves as a Middle East tax haven comparable to the Cayman Islands or Liechtenstein. Observers have predicted the UAE will become the world center for Islamic finance. With a GDP per capita in 2008 of US$40,000, it ranks with the U.S. and Liechtenstein in personal income.

Dubai's evolution has been dramatic, with modern skyscrapers and gleaming office blocks springing up on the banks of Dubai Creek. Development has been well managed and oil wealth well channeled. The rulers of Dubai have a penchant for grand projects — a new extension to port facilities, the world's tallest hotel, the Palm Islands, a massive project with 62 miles of new beachfront as well as hotels, villas, shopping malls, cinemas and Dubai's first marine park. The global recession has slowed much of this development.

Land-hungry Dubai is increasingly looking to the waters of the Arabian Gulf in search of new land on which to develop, as shown by yet another huge project, "The World," which plans to build 300 islands in the shape of the world's countries. Dubai signed a deal with the Louvre Museum in Paris to establish a branch of the museum there — a claim no other nation can make.

Dubai International Financial Centre (DIFC): The DIFC is the world's newest international financial center with an announced aim of rivaling New York, London and Hong Kong. It primarily serves the vast region of the Middle East between Western Europe and East Asia. Since it opened in 2004, the DIFC has attracted leading global firms as well as regional firms. A world-class stock exchange, the Dubai International Financial Exchange (DIFX), opened in 2005. The DIFC is a 110-acre free zone, part of the larger government vision of a free environment for progress and economic development in the UAE.

The DIFC focuses on several sectors of financial activity: banking services, (including investment, corporate and private banking); capital markets (equity, debt instruments, derivatives and commodity trading); asset management and fund registration; insurance and re-insurance; Islamic finance; business processing operations and ancillary services. Financial institutions may apply for licenses in these sectors. Firms operating in the DIFC are eligible for benefits such as a zero tax rate on profits, 100% foreign ownership, no restrictions on foreign exchange or repatriation of capital and full modern operational support and business facilities.

UAE Commercial Center

The United Arab Emirates (UAE) is a union of seven sovereign sheikdoms formed when the British withdrew from the Arabian Gulf in 1971. Dubai is located on the Eastern coast of the Arabian Peninsula, in the southwest corner of the Arabian Gulf. It boasts mountains, beaches, deserts, oases, camel racing, markets and the renowned duty-free shopping, all packed into a relatively small area, home to 1.7 million people, a majority of them foreigners, especially south Asians. Dubai was also home to some 100,000 British and other Western expatriates, with Brits as leaders in the offshore financial sector, many of whom moved here from banks and investment firms in the City of London. The global recession caused an exodus of expats in 2009. A quarter of the people trace their origins to neighboring Iran.

This diversity discourages any real ethnic tensions and while conflict rages further north in Iraq, Dubai has remained trouble-free. The UAE government does not offer naturalization or permanent residence to expatriates. However, foreigners are permitted to purchase and own specifically designated property without a local partner or sponsor ("freeholds," as they are called).

Review its history and it's difficult to believe today, when Dubai has emerged as a global economic player and a major tourist destination, was little more than a desert settlement where Bedouin tribes roamed the sands and a huddle of settlers crowded around the banks of Dubai Creek less than a century ago. Only decades ago, Dubai had no running water, no roads and the main transport was the camel. But just before British colonial rule ended, oil was discovered in 1966 and Dubai blossomed.

Zero Taxes

Dubai also has one of the world's largest free trade zones and first-class Internet, media and communications infrastructure, much of it brand-new. All this and zero taxes, too. And Dubai has no Mutual Legal Assistance Treaties (MLATs) or tax information exchange agreements with the United States. Dubai stoutly resisted the Organization for Economic and Community Development's "harmful tax competition" initiative, preferring to keep its attractive zero tax regime. In 2009, Dubai agreed to apply the OECD's Article 26 standards for tax information exchange, thus avoiding the G-20 blacklist.

Dubai is a good choice for companies setting up distribution channels in Europe, the Middle East, Africa and Asia. It's worth considering for a bank account, although the banks tend to cater to rich Arabs and Dubai's large expatriate community. Residence permits are easy to acquire, especially if you're hired by a local company.

Dubai seems to know no end to its ambition, nor does it have any inhibitions, with new plans, such as those for the Middle East's largest shopping mall, the new airport at Jebel Ali and the world's tallest tower in Burj Dubai on the drawing board.

Dubai might be just what you or your business needs as a base of tax-free operations in an important part of the world.

It is one free market Arab country that is friendly to America and the West and one that offers real possibilities for offshore investment, banking and commerce of all kinds. And it could very well offer you a firm basis for investment in real estate, stocks and as a base for your business in the Mid-East and worldwide.

Contacts

U.A.E. Embassy, 3522 International Court, NW, Washington, D.C., 20008; tel. 202-243-2400. Website: http://www.uae-embassy.org/; Email: http://www.uae-embassy.org/contact-embassy.

U.S. Embassy mailing address: P.O. Box 4009, Abu Dhabi; Tel.: + 971 2 414-2200; Commercial Office: 971 2 414-2304; Website: http://uae.usembassy.gov/; Consul General in Dubai, P.O. Box 9343; Tel.: + 971 4 311-6000; Commercial Office: + 971 4 311-6149; Website: http://dubai.usconsulate.gov/.

For more about Dubai, see:

Dubai International Financial Center (DIFC); http://www.difc.ae/.

Dubai Government Information: http://www.dubai.ae/en.portal.

Dept. of Tourism & Marketing: http://www.dubaitourism.ae/.

Chapter Nine

The Atlantic/Caribbean Havens

The wide arc from Bermuda in the mid-Atlantic to Panama in Central America, including the adjacent Caribbean, is home to several tax and asset havens. Some are British colonies and, as such, have yielded to pressure from London to restrict their tax haven status, especially curtailing what was once strict financial privacy. In the past, these small jurisdictions built a reputation of protecting the wealth of offshore persons from many nations. But circumstances are changing rapidly in this area and you must be wary. Check their current status before you act.

Park Your Money in a Sunny Tropical Clime

High finance generates far more money than agriculture, tourism and fisheries combined — especially among the Atlantic and Caribbean havens.

During the last half of the 20th century, many of the sunny islands of the Caribbean realized this economic fact and purposefully transformed themselves into international tax and asset protection havens. Some of them, as British colonies, did so with encouragement from their colonial masters in London. At the time, the U.K. Foreign Office saw this transformation as a way to reduce the need for colonial subsidies from the British Treasury. In a far freer international atmosphere decades ago, London was not much bothered by far-off colonies where foreigners paid no taxes and bank accounts could be opened in fictitious names.

A Basic Change in Policy

By the end of the 20th century, the tax collectors at the Her Majesty's Revenue and Customs began to imagine that vast sums of unpaid taxes were hidden in what London now officially calls "British overseas territories." The socialist welfare states of Europe, joined by the United States, began to see tax havens, in general, as a vast sink of tax evasion. As I noted in Chapter 3, tax havens came under siege from a diverse group of leftist antagonists including the European Union, the Organization for Economic Cooperation and Development (OECD), the Financial Action Task Force (FATF) and even the United Nations.

The U.S. "war on drugs" played right into the hands of the IRS and other national tax collectors, since much of the illegal drug traffic originated in Latin America. Caribbean jurisdictions, where banking secrecy had always been a positive selling point, now found themselves accused of hiding millions in illicit drug money. Anti-money laundering laws became the new standard of international finance. The major nations, especially the U.S. and the U.K., ignored the fact that their own domestic banks laundered most of the criminal cash in the world. The drug war became a politically useful public relations ploy and an easy, shorthand way for politicians to accuse tax havens of being criminal cash conduits. In most cases, a lazy news media cooperated in this tax haven smear with little concern for the truth.

This anti-tax haven campaign only intensified after the terrorist attacks in New York and Washington, D.C. on 9/11. In the confused aftermath of these earthshaking events, leftist politicians raised the false accusation that haven nations had served as hiding places for terrorist cash. That this later proved untrue, after extensive investigations, mattered little to the major nations who saw an opportunity to push their anti-tax evasion plans. These plans called for an end to financial privacy, automatic tax information exchange and abolition of haven tax exemptions for foreigners who dared to use them.

The high-tax Labor government that took over in London in 1997 was among the strongest proponents of this new onslaught against tax havens, even though many of the leading havens were under British jurisdiction. Labor had strong allies in the City of London, where many financial firms viewed far off tax havens as a drain on their business. This sharp reversal of policy harmed the British overseas territories in the Atlantic and Caribbean for a time, but ultimately brought about needed reforms that produced net business gains in many jurisdictions.

The British Labor Party views the U.K.'s colonial offshore tax havens with disfavor. To protect yourself, you must be very careful in dealing with any of these havens. In every one of these jurisdictions, financial privacy and banking secrecy has been diminished. Beginning in 2009, all of these jurisdictions applied the OECD Article 26 standard for tax information exchange I previously discussed. In addition, where foreign tax evasion was not formerly considered a crime, it is now. And many of these jurisdictions now have signed Tax Information Exchange Agreements with the United States, a crucial step they had resisted for decades.

Nevertheless, in my opinion, several of these haven nations remain well-developed offshore financial centers that continue to offer good professional, legal, banking, trust and corporate services. Insurance and annuities are also specialties. As an added attraction, some offer attractive, tax-free residential retirement programs for foreigners. But if financial privacy is your major concern, you must move carefully in this area.

These definite pluses must be weighed against the rapidly changing political and legal climate in these havens, but I warn you to obtain the latest facts before you make decisions.

ATLANTIC-CARIBBEAN HAVENS

In a broad arc stretching southward from the mid-Atlantic to Central America are independent countries and some British overseas territories that specialize in offshore banking and finance. Each offers varying degrees of financial privacy and friendly, no-tax or low-tax special programs designed for foreigners.

Each of the sovereign nations in this group is a member of the United Nations and the more-or-less toothless Organization of American States (OAS). Some are also members of the British Commonwealth and others, by their U.K. association, enjoy special participation rights in the European Union. Most are members of the Caribbean Community (CARICOM), an area-wide economic and trading group of 15 nations. Created in 1973, the CARICOM groups Antigua and Barbuda, The Bahamas, Barbados, Belize, Dominica, Grenada, Guyana, Haiti, Jamaica, Montserrat, Saint Kitts & Nevis, Saint Lucia, Saint

Vincent and the Grenadines, Suriname and Trinidad and Tobago. Anguilla, Bermuda, the British Virgin Islands, the Cayman Islands and the Turks & Caicos Islands are all associate members of CARICOM.

Anyone with investments, banking or offshore entities located in the United Kingdom's overseas territories — **Bermuda**, the **British Virgin Islands**, the **Cayman Islands, Anguilla** and the **Turks & Caicos Islands** — should have serious concerns about the direction in which these havens are being forced to go by London.

The U.K. Foreign Office ordered the above overseas territories to amend local laws to permit the enforcement of foreign tax judgments, something none of them previously allowed. Since the U.K. has ultimate colonial jurisdiction over the territories, their only alternative to compliance with the U.K. demands is to declare independence from the U.K., a step none of them seems willing to take. Although independence groups developed in some places most never got off the ground.

There were rumblings about possible independence in Bermuda but they faded fast. At least one territorial head of state minced no words: "You have one option; independence or serfdom." The then-former Chief Minister of Anguilla, Hubert Hughes, made this blunt statement in a letter to all Anguillans in direct response to the U.K. Foreign Office demands. Hughes said London was bestowing dictatorial powers on the official Crown-appointed governor who, with agreement of the U.K. Foreign Secretary, was amending, vetoing and introducing legislation without consulting the Anguillan parliament. Similar directives were issued to Bermuda, the Cayman Islands, the British Virgin Islands and the Turks and Caicos Islands. This sort of control from London reached a zenith in 2009 when the Foreign Office revoked the right of self-government of the Turks & Caicos and took over control of the islands after a major corruption scandal.

Sir Ronald Sanders, formerly Antigua and Barbuda's High Commissioner to the United Kingdom, has been a vociferous critic of the OECD. Concerning the G-20/OECD gray list that emerged after the April 2009 London meeting he wrote: "Conspicuously absent from the meeting were small island states, the world's poorest states, and countries regarded as 'tax havens'. There is no evidence whatsoever that public finances and financial systems were threatened by jurisdictions with offshore financial services. Yet, without one of these accused jurisdictions present to argue the unfairness of the statement, it was made by the G20..."

Independence does not seem to be a real option for the smaller U.K.-dependent territories, some of which, like the Turks & Caicos, would find it difficult to survive without ties to the "mother country" and the subsidies that brings. That cannot be said of places like Bermuda and the Cayman Islands that can stand on their own considerable financial feet, just as The Bahamas has done more-or-less successfully since they became independent from the U.K. in 1973. What seems to be lacking in the Caymans and in Bermuda is both the leadership and the collective political will to act. The colonials seem comfortable with the chains that bind them to their London masters.

RATIONALIZED JUSTIFICATION

Defending this fundamental change in its attitude

towards its offshore financial centers, the U.K. claimed it was acting to meet its obligation to comply with the European Union's anti-money-laundering directives. Then the excuse was a need to fight international terrorism. In 2008-2009, the global recession became the latest excuse, with U.K. leaders falsely claiming that offshore jurisdictions somehow were responsible for the mess that originated in Wall Street and the City of London.

The Labor Party aimed their high tax attacks squarely at the British people with offshore investments, banking, trusts and asset protection plans. U.K. banks were forced to reveal accounts of all U.K. residents with offshore financial activity. Tax collectors hounded those named. Indeed, her Majesty's Revenue and Customs (aping the U.S. IRS), now seems to assume that any Brit with offshore financial activity is evading taxes.

As expected, the result has been to dampen foreign interest in using some of these places as offshore havens. The resulting outflow of funds from places such as the Cayman Islands has benefited other haven nations such as Switzerland. Other major beneficiaries have been Far Eastern financial centers such as Hong Kong, Singapore and Dubai.

What London did not expect were the major "clean house" policy changes these U.K. offshore havens adopted on their own. As did the U.K. havens in the Channel Islands and the Isle of Man, the Caribbean havens adopted stricter anti-money laundering, tough know-your-customer rules and much stronger criminal investigations aimed at financial fraud and terrorist cash. Indeed, these jurisdictions now have tougher laws and better financial law enforcement than the U.K. itself.

The written constitutions provided to overseas territories pursuant to the U.K.'s Statute of Westminster (1931) allow the British Crown (i.e., the government of the moment) to bypass local legislatures by declaring an emergency and imposing its own rules. These extraordinary powers were invoked in the Caribbean area dependent territories in January 1998 after they initially refused London's demand to enact "all crimes" anti-money laundering statutes that would enforce foreign tax claims. Until this threat loomed, these havens traditionally had imposed no taxes on income and did not recognize foreign tax avoidance or tax evasion as a criminal matter.

All four territories (Bermuda, the British Virgin Islands, Anguilla and the Turks and Caicos Islands) already had adopted tough money laundering laws that permitted enforcement of foreign confiscation orders in money laundering cases from "designated countries" — only the U.S. and the U.K. at the time. However, contrary to U.K. demands, they all included in their statutes a "fiscal offense" exemption that precluded enforcement in case of tax and customs violations alleged by a foreign government. In 1998, the Cayman Islands government was the first to remove the fiscal offense exemption. London said it expected all the territories to follow orders and each one did.

In the eyes of many, once these anti-privacy demands of London were met, the U.K. overseas territories diminished their value as asset havens. They are being pressed by London to repeal laws allowing a tax-free status for foreign investors and to reveal beneficial ownership of all trusts and international business corporations (IBCs). When and if that comes to pass, they will be tax havens no more.

I have serious concerns about the Labor government's continued crackdown on all overseas territories, but at this writing it appears Labor may be defeated in the 2010 parliamentary elections — not that the British Conservative Party would be much better. However, these islands still offer a great deal of financial services that you can invest in without worrying about U.K. government intervention.

What this recent U.K. history means to the average offshore investor is less financial privacy. For those trying to hide funds abroad, it means, as it should, an increased probability of discovery and prosecution.

The danger lies in a middle area in which foreign tax collectors try to conduct "fishing expeditions." They're looking for possible tax evasion simply because their citizens are financially active offshore. The TIEAs with the United States may lend themselves to just this sort of tax overreaching. However, this depends on how the island governments administer the TIEA terms, although each has denied that they will allow IRS fishing expeditions.

Because these islands are under ultimate control of the United Kingdom, they lack the somewhat greater privacy and freedom to act as independent tax havens, such as Panama, Singapore, Hong Kong or Switzerland.

Five years ago, I wrote, "As long as the British Labor government continues in power, you can expect it will continue its unrelenting efforts to curb tax and asset havens, including those under its colonial domination." At this writing, it appears that Labor's tenure may end in the elections of 2010.

ANGUILLA

This luxury tourist destination has high-priced villas and upscale resorts. The most northerly of the British Leeward Islands, it retains the laid-back character of a sleepy backwater. Goats still wander the streets and reggae music blares from passing cars. However, it offers a unique electronic Internet system (ACORN) for instant registration of IBCs, trusts and other legal entities.

Anguilla (population 14,000) is located in the Caribbean Sea, the northern-most island in the Leeward Island chain. It was first colonized by English settlers from St. Kitts, beginning in 1650. The island was administered by England until the early nineteenth century, when, against the wishes of the inhabitants, it was incorporated into a single British dependency along with St. Kitts & Nevis. After a 1967 rebellion and brief period as a self-declared independent republic, it became a separate British "dependency" (now termed a British overseas territory) in 1980.

Anguilla has few natural resources, and the economy depends heavily on luxury tourism, offshore banking, lobster fishing, and remittances from emigrants. Increased activity in the tourism industry has spurred the growth of the construction sector contributing to economic growth. Anguillan officials have put substantial effort into developing the offshore financial sector, which is small but growing. In the medium term, prospects for the economy will depend largely on the tourism sector and, therefore, on revived income growth in the industrialized nations as well as on favorable weather conditions.

ELECTRONIC OFFSHORE

Anguilla's Commercial Online Registration Network (ACORN) came into existence in 1998 allowing electronic filing of documents and signatures in electronic form. Today, 95% of all documents, including new registrations, are filed electronically by locally licensed service providers and their approved overseas agents, who are given direct access to ACORN. Using the latest technology, ACORN enables instant and secure electronic incorporation and registration of Anguillan domestic companies, IBCs, limited liability companies (LLCs), limited partnerships and trust companies. In addition to English, ACORN has been able to incorporate electronically companies with Chinese characters and in French, Spanish and Russian (Cyrillic).

Anguilla has enacted numerous laws authorizing offshore insurance, mutual funds, trusts and private interest foundations, but with a small professional sector and limited personnel, it will be a while before the island can compete fully with the established offshore big boys.

CONTACTS

Government of Anguilla: http://www.gov.ai/.

Anguilla Financial Services Commission, PO Box 1575, The Valley, Anguilla. Tel.: + 1 264 497 5881, Email: info@fsc.org.ai; Website: http://www.fsc.org.ai.

ACORN (Anguilla Online Commercial Registration Network) PO Box 60, The Valley, Anguilla, Tel.: + 264497 5881, Email: anguillafsd@anguilla.net,

Website: http://www.axafsc.com/.

OFFICIAL

There is no U.S. embassy in Anguilla. Relations are conducted through the U.S. Embassy in London and the Embassy of the United Kingdom, 3100 Massachusetts Avenue NW, Washington, D.C. 20008; Tel.: 202-462-1340; Website: http://www.britainusa.com/.

Commonwealth of The Bahamas

During the 20th century, these islands off the southeast coast of the U.S. blossomed into a major tax and asset protection haven, especially for nearby Americans. It offered tax exemption for foreigners and a series of well-crafted laws allowing IBCs, trusts, offshore banks and insurance — all wrapped in maximum financial privacy protected by law.

Because so many Americans used The Bahamas as their favorite offshore haven, the islands came under heavy pressure from the U.S. government and the IRS because of suspected tax evasion. Then there is the issue of drug smuggling and money laundering. Starting in 2000, the then-Bahamian government adopted a series of U.S.-demanded laws that largely disrupted these cozy arrangements and seriously diminished the islands role as an offshore haven. These changes were topped off with a Tax Information Exchange Agreement with the U.S., which meant goodbye financial privacy!

It's still a nice place to retire, vacation, or have a second home, but more secure banking, investment, tax and asset havens can be found elsewhere.

Geography Determines History, Then and Now

Geography has always played a major part in determining Bahamian history. Located at the northern edge of the Caribbean, this chain of hundreds of islands lies in the North Atlantic Ocean, southeast of Florida and northeast of Cuba. The Bahamas archipelago at its nearest point is about 50 miles east of the United States.

Arawak Indians inhabited the islands in 1492 when Christopher Columbus made his first landfall in the New World on the island of San Salvador in the eastern Bahamas. After observing the shallow sea around the islands, it is reported that he said, "baja mar" (low water or sea) and thus named the area The Bahamas, or The Islands of the Shallow Sea. (By the way, this nation's official name is two words — "The Bahamas," and that's with a capital 'T'.)

English settlement began in 1647 and the islands became a British colony in 1783. Its population now is about 304,000. Since attaining independence from the U.K. in 1973, The Bahamas have prospered through tourism, international banking and investment management. But because of its geography, the country is a major transshipment point for illegal drugs to the U.S. and for smuggling illegal migrants into the U.S. And, as you will see, having the United States as your next-door neighbor has not been easy for The Bahamas.

AN OFFSHORE POWERHOUSE NO MORE

Start with these facts. The Bahamas grew from a tiny offshore tax haven comprising a few branches of foreign banks in the mid 1960s to a world banking powerhouse by the year 2000. The country's legislation and regulatory structure, comparatively highly skilled workforce and its friendly, pro-business government attracted some of the most prestigious financial institutions from around the globe.

The Bahamas is, and has been for several decades, home to a well-developed offshore financial center. Until a few years ago, it had more than 400 banks and trust companies, 580 mutual funds and 60 insurance companies operating here. It also had registered approximately 100,000 IBCs, mostly for nonresidents.

The asset base of The Bahamas' banking center was in excess of US$200 billion, positioning it among the top 10 countries in the world, behind Switzerland, the U.S., the U.K., Japan and the Cayman Islands, among others. Private banking, portfolio management and mutual fund administration are important. In those days, banks from 36 countries were licensed to conduct business within or from The Bahamas. Licensees included about 100 euro currency branches of international banks and trusts, as well as 168 Bahamian incorporated banking institutions. Sixty percent of all licensed banks offered trust services in addition to their regular banking operations.

After tourism, financial services constitute the second-most important sector of the Bahamian economy and, when combined with business services, account for about 36% of GDP. However, since December 2000, when the government enacted new regulations on the financial sector, many international businesses have left The Bahamas. Nevertheless, largely due to increased offshore financial activity, the GDP more than doubled from US$3.2 billion in 1992 to US$8.8 billion in 2008.

And The Bahamas is still a tax haven. There are no business taxes or income taxes, although various registration and transfer fees amount to a tax estimated by some to approach 20%, depending on the nature of the transactions.

Since 2000 and the adoption of new, stricter laws, 200 of the 223 private banks in The Bahamas have closed and 30,000 international business companies have been stricken from the official register. The local news media attributed these departures, at least in part, to stricter money laundering legislation and a weakening of banking and financial secrecy.

Drastic, Unnecessary Changes

Therefore, until the year 2000, The Bahamas stood out as one of the world's premier asset and tax haven nations.

But in June 2000, the former Free National Movement (FNM) government (later defeated for re-election in May 2002) systematically began to dismantle and dilute the islands' offshore legal framework that had been carefully designed to protect financial privacy and offshore wealth brought into the islands.

This signaled retreat from tax haven status by the FNM government was a defeatist response to the double "honor" of being listed on two tax haven blacklists issued by the FATF and the OECD. These outsiders charged The Bahamas with damaging "international financial stability," being uncooperative in combating money laundering and engaging in "harmful tax competition," meaning levying no taxes on foreigners. They were threatened with undefined "stern countermeasures" if they failed to open bank and other financial records to foreign tax and criminal investigators and to make numerous other changes in their offshore laws.

Pressure from Washington

Instead of fighting back and telling these outsiders to "buzz off," the FNM government rapidly pushed through

Parliament, over strong minority opposition, a host of statutory changes that substantially weakened the very financial privacy and asset protection that had attracted to the islands tends of thousands of offshore bank accounts, international business companies and asset protection trusts. These new laws admittedly were drafted with the direct assistance of "financial experts" from London and Washington, D.C. The government also said it had accepted "a generous offer" of technical assistance from the U.S. Treasury Department, no doubt including IRS agents.

This capitulation to Washington's demands echoed a crisis in the early 1980s when the late Prime Minister, Lynden O. Pindling, accused of drug dealing, was confronted by an angry U.S. government that threatened sanctions against The Bahamas. Although Pindling was cleared, he was forced to grant U.S. law and drug enforcement officers diplomatic immunity and free passage through the archipelago, plus some limited access to secret offshore banks of some accused criminals.

The Progressive Labor Party (PLP) parliamentary opposition rightfully argued that repeal or change of most of the offshore laws that brought huge investments and assets to The Bahamas would indeed result in capital flight, as individual offshore bank accounts were closed and financial activity fled elsewhere.

Subsequently, many private banks and offshore financial firms announced their departure, citing the new laws as reason for their exodus. PLP opposition members of parliament called on the government to resign over the OECD and FATF debacle, claiming that the blacklisting was directly related to the government's prolonged inability to deal with drug trafficking. Privately, Bahamian sources said government figures were implicated in numerous questionable, but highly profitable, financial activities, a situation the U.S. was holding over their heads unless they acted as Washington demanded.

In May 2002, the PLP opposition won control of parliament and a new PLP Prime Minister, Perry Christie, took office. All these new laws became a major political issue with the PLP, charging they had damaged the offshore financial community. Although Perry and the PLP promised to review and reverse many of these laws, they failed to do so. Indeed, they went ahead with the U.S. Tax Information Exchange Agreement initiated by the defeated FNM government.

Since then, the FNM has regained political control and all the laws that drove away much of the offshore business remain in place.

New Laws, Amendments to Old Laws

Among the many laws, the "Evidence Act 2000" removed the requirement that requested evidence could not be released to another country until a court proceeding had begun in the requesting nation. Evidence can now be released for foreign preliminary investigations. This law appears to permit Bahamian enforcement of U.S. civil forfeiture orders. Another law allows confiscation of cash and assets under a U.S.-style civil forfeiture procedure that permits freezing of bank and other accounts. Still another law empowers Bahamian courts to extradite criminal suspects during investigations before trial. It should be noted that The Bahamas already had in force mutual legal assistance treaties with the U.S., U.K. and Canada.

Tougher Money Laundering Laws

Existing anti-money laundering laws were toughened to make violations punishable by a possible sentence of 20 years in jail and/or a US$100,000 fine for each instance. A "Currency Declaration Act" requires reporting of all cash or investment transfers, in or out of the islands in excess of US$10,000. The Central Bank also has broad powers to regulate offshore banks, their registration, operation and reporting. The law allows foreign bank inspectors to conduct on-site and offsite examinations of the accounts in bank branches or subsidiaries located in The Bahamas.

The Bahamas "financial intelligence unit" was modeled after the U.S. Treasury Financial Crimes Enforcement Network (FinCEN). Opposition members of parliament criticized the FIU's powers as far too broad, charging there are no provisions to prevent political "fishing trips" or "witch hunts" by government police. This unit can request ("order" might be a better word) a bank to freeze any funds suspected of being part of criminal activity for up to 72 hours, while a secret "monitoring order" is sought by police to confiscate money or block transactions. In such cases, all other financial confidentiality laws are waived. The FIU issued U.S.-style rules requiring "suspicious activity reporting" by all financial institutions.

Still other laws require all banks to verify the true identity of customers for whom Bahamian intermediaries open accounts. Bahamian banks now use special U.S. cash flow analysis software to detect possible money laundering. Offshore financial trustees and attorneys are required to maintain records of beneficial owners of offshore trusts and international business corporations. Previously, professional attorney-client privilege rules prevented revealing such information.

IBCs Under Fire

Until 2002, IBCs had not been required to disclose the identities of shareholders or other detailed business information unless under a court order. Now, the right of IBCs to issue and use bearer shares has been repealed and all IBCs are required to submit to the government the true identities and addresses of directors. There are currently more than 100,000 international business corporations in The Bahamas, with about 16,000 added each year. Secrecy of ownership undoubtedly was a large factor in attracting these IBCs and now that has ended.

Conclusion

Even though The Bahamas is still an offshore tax haven, it remains in considerable internal governmental and political turmoil. The mass exodus of so many Bahamian financial community members speaks volumes about those who judge events first-hand. The best financial and investment climates are those that enjoy some degree of predictability and that's not The Bahamas.

My advice is to scratch The Bahamas off your list of offshore tax and asset haven nations. Things may change someday, but if you were thinking of using the islands as a base of offshore operations, forget it.

CONTACTS

Government

Securities Commission of The Bahamas, Charlotte House, Charlotte Street, P.O. Box N-8347, Nassau, The Bahamas; Tel.: +242-356-6291. Website: http://www.scb.gov.bs/.

Central Bank of The Bahamas, P.O. Box N-4868, Nassau, The Bahamas; Tel.: +242-322-2193, Website: http://www.centralbankbahamas.com/.

Official

Embassy of The Bahamas, 2220 Massachusetts Ave., NW, Washington, D.C. 20008 (tel: 202-319-2660). Consulates General: 231 East 46th Street, New York, NY 10017 Tel.: 212-421-6420; Suite 818, Ingraham Building, 25 SE Second Ave., Miami, FL 33131; Tel.: 305-373-6295.

U.S. Embassy, 42 Queen Street, Nassau, The Bahamas; Tel.: + (242) 322-1181 or after hours: + (242) 328-2206; Email: embnas@state.gov; Website: http://nassau.usembassy.gov/.

BARBADOS

This Caribbean island is not a full-fledged tax haven, but its low business and professional taxes, combined with a network of bilateral double tax treaties with major nations, makes it a favorite for foreign investment, especially among Canadians.

HISTORY

Barbados is the most easterly of the Caribbean islands, northeast of Venezuela, 166 square miles (430 square kilometers), located 1,200 miles southeast of Miami, about four and a half hours by air from New York and eight hours from London.

Although it only achieved independence in 1966, the country has one of the oldest Westminster-style parliaments in the western hemisphere, one that has existed for almost 360 years. Ninety percent of the population of 285,000 is of African descent and more than 80% of the people live in urban areas. The education system is excellent with a literacy rate of almost 100% providing a highly trained workforce for both professional and skilled workers. English is the official language, which helps to make Barbados a good place to do business.

The island was uninhabited when first settled by the British in 1627. Slaves worked the sugar plantations established on the island until 1834 when slavery was abolished. The economy remained heavily dependent on sugar, rum and molasses production through most of the 20th century. The gradual introduction of social and political reforms in the 1940s and 1950s led to complete independence from the U.K. in 1966. In the 1990s, tourism and manufacturing surpassed the sugar industry in economic importance.

Historically, the Barbadian economy had been dependent on sugarcane cultivation and related activities, but production in recent years has diversified into light industry and tourism.

OFFSHORE FINANCIAL CENTER

Offshore finance and information services are important foreign exchange earners. International business and financial services employ about 3,000 Barbadians and by some unofficial estimates contribute 7.5% of the country's GDP. The major appeal as an offshore financial center is the country's low corporate and business taxes, plus a network of bilateral double tax treaties with major nations that allow tax credit for foreign taxes paid. Double taxation treaties exist with Canada, CARICOM, China, Cuba, Finland, Norway, Malta, Mauritius, Sweden, Switzerland, U.S., U.K., Venezuela, and Botswana.

The country enjoys one of the highest per capita incomes ($9,800) in the region. Offshore finance and information services are important foreign exchange earners and thrive from having the same time zone as eastern U.S. and Canadian financial centers and a relatively highly educated workforce.

Barbados has avoided OECD and FATF blacklists by having low tax rates, double taxation agreements and exchange of information treaties as a way to attract business. It has a strict anti-money laundering law and is serious about applying "know your customer" and suspicious activity rules. Its no-nonsense, clean business image undoubtedly accounts for its popularity among foreign investors and businesses who choose to locate here.

The Barbados dollar has been pegged to the U.S. dollar since 1975 at a rate of two Barbados dollars to US$1.00 and this stability has proven attractive to foreign business. The country has some exchange control regulations but international business corporations and financial services, including insurance companies, international banks and international trusts are exempted. A special tax break allows 35% of the paychecks of qualified foreign employees working in IBCs, international banks, international societies with restricted liability, qualifying insurance companies and exempt insurance companies can be paid free of Barbadian income tax and in any foreign currency.

The government has established a separate ministry to facilitate the development of the international business sector. Some of the incentives include reduced tax rates between 1% and 2.5%, exemption from withholding tax on dividends, interest, royalties or other income paid to non-residents and freedom from exchange controls.

CONTACTS

Barbados Investment & Development Corp. Pelican House Princess Alice Highway, Bridgetown, Barbados. Tel.: + 1 246 427 5350, Email: asobers@bidc.org, Website: www.bidc.com

Central Bank of Barbados, Tom Adams Financial Center, Spry Street, Bridgetown Barbados, West Indies. Email: info@centralbank.org.bb, Website: http://www.central-bank.org.bb/

Invest Barbados, Trident Insurance Financial Center, Hastings, Christ Church, BB15156, P.O. Box 1009 Bridgetown, St. Michael, BB11142 Tel.: (246) 626-2000; Email: info@investbarbados.org, Website: http://www. investbarbados.org/

Offices in the U.S., U.K. and Canada

Official

Embassy of Barbados, 2144 Wyoming Avenue, N.W., Washington, D.C. 20008; Tel.: (202) 939-9200; Website: http://barbadosembassy.org/, Email: washington@foreign. gov.bb.

U.S. Embassy, Wildey Business Park, Wildey, St. Michael, Barbados; Tel.: 246-436-4950; Fax: 246-429-5246. Website: http://barbados.usembassy.gov/

Belize: Caribbean Gem

Belize, the only English-speaking nation in Central America, has had in place for almost two decades a series of offshore laws allowing asset protection trusts, IBCs, maritime registration, insurance and banking — plus maximum financial privacy. Its parliament, courts and government are very pro-offshore and cultivate foreign business and investments. An unusual feature is a special, tax-free retirement residency program for foreigners. But having said all that, this is definitely a Third World country, with all the problems that entails.

In the Caribbean region after Panama and Nevis, Belize is a close third for banking privacy, low and no taxes and a business-friendly government. It should be on everyone's list of possible offshore financial bases, but you need to understand its limitations as well.

Having visited Belize twice, I can attest that it's definitely "Third World," but people there are very friendly and oceanfront real estate is still relatively cheap. Belize is one of the few remaining independent nations proud to hold itself out as a tax and asset protection haven.

Belize is the only English-speaking country in Central America. Its mixed population of 304,000 includes descendants of native Mayans, Chinese, East Indians and Caucasians. Independent since 1981, its language came from its colonial days when it was known as "British Honduras." Situated south of Mexico and to the east of Guatemala, Belize is on the Caribbean seaboard. It has the largest barrier reef in the Western Hemisphere and great deep-sea diving. To the east, there's a sprinkle of Caribbean tropical islands included within the nation's borders. A few years ago, American television viewers discovered

Belize as the locale for one of the first reality TV shows, "Temptation Island."

Belize retains many of the colonial customs and features familiar in places such as the Cayman Islands and Bermuda, although it is far less developed. The first settlers were probably British woodcutters, who in 1638, found the valuable commodity known as "Honduran mahogany." Bananas, sugar cane and citrus fruit are the principal crops. Like many small countries dependent on primary commodities, Belize more recently recognized the benefits of introducing offshore tax haven financial services to boost its income.

CLEAN MONEY

American government officials have had a case of nerves over Belize. Some feared that the sleepy little capital town of Belmopan would become a prime site for U.S. tax evasion and money laundering. But the Belizean government has cooperated with the U.S. in drug and money laundering cases, although extradition from Belize is still difficult. The nation's clean money reputation was also boosted by adoption of a strong anti-money laundering law that is enforced vigorously.

In 1992, the Belize National Assembly enacted modern legislation seeking to make the country a competitive offshore financial center. Drafters combed tax haven laws worldwide and came up with a series of minimal corporate and tax requirements that could well fit your business needs. The new laws include the Trust Act, which allows a high level of asset protection, great freedom of action by the trustee and no taxes on income earned outside Belize.

There is also a statute allowing the creation of international business companies that can be formed in less than a day for less than US$1,000. You only need one shareholder and/or director, whose name can be shielded from public view.

There are no local income taxes, personal or corporate and no currency exchange controls. Since 1990 when the International Business Companies Act became law, foreigners have registered about 5,000 IBCs. That's a relatively small number compared to a place like the British Virgin Islands, but the number is growing. Belize is also witness major growth in the shipping registry business. Other laws favor offshore insurance companies, limited liability partnerships and banking.

Over the last decade, the government of Belize has carefully and systematically established the nation as an offshore haven that welcomes foreign investment and foreign nationals. It has enacted a series of laws crafted to protect financial privacy and promote creation of offshore trusts and international business corporations (IBCs). It has an attractive special residency program aimed at retirement-bound foreign citizens.

LONDON PRESSURES

A member of the Commonwealth and a former British colony, independent since 1981, Belize still has strong ties with London and is thus susceptible to U.K. Foreign Office pressures. In 2000, shortly after the OECD "harmful tax competition" blacklisting of Belize, London made known that future aid of all kinds, including debt forgiveness, would depend in part on Belize's willingness to cooperate in modifying some of its tax-haven attractions. At one point, London suspended debt relief to Belize in response to alleged tax breaks for favored offshore investors in Belize.

Belize bowed to the pressure by promising to somewhat tighten its offshore regulations. This subsequently included repeal of the Belize instant economic citizenship program and limitations on the issuance and use of bearer shares.

Offshore Industry Expands

In spite of OECD's and London's carping, Belize's small offshore industry continues to grow, providing financial services to a largely nonresident clientele. These services include international business company and offshore trust formation and administration; international banking services, including foreign currency bank accounts and international VISA cards; fund management, accounting and secretarial services; captive insurance; and ship registration.

A sympathetic government continues to work closely with the Belize Offshore Practitioners Association in drafting future legislation covering offshore banking, captive insurance, limited duration companies, protected cell companies and limited partnerships. All professional trust providers now must register with, and be licensed by, the government.

The Belizean banking sector is small but secret by force of law. There are only five commercial banks. Privacy protection here rivals even that of airtight Nevis. In 2009, Belize was placed in the OECD "gray list" of those countries allegedly failing to meet international standards concerning tax information exchange. It has indicated that it will do so.

Some banking clients here have complained about a Third World attitude on the part of Belize bankers, with slow service and failure to protect client privacy due to sloppy work.

Tax Free Residency

A good example of a Belize welcome of offshore persons is the Retired Persons Incentive Act that is implemented by the Belize Tourism Board. The program, which resembles the popular pensionado program in Panama, is designed to attract foreign retirees and foreign capital.

Known as the "qualified retired persons" (QRP) Program, the law offers significant tax incentives to those willing to become permanent residents, but not full citizens. The program is aimed primarily at residents of the U.S., Canada and the U.K., but is open to all.

A "qualified retired person" is exempted from all taxes on income from sources outside Belize. QRPs can own and operate their own international business based in Belize exempt from all local taxes. Local income earned within Belize is taxed at a graduated rate of 15% to 45% and QRPs need a work permit in order to engage in purely domestic business activities. For QRPs, import duties are waived for personal effects, household goods and for a motor vehicle or other transport, such as an airplane or boat. There is no minimum time that must be spent in Belize and QRPs can maintain their status so long as they maintain a permanent local residence such as a small apartment or condominium.

To qualify for the QRP Program, an applicant must be 45 years of age or older and prove personal financial ability to support oneself and any dependents. A spouse and dependents (18 and younger) qualify along with the head of household at no extra fee. Initial fees for the program are US$700, plus US$100 for an ID card upon application approval. Minimum financial requirements include an annual income of at least US$24,000 from a pension, annuity or other sources outside Belize.

For more information about the QRP Program, contact the following agency:

Belize Tourism Board, 64 Regent Street, P.O. Box 325, Belize City, Belize. Tel.: 501-227-2420, Toll-free (from the US): 1-800-624-0686, Email: info@travelbelize.org, Website: http://www.belizeretirement.org; http://www. travelbelize.org.

CONCLUSION

In spite of British, U.S. and OECD pressures, Belize is not about to enact income or corporate taxes that would drive away foreign investors and residents. In this relatively impoverished country, the offshore sector is a needed and highly valued source of foreign capital that has strong government support. Any modifications to offshore laws are likely to be minimal and mainly window dressing to silence foreign critics.

The offshore professional sector in Belize certainly is not comparable to a highly developed nation such as

Panama as an offshore haven, but it also has not sold out to outside pressures, as have the British overseas territories. Its laws offer a full array of offshore entities for asset protection and as investment vehicles, trusts, IBCs and limited liability companies. Its one weakness is its small banking community, but you can just as easily locate your Belize IBC bank account in Vienna or London, where private banking is an art.

CONTACTS

Official

Government of Belize, http://www.governmentofbelize. gov.bz/.

Belize Embassy, 2535 Massachusetts Avenue, N.W., Washington, D.C. 20008; Tel.: (202) 332-9636; Fax: (202) 332-6888; Website: http://www.embassyofbelize. org; Email: ebwreception@aol.com, Belize travel information office, New York City; Tel.: 1 (800) 624-0686.

U.S. Embassy, Floral Park St., Belmopan, Cayo Belize; Tel.: + (501) 822-4011; Email: embbelize@state.gov, Website: http://belize.usembassy.gov/.

BERMUDA: CROWN JEWEL OF THE ATLANTIC

This mid-Atlantic island is the world's leading place for "captive" self-insurance used by businesses and for re-insurance and it offers excellent asset protection trusts and IBCs. Its respected banks have worldwide branches and investment services. But Bermuda has signed a TIEA with the U.S., made foreign income tax evasion a local crime and curbed its former financial privacy laws. Of equal concern, as a U.K. colony, it is forced to take orders from London and the British Labor Party.

WORLD CLASS OFFSHORE CENTER

Bermuda is located in the mid-Atlantic, 750 miles southeast of New York City, 3,445 miles from London. The island (68,000 people, 21 square miles) has a long history as a tax and banking haven. This is a world-class financial outpost, not to mention a very pleasant place to visit or live in any season.

The islands were first settled in 1609 by shipwrecked English colonists heading for Virginia. Bermuda has remained in British hands ever since and today is a British overseas territory with internal self-government. A referendum on independence was defeated in 1995 but sporadic independence talk continues. The present government says it has reopened debate on the issue, but not very seriously.

Bermuda enjoys the third-highest per capita income in the world (US$70,000), more than 50% higher than that of the US. Its economy is primarily based on providing financial services for international business and luxury facilities for tourists.

Because of its liberal regulatory laws, a number of U.S. reinsurance companies relocated to the island following the 9/11 attacks and again after Hurricane Katrina in August 2005 contributing to the expansion of an already booming international business sector. Bermuda's tourism industry, 80% of its visitors from the U.S., continues to struggle but remains the island's second industry. Most capital equipment and food must be imported. Bermuda's industrial sector is small, although construction continues to be important; the average cost of a house in 2003 had risen to $976,000. Agriculture is limited with only 20% of the land being arable.

A self-governing British overseas territory, Bermuda is a major international financial center. In the early days, the focus was based largely on re-insurance companies. About 30% of the world's 5,000 captives are domiciled in Bermuda. The insurance industry includes more than 1,400 insurance and reinsurance companies, with active companies having US$172 billion in assets and writing almost US$50 billion in annual gross premiums.

Tax-Free Business, Expensive Real Estate

Bermuda imposes no corporate income, gift, capital gains, or sales taxes. The income tax is extremely low — 11% on income earned from employment in Bermuda. More than 13,000 international business corporations call Bermuda home. They are drawn by the island's friendly, tax neutral environment, established business integrity and minimal regulation. Over 60% of these companies operate as "exempted," meaning their business is conducted outside Bermuda (except for the minimal contacts needed to sustain an office on the island).

Bermuda is also home to more then 600 "collective investment schemes" (mutual funds), unit trusts and limited partnerships. The net asset value of these funds licensed in Bermuda rose by 37% in 2005, reaching US$158 billion. Under the strong protective umbrella of the U.K. Copyright Act of 1965, also applicable in Bermuda, many collective investment schemes with intellectual property and software interests use the island as a legal home port. With a statutory structure for protection, Bermuda also has become a center for offshore trust creation and management. The island offers a wide variety of trusts to meet every need, including offshore asset protection.

The "jewel of the Atlantic" is also a great place to live, but be aware of tough real estate restrictions. Demand is high and supply short. In general, non-Bermudians are permitted to own only one local property. Acquisition is allowed only after careful background checks (at least one bank reference and two or more personal references). Out of 20,000 residential units on the island, only 250 detached homes and 480 condominiums qualify for non-Bermudian purchasers based on government set values.

In January 2009, the average price in Bermuda for a modest two-bedroom, single-family house without water views was $1.65 million. The average price of a condominium was above $1 million. In addition to the purchase price of a home or condominium qualified for sale to non-Bermudians, there is a 25% government upfront purchase tax on homes and 18% on condominiums. Purchase licenses are granted by the Department of Immigration and require six months or more for approval.

BERMUDA BANKING

Over many decades, Bermuda has achieved a global reputation as a world-class business center. It has set high standards with the best laws and infrastructure with continuing improvements based on experience. There is a spirit of cooperation between business and government in support of the offshore sector. Bermuda as an offshore financial center dates to the 1930s, but began to grow significantly after 1960, initially concentrating on Canada, the U.K. and countries in the sterling area. When Bermuda moved to the Bermuda dollar on a par with the U.S. dollar in 1970, focus shifted from the U.K. to the United States.

Such extensive worldwide finance and insurance activity requires a highly sophisticated banking system. Bermuda provides this with up-to-date services and fiber-optic connections to the world. The four local banks clear over US$3 billion daily. Under the Banking Act of 1969, no new banks can be formed or operate in Bermuda unless authorized by the legislature. The chances of that happening are slim. However, international banks may form exempted companies engaged in non-banking activities and many have done so. Perhaps the biggest local banking news in years occurred in 2003, when the world's second largest bank, HSBC, purchased control of the Bank of Bermuda.

Bermuda's four banks follow very conservative, risk-averse policies. They hold an average of 85% of customer liabilities in cash and cash equivalents. For example, the Bermuda Commercial Bank recently had a weighted "risk-asset ratio" of 32%. Eight percent is the minimum required by Basle International Banking Agreement standards.

Bank of Bermuda, founded in 1889, has assets exceeding US$7 billion and offices in the Cayman Islands, Guernsey, Hong Kong, the Isle of Man and Luxembourg and an affiliate in New York City. Butterfield Bank (founded in 1859) also has offices in all of those havens, except the Caymans.

The Bermuda dollar circulates on par with the U.S. dollar. U.S. currency is accepted everywhere. There are no exchange controls on foreigners or on exempt companies, which operate freely in any currency, except the Bermuda dollar.

Unlike Panama, the Cayman Islands or The Bahamas, Bermuda has no bank secrecy laws officially protecting privacy, but bank and government policies make it difficult to obtain information in most cases. To do so requires judicial process. A 1988 tax treaty with the U.S. allowed for governmental exchange of limited information in certain cases, but a more recent Tax Information Exchange Agreement (TIEA) with Washington opened the door to free exchange of information with the IRS. In my opinion, on a comparative 1-to-10 international banking privacy scale, Bermuda now ranks about five or less.

For your personal and business purposes, a Bermuda bank account can offer a tax-free means for global financial activity and vast investment possibilities. If you have need for an offshore-based business locale, Bermuda, with its IBC creation laws and its modern digital Internet connections, may be a good bet.

FOREIGN TAX EVASION A CRIME

In recent years, Bermuda has adopted proposals to toughen the provisions of the U.S. Bermuda tax treaty.

It also upgraded anti-money laundering laws, as well as financial management laws governing the chartering and operation of banks and trust companies. These laws were seen as Bermuda's calculated response to demands from the Foreign Office in London, the OECD and FATF.

The rewrite of the 1986 U.S. Bermuda tax agreement in 1995 toughened the existing agreement at Washington's request. It clarified and expanded the types of information that Bermuda can now give the IRS "relevant to the determination of the liability of the [U.S.] taxpayer." For the first time, Bermuda also permitted on-site inspections of records by foreign tax authorities. The Proceeds of Crime Act fiscal offences list was broadened to include tax fraud. In effect, this meant that by proxy, American tax laws and their enforcement mechanisms were adopted by Bermuda.

Most importantly, the fraudulent evasion of foreign taxes was a made a crime, a major reversal of prior Bermuda policy and law. This made Bermuda the first major tax haven (and the first British overseas territory) to adopt such legislation. Together, these laws allow the U.S. IRS and the U.K. Inland Revenue (as well as other nations' tax collectors) to pursue their alleged tax-evading citizens with the assistance of Bermuda prosecutors and courts.

In 2002, Bermuda became an "approved jurisdiction" of the U.S. IRS for tax reporting purposes under the IRS Qualified Intermediary (QI) program described in Chapter 3. That means that the island's banks, investment advisors and other financial services that deal in U.S. securities agree to disclose to the IRS the names of their U.S. clients, or to impose a 30% withholding tax on investment income paid to such U.S. persons. This agreement was said to show IRS approval of Bermuda's stricter know-your-customer and suspicious activity reporting rules.

BERMUDA BUSINESS

Because of the large number of international companies that conduct insurance operations from Bermuda, the island does not rely as heavily on personal offshore services and banking as do most other havens. In 2009, over 13,400 international businesses maintained registration in Bermuda and over 3,300 locally. Total income generated by international companies was nearly US$2 billion. The number of business permits surged as the island promoted itself as an e-commerce haven and opened its shores to licensed investment services providers for the first time. Bermuda has long been a haven for offshore businesses. There is no income tax in Bermuda and international companies pay vastly reduced corporate taxes compared to the United States and Europe.

The Bermuda Stock Exchange, established in 1971, was intended as a domestic equities market. With the growth in international financial business, the exchange was restructured into a for-profit entity owned by the Bermuda banking institutions. It offers fully electronic clearing, settlement and depository services. The BSX has become the world's largest offshore fully electronic securities market offering a full range of listing and trading opportunities for global and domestic issuers of debt, equity, depository receipts, insurance securitization and derivative warrants.

WHY BERMUDA?

In my opinion, Bermuda is a prime candidate if you are

looking for a tax-free offshore base for your international business operations. An IBC registered here allows world-wide business and banking activity, even though you may live elsewhere. The IBC law allows great flexibility in operation with minimal reporting requirements. And IBCs and their profits are tax exempt locally. Another plus for Bermuda incorporation is the island's squeaky-clean reputation.

In recent years, Bermuda became an object of attack for American politicians who loudly denounced U.S. companies who re-incorporated there. The reason companies did this is easy to understand. Under U.S. tax law, a corporation pays 35% or more in federal and state taxes, one of the highest corporate taxes in the world. Once that company changes its corporate registration to Bermuda, its profits from foreign operations are tax-free if the funds are kept offshore. It's easy for U.S. politicians to dema-gogue this issue, rather than do the hard work of reform-ing and lowering U.S. corporate tax laws.

One of the main parts of President Obama's 2009 tax proposals was abolition of this offshore corporate tax break, but without any compensating reduction in the U.S. 35% tax. At this writing, he wants to tax all income from corporations whose main operations are in the U.S. wherever the income is earned or located. In 2006, the U.S. Congress curtailed somewhat the ability of U.S. corporations to re-incorporate in Bermuda after that date, imposing tax penalties for such moves.

EARLY SURRENDER TO THE OECD

Bermuda was one of only six offshore financial centers, which gave a written pledge to the OECD before publication of its 2000 blacklist of "harmful tax competition" nations. Each promised to meet OECD tax requirements in the future. Even after the adoption of criminal tax evasion and tax information exchange laws, Bermuda's tax agreement with the OECD was still a surprise. In essence, that meant that Bermuda eventually might impose taxes on tax-exempt foreigners who do business there. But this commitment was based on the OECD guarantee that all nations would adopt the same tax laws, the so-called "level playing field" rule. That this has not happened is hardly surprising.

Essentially, the Bermuda government pledged to the OECD to exchange all tax information with other nations; to require local and international companies to file publicly audited annual accounts; to maintain its current tax system.

For all its pains trying to placate the OECD, in 2009 when the G-20 issued its list of tax havens allegedly deficient in tax information exchange much to officials chagrin, Bermuda was relegated to the "gray list." It immediately mounted a major public relations effort in the U.S. and U.K. aimed at getting de-listed, pledging to follow the OECD Article 26 on tax information exchange that its stunned leaders thought it had been doing. By June 2009, Bermuda had reached the OECD-ordained magic number of 12 TIEAs, the number that supposedly indicates compliance with the new international tax information exchange standards. When Finance Minister Paula Cox dutifully signed the Island's 12th TIEA with the Netherlands, the OECD moved the island onto its "white list" of countries considered to have substantially implemented international tax transparency standards.

CLEAN MONEY

Not only did Bermuda evade the OECD "tax harmonization" hit list but also it escaped the FATF list of jurisdictions alleged to indulge dirty-money laundering through banking secrecy and lack of "transparency." Bermuda's four banks all work diligently to maintain clean reputations, although several money laundering cases have occurred, but without any overt bank complicity.

The former Bermuda Financial Secretary, Peter Hardy, argued that endorsement from the FATF and OECD "enables those major companies that want to set up in Bermuda to demonstrate they are, in fact, able to move to jurisdictions where international standards are upheld. We are able to say Bermuda is an upstanding and clean jurisdiction." That may be true, but in my opinion, it is also a jurisdiction no longer able to guarantee a high degree of financial privacy for those who do business on the island.

In 2009, some major corporations that had previously moved their corporate headquarters from the U.K. to Bermuda began to have second thoughts. Reacting to heavy handed attacks by the Labor government on tax havens and concerned about what London might do, these companies moved to Switzerland where a network of over 70 double tax treaties offers a more secure tax environment.

BRAGGING RIGHTS

This financial housecleaning and its strict laws led to a government claim that the island was now "the business leader among the British overseas territories," ready to meet and exceed international financial standards and regulation.

The British Westminster system confers an immensely important constitutional right on each U.K. overseas territory, that of declaring independence. Until 2004, most local political leaders avoided the issue of Bermuda's possible independence from the United Kingdom. But then-Prime Minister Alex Scott called for a national debate on the subject, looking towards the possibility of ending London's control over the island. Independence is a possibility, but a remote one. Nothing came of the debate, such as it was.

CONCLUSION

Bermuda remains a good, basic, no-tax asset protection jurisdiction for the location of offshore trusts, IBCs and is great for insurance. Its banks are first-class. But its willingness to cooperate with tax-hungry governments in Washington and London has diminished what was formerly a policy of strict financial privacy.

CONTACTS

Government

Bermuda Corporation Registry, Tel.: + 441 297-7753 Website: https://www.roc.gov.bm/.

Bermuda Monetary Authority, BMA House 43 Victoria Street. Hamilton HM 12; Bermuda Tel.: +441-295-5278; E-mail: info@bma.bm, Website: http://www.bma.bm.

Official

Bermuda's interests in the U.S. are represented by the Embassy of the United Kingdom, 3100 Massachusetts

Avenue, N.W., Washington, D.C. 20008; Tel.: (202) 588-6500; Website: http://www.britainusa.com/.

U.S. Consulate General, Crown Hill, 16 Middle Road, Devonshire DV03, Tel.: +1-441 295-1342 or after hours: + 441 235-3828.

British Virgin Islands

BVI, as it's known, has a bit more than 24,000 people — but more than 400,000 registered IBCs, second only to Hong Kong in total number. That's because the BVI specializes in creating, servicing and promoting offshore corporations for every purpose. The BVI can truthfully say, "IBCs R Us." And don't overlook their asset protection trusts, international limited partnerships and insurance. But remember: they take orders from London.

The British Virgin Islands, with about 24,000 people, consists of more than 60 islands, only 16 inhabited, at the eastern end of the Greater Antilles in the Caribbean, 25 minutes flying time east of Puerto Rico. Its economy is closely integrated with the nearby (to the west) U.S. Virgin Islands. The currency, since 1959, has been the U.S. dollar and there are no exchange controls. First settled by the Dutch in 1648, the islands were annexed in 1672 by the English.

The capital, Road Town, located on Tortola, is the financial center and the seat of government and courts. As a British overseas territory, the BVI has a long history of political stability with a measure of self-government, but London calls the shots. There is a ministerial system of government headed by a chief minister, with an executive council chaired by the U.K. appointed governor and a legislative council. The BVI is one of the world's most popular offshore jurisdictions for registering international companies and is a growing, but much lesser force in offshore hedge funds (currently about 2000), trust administration and captive insurance markets.

The economy, one of the most stable and prosperous in the Caribbean, is highly dependent on tourism, generating an estimated 45% of the national income. An estimated 850,000 tourists, mainly from the U.S., visit the islands each year.

IBCs R Us

The BVI adopted its successful International Business Company (IBC) Act in 1984. By the time the Act was superseded by the BVI Business Companies Act 2004, which removed the distinction between 'offshore' and 'onshore' companies, well over 400,000 had registered. Hong Kong and Latin America have been the main sources of clients, which is ironic, since Hong Kong leads all jurisdictions in registration of offshore corporations. (Many of BVI's Hong Kong clients are newly rich Chinese seeking to avoid taxes on the mainland.)

The IBS Act allows quick and cheap formation of tax-free corporations to hold assets and execute offshore transactions. The IBCs are used as holding companies, for consultancies, royalty income, foreign real estate, equipment leasing and ownership of moveable assets, such as airplanes and yachts.

The BVI has significant mutual fund and captive insurance sectors. Banking activity is, by design, minor. The BVI has tried hard to exclude money laundering, mostly with success, and has a relatively good reputation.

There is no statutory duty of confidentiality or privacy under BVI laws. However, confidentiality is imposed under the British common law and also may be imposed by contract. A breach, or threatened breach, of confidence is actionable in court, which may grant an injunction or award damages for an actual breach. Several laws waive confidentiality for criminal investigations.

In the past, one of the major attractions for BVI corporate registration was that true beneficial ownership was not a matter of public record. That has now changed. Under pressure from the Labor government in London the BVI colonial government enacted numerous laws that compromised this former strict corporate privacy.

In 2002, the BVI signed a tax information exchange agreement with the United States. In 2009 the BVI was one the G-20/OECD "gray list" of tax havens judged by them to be deficient in tax information exchange policies. BVI promptly announced that it would adopt the Article 28 OECD guidelines for tax information exchange. Its leaders also raced around the world signing new TIEAs. Within months it had reached the OECD-ordained magic number of 12 TIEAs, the number that supposedly indicates compliance with the new international tax information exchange standards.

Anti-money laundering laws cover reporting of suspicious activities and apply know-your-customer rules. The use of bearer shares (freely transferable corporate shares with the owner designated only as "bearer") has been so restricted that they remain "bearer shares" in name only.

BVI companies still are not subject to withholding tax on receipts of interest and dividends earned from U.S. sources. There are no capital gains or asset taxes. Use of a standard domestic BVI corporation can be more profitable than an IBC, particularly if one wants to take advantage of the BVI double tax treaties in effect with Japan and Switzerland. The U.S. canceled a similar BVI tax treaty more than a decade ago.

CONCLUSION

The BVI suffers somewhat as an offshore center because of its status as a U.K. offshore territory under the control of the Labor government in London. That's where its orders come from and it follows them.

But the colonials are growing restless. With all the attacks on tax havens, especially coming from London, BVI people fear their economic lifeline could disappear. The revenue from registering foreign companies has paid for a community college and a hospital. The Premier, Ralph O'Neal, 75, a former schoolteacher who leads the archipelago, says it smacks of colonialism when developed nations dictate standards for financial operations, especially when they don't comply with the rules themselves. "Why is it that we now in the colonies, because we are still a colony, can't have a financial centre?" Mr. O'Neal said. "If you are doing something and you are saying I can't do it, are you saying that I am inferior?"

But if you need an IBC to conduct your worldwide business, the British Virgin Islands will provide it efficiently — and all the service and maintenance you will ever need. And they also offer trusts and limited partnerships.

CONTACTS

Government

Ministry of Finance, 3rd Floor West Atrium, Central Administration Building, 33 Admin Drive, Road Town, Tortola, BVI VG1110. Tel.: (284) 494-3701 ext. 2144, Email: finance@gov.vg, Website: http://www.finance. gov.vg/.

BVI International Finance Center 1 Haycraft Bldg, 2nd Floor, Pasea Estate, Road Town, Tortola, BVI. Tel.: 1 284 468 4335, Email: ortizs@bvifsc.vg, Website: www.bviifc.vg.

BVI Government, Central Administration Complex, Road Town, Tortola, Website: http://www.bvi.gov.vg/default.asp.

Official

BWI is represented in the United States by the Embassy of the United Kingdom, 3100 Massachusetts Avenue NW, Washington, D.C. 20008; Tel.: 202-462-1340; Website: http://www.britainusa.com/.

The U.S. has no embassy in the BVI. The nearest is U.S. Embassy Barbados, Wildey Business Park, Wildey St. Michael Tel.: +246-436-4950, Website: http://barbados.usembassy.gov/. The U.S. Consular Agent in Antigua is closer to the BVI; Suite #2, Jasmine Court, Friars Hill Road, St. John's, Antigua; Tel.: +(268) 463-6531; Cell: +(268) 726-6531; Email: ANUWndrGyal@aol.com, Mailing address: P.O. Box W-1562, St. John's, Antigua.

CAYMAN ISLANDS

Some years ago, the Cayman Islands could claim that its financial institutions stood fifth in the entire world in the total of billions of dollars of assets under management. It was the jurisdiction of choice for tax free international banks and businesses that wanted (and got) ironclad secrecy guaranteed by law. But a series of highly publicized cases involving drug and other criminal money laundering, plus a major case in which a local bank was used for wholesale U.S. tax evasion, contributed to ending this haven's secrecy.

More recently this U.K. colony, under extreme pressure from London and Washington, weakened its financial and bank secrecy laws. The result: an outflow of billions in assets to other, more privacy-oriented, havens. But the Caymans are still an efficient, tax-free haven for offshore bank accounts, trusts and international business corporations, as well as hedge funds, mutual funds, insurance and annuities. Its name also is a red flag for foreign tax collectors and anti-tax haven politicians everywhere.

Let's face it: the major reason the Cayman Islands originally became a world-renowned tax-free haven was its strict bank and financial privacy — not just privacy, but near absolute secrecy. Guaranteed by law and zealously enforced by local courts, any foreigner doing business here was shielded from scrutiny — unless it was shown that he was engaged in overtly criminal acts. Even then, a lengthy judicial process often was needed to pierce this wall of secrecy. Secrecy sold and the Caymans sold it well.

That was the old Cayman Islands before it was forced, under orders from its colonial masters in London, to compromise its bank and financial secrecy, instead to become a potential proxy tax collector for other nations.

Many Caymans residents do not agree with what has happened. Michael Alberga, a Caymans lawyer with a long list of foreign clients, accuses the world's richest nations of practicing "economic terrorism" against the Caymans. We are simply "practicing pure capitalism; few or no taxes and little regulation," he claims, asking to be left alone.

GOVERNMENT & HISTORY

The Cayman Islands is a parliamentary democracy with judicial, executive and legislative branches. The present 1972 constitution provides for governance as a British Dependent Overseas Territory, meaning ultimate power rests with London.

The territory consists of three islands in what was known as the British West Indies, Grand Cayman (76 sq. mi.), Little Cayman (10 sq. mi.) and Cayman Brac (14 sq. mi.). Administered by Jamaica from 1863, they remained a British dependency after 1962 when Jamaica became independent. Grand Cayman is located directly south of Cuba, approximately 500 miles south of Miami, Florida. The capital, located on Grand Cayman, George Town, serves as the center for business and finance.

The Cayman Islands is an English-speaking common-law jurisdiction with no direct taxation on income, profits, wealth, capital gains, sales, estates or inheritances. Described as being "one of the more mature jurisdictions … in terms of regulatory structure and culture," the traditionally impenetrable confidentiality of the Cayman

Islands ended finally, in 2001, when it signed a tax information exchange treaty with the United States. Among other things, that treaty gave the U.S. Internal Revenue Service permission to examine accounts of Cayman financial institutions.

OFFSHORE BUSINESS LEADER

The Cayman Islands financial services industry includes banking, mutual funds, captive insurance, vessel registration, companies and partnerships, trusts, structured finance and the Cayman Islands Stock Exchange.

As of 2009, there were 270 banks (74 of them U.S. branches) licensed under the Banks & Trust Companies Law, representing 45 countries, including 40 of the world's 50 largest banks, with a combined total all of $1.6 trillion in assets. The Caymans is home to over 80,000 international business corporations (IBCs), 9,705 mutual funds, 239 trust companies, 815 insurance companies, 777 captive insurance companies and thousands of closed-end funds — plus the latest financial schemes dreamed up by cutting edge lawyers and investors as the Enron scandal showed. (Enron's creative managers created scores of IBCs used to conceal company debts, leading to the company's collapse and further hurting the Cayman's reputation.)

As of 2008, there were over 10,000 hedge funds registered here with assets of more than US$600 billion. Cayman dominates offshore hedge funds with approximately a 65% world market share. It has excellent communications facilities and extensive professional services.

At one time, the Caymans ranked as the world's fifth-largest financial center behind New York, London, Tokyo and Hong Kong. In 2009, it had slipped to number 10. Offshore business accounts for roughly 30% of the territory's gross domestic product of nearly US$2 billion. Many of the world's most reputable companies, including many American companies, do business through subsidiaries registered in the islands, to take advantage of the favorable, tax-free laws.

POLITICS AS USUAL

The Caymans, even more than Bermuda, became a major punching bag for U.S. politicians, what with Enron having used it for corporate subsidiaries, and Hollywood movies such as The Firm depicting the islands as a sinkhole of fetid corruption and billions in illicit cash.

Many U.S. firms have subsidiaries registered in the Cayman Islands. Big energy companies such as El Paso Corp., Transocean Inc. and GlobalSantaFe Corp. have subsidiaries there. Most U.S. companies have corporate units offshore for strategic, financial and tax reasons and they make no attempt to hide them because, at least at this writing, they are fully legal, although President Obama and the U.S. Congress may change that.

On the 2008 presidential campaign trail, then-candidate Barack Obama made his hostility toward offshore jurisdictions clear. He repeatedly scored points with crowds when he said, "There's a building in the Cayman Islands that houses supposedly 12,000 U.S.-based corporations. That's either the biggest building in the world or the biggest tax scam in the world, and we know which one it is."

It made no difference to him that a similar building in Wilmington, Delaware, home of his vice president,

Joe Biden, houses more than 50,000 American corporations as a means to legally escape state taxes in other American states. Ugland House, on South Church Street near the center of George Town, is indeed home to Cayman's largest law firm, Maples and Calder that serves a registered agent for these all those corporations that it represents.

TALKING SURRENDER

In 2000, the Cayman Islands government, at the insistent urging of London, began secret negotiations with the OECD and FATF. Discussion centered on demands to stop alleged foreign tax evasion and to increase transparency in the islands' financial institutions. The government was threatened with OECD/FATF blacklisting plus possible undefined "sanctions."

Demands also included expansion of existing mutual legal assistance treaties (MLATs) with the U.S. and the U.K. to include, for the first time, criminal tax evasion. The 1990 U.S. MLAT already had been used 170 times to exchange information. Traditionally, the Caymans had not viewed foreign tax evasion as a crime since its law imposed no income taxes.

As the law stands now, a Caymans court can confiscate all assets of a convicted person up to the amount by which he benefits from the crime. While the law requires the government to have prima facie evidence of a crime in order to seize cash or property, there is little recourse for a falsely accused person. An innocent defendant is ineligible for compensation unless he can prove "serious default" on the part of prosecuting authorities. Some Cayman legal experts said this lack of restraint could result in the law being used oppressively for "fishing expeditions." The legal situation now is virtually identical in the other U.K. overseas territories.

Money Laundering Crackdown

The Cayman Islands viewed themselves at the forefront of the fight against money laundering in the Caribbean. Drug money laundering was made a serious crime in 1989 and so called "all crimes" anti-money laundering legislation took effect in 1996.

In 2000, the government issued a new code of conduct for financial institutions aimed at further curbing money laundering, supplementing the 1996 landmark law that had criminalized money laundering in all serious crimes. The new code encouraged reporting of suspicious transactions by providing a safe harbor from liability for those who reported suspected crimes.

In spite of all these new laws, in 2000, the Financial Action Task Force listed the Caymans along with 15 other "dirty money" nations as being uncooperative in fighting criminal money laundering. Cayman's government officials, who had been quietly negotiating with FATF and the OECD for months, were vocal in their condemnation of the FATF blacklisting. Within days of the FATF blacklisting, undoubtedly by prearrangement, the U.S., U.K. and Canadian governments issued "advisory warnings" to their respective banking and financial institutions about dealings with the newly accused dirty-money Caymans.

Surrender of Financial Secrecy

Undeterred by the FATF blacklisting, in 2000, the government proudly announced what its politicians repeatedly had said they would never do. They had reached an agreement with the OECD on the issue of future "transparency." Thus, the government officially embraced the OECD's demand for an end to the Caymans' traditional bank and financial secrecy, guaranteeing it would provide financial information about Caymans' clients to foreign tax collecting authorities. In return for this major surrender, the OECD promised the Caymans would not appear on the OECD blacklist of tax havens allegedly engaged in "harmful tax practices" published in 2000.

Within three weeks of the FATF report, all the primary legislation necessary to address every one of the FATF's concerns was on the statute books. Within a further few weeks, more anti-money laundering rules were introduced to complete the legislative framework. The Islands now have a regime considerably tougher than that which exists in many of the FATF's 29 member countries.

The new laws allow the Cayman Islands Monetary Authority to obtain information on bank deposits and bank clients without a court order and ended existing restrictions on sharing information with foreign investigators. A new provision made it a crime to fail to disclose knowledge or suspicion of money laundering. Previously, it had been a crime for financial sector workers to disclose any private financial information without a court order. The Caymans government even went so far as to guarantee that it would stop island financial services providers from "the use of aggressive marketing policies based primarily on confidentiality or secrecy."

As was the case with Bermuda, for its pains trying to placate London and the OECD, in 2009 when the G-20 issued its list of tax havens allegedly deficient in tax information exchange the Cayman Islands also was relegated to the "gray list."

RECOMMENDATION

Regardless of the end of financial secrecy here, enormous amounts of money have flowed through these islands over many years. That has created an impressive financial and professional community from which you and your businesses can benefit. These professionals can provide first-class investment advice, a variety of offshore legal entities, trusts and IBCs, annuities and life insurance. There are many mutual and hedge funds in which to invest.

If you value financial privacy and are considering or have financial dealings in the Cayman Islands, as with any British overseas territory haven, plan accordingly. But don't overlook what they have to offer — even if everything these days is out in the open.

CONTACTS

Official

U.S. Consular Agent, Unit 222, Micro Center, North Sound Road, George Town, Grand Cayman; Tel.: (345) 945-8173. The United States does not maintain diplomatic offices in the Cayman Islands. Relations are conducted through the U.S. Embassy in London and the British Embassy in Washington, D.C.

The Cayman Islands are represented in the United States by the Embassy of the United Kingdom, 3100 Massachusetts Avenue NW, Washington, D.C. 20008; Tel.: 202-462-1340; Website: http://www.britainusa.com/.

Cayman Islands Monetary Authority, P.O. Box 10052 APO, Elizabethan Square, Grand Cayman, Cayman Islands; Tel.: +345-949-7089, Website: http://www.cimoney.com.ky/.

NEVIS: AIRTIGHT PRIVACY AND FAST SERVICE

While it is not well known outside offshore financial circles, Nevis is a leading tax-free asset haven jurisdiction. That's because it has had in place for 30 years asset protection friendly laws allowing trusts, IBCs and limited liability companies. Its government and courts have enviable records of support for offshore business. It has few banks, but you can bank elsewhere. And any legal entity you need can be set up in a matter of a few days at minimal cost.

If there is any one haven country that has all the things you need for smooth offshore financial operations, it's the eastern Caribbean island of Nevis (pronounced KNEE-vis). Best of all, Nevis has a no-nonsense banking and business privacy law that even the U.S. government can't crack. Its pro-offshore laws have existed for three decades — so there is plenty of experience and precedent in the local courts — and the legislative assembly keeps the applicable laws current. There are well-established service companies that can do what you want and several have U.S. branch offices for your convenience.

The two island "sovereign democratic federal state" of St. Christopher-Nevis (as its 1983 constitution ceremoniously describes it), has a governmental form and name almost larger than its population (40,000) and total land area (103 sq. miles) It is part of the chain of islands known in colonial days as the British West Indies, but now known without the "British" part of that title.

But this tiny West Indies two-island nation, known to the natives as "St. Kitts-Nevis," has earned prominence in offshore financial circles. That's because Nevis has no taxes, extremely user-friendly, quick incorporation and trust laws and an official attitude of hearty welcome to foreign offshore corporations and asset protection trusts.

The islands are located 225 miles east of Puerto Rico and about 1,200 miles south of Miami. Until their 1983 declaration of independence, both were British colonies. They are still associate members of the British Commonwealth. Her Majesty, Elizabeth II, as the titular head of state, still appoints the Governor General. The elected unicameral parliament sits in the capital of Basseterre on St. Kitts (population 30,000). The population of Nevis is about 10,000.

VERY INDEPENDENT NEVIS

St. Kitts & Nevis suffer under none of the restrictions inflicted by London on British overseas territories. Their national sovereignty allows them to enact their own laws and make their own policies, free from outside pressures.

Nevis also has its own Island Assembly and retains the constitutional right of secession from St. Kitts. For years, there were heated demands for separation. Then in 1998, defying international pleas, residents of the seven mile long island of Nevis voted on whether to secede from St. Kitts and become the smallest nation in the Western Hemisphere. Approval of two thirds of the island's voters was required for secession. The vote was 2,427 for secession and 1,418 against, falling just short of two thirds.

The vote was the culmination of a struggle that began with Britain's colonization in 1628. In 1882, Britain stripped Nevis of its legislature and wed it to St. Kitts. When the islands became independent in 1983, Nevis reluctantly joined in a federation with neighboring St. Kitts, but Nevisians insisted on a constitutional clause allowing them to break away. After years of complaining that they are treated like second class citizens by the federal government on St. Kitts, they invoked that right with the failed referendum.

St. Kitts and Nevis is already the smallest nation in the Western Hemisphere and retains the right to secede and proponents vow they will try again.

AN OFFSHORE CORPORATE HOME

Based on the Island Assembly's adoption of the Business Corporation Act of 1984, Nevis has an established record of catering to offshore corporations. The statute contains elements of the American State of Delaware's extremely liberal corporation laws, along with English commercial law. As a result, both U.S. attorneys and U.K. solicitors are comfortable navigating its provisions.

The corporation statute allows complete confidentiality for company officials and shareholders. There is no requirement for public disclosure of ownership, management, or financial status of a business. Although they must pay an annual fee of US$450, international business corporations are otherwise exempt from taxes — no withholding, stamps, fees, or taxes on income or foreign assets. Individually negotiated, government guaranteed tax holidays are available in writing, provided the IBC carries on no business locally. Official corporate start-up costs can be under US$1,000, including a minimum capitalization tax of US$200 and company formation fees of US$600. These low government levies compare very favorably with those imposed by other corporate-friendly havens like the high profile, high-cost Cayman Islands.

UNDER OECD PRESSURES

There are no exchange controls and no tax treaties with other nations. In 2000, St Kitts & Nevis was name on the OECD and FATF blacklists, but was removed from both after adopting anti-money laundering laws in 2001-2003. As a matter of official policy, until 2009 the government of Nevis did not exchange tax or other information with any other foreign government. However, in 2009 St. Kitts & Nevis was placed in the G-20/OECD "gray list" of countries allegedly failing to meet international standards concerning tax information exchange. Its officials took great offense at this listing and publicly denounced the OECD and larger nations for ganging up on small countries. Nevertheless, in 2009 it adopted a law containing the tax information exchange standard of OECD Article 26, allowing information to be provided in individual cases of alleged foreign tax evasion. It also negotiated a series of TIEAs with several nations in an effort to appease the G-20 and OECD critics.

Nevis corporate law is somewhat unique in that it contains a very modern legal provision. It allows the international "portability" or transfer of an existing foreign company from its country of origin to the island. Known as the "re-domiciling provision," this allows the smooth and instantaneous transfer of an existing corporation from any nation and retention of its original name and date of incorporation. This is all done without interruption of business activity or corporate existence. The only requirement is the amendment of existing articles of incorporation to conform to local laws. Principal corporate offices and records may be maintained by Nevis companies anywhere in the world.

New company creation and registration is fast in Nevis. It's accomplished simply by paying the capitalization tax and fees mentioned earlier. Using Nevis corporate service offices in the U.S. (see the list below), your corporation or limited liability company can be registered and ready to do business within 24 or 48 hours. You can do everything by phone, fax, wire and FedEx. Your confirmation papers can be sent to you overnight from Nevis. Formal incorporation documents must be filed within 10 days of receiving the confirmation papers. Corporate service firms will assist you with ready-made paperwork.

Small wonder, that in 25 years since the corporation law's original adoption thousands of foreign corporate owners have established their companies in Charles Town, Nevis.

Asset Protection Trusts

Building on their reputation for statutory corporate cordiality, in 1994 the Island Assembly adopted the Nevis International Trust Ordinance, a comprehensive, clear and flexible asset protection trust (APT) law. This law is comparable and, in many ways superior, to that of the Cook Islands in the South Pacific, already well-known as an APT world center.

The Nevis law incorporates the best features of the Cook Islands law, but is even more flexible. Its basic aim is to permit foreign citizens to obtain asset protection by transferring property titles to an APT established in Charlestown, Nevis.

Nevis also is taking advantage of the worldwide explosion in medical, legal and professional malpractice lawsuits. Legislative and judicial imposition of no-fault personal liability on corporate officers and directors has become a nasty fact of business life, especially in the U.S. A Nevis trust places personal assets beyond the reach of foreign governments, litigious plaintiffs, creditors and contingency-fee lawyers.

Under the 1994 law, the Nevis judiciary does not recognize any non-domestic court orders regarding its own domestic APTs. This forces a foreign judgment creditor to start all over again, retrying the case in Nevis courts and with Nevis lawyers. A plaintiff who sues an APT must first post a US$25,000 bond with the government to cover court and others costs before a suit will be accepted for filing. And the statute of limitations for filing legal challenges to a Nevis APT runs out two years from the date of the trust creation. In cases of alleged fraudulent intent, the law places the burden of proof on the foreign claimant.

All these factors combine to create an atmosphere in which a claimant confronted with a Nevis APT may settle for cents on the dollar, rather than attempt to fight an entire new battle in Nevis at great cost. This is especially useful to American doctors or other health providers who can shield their personal assets in an APT and may use the trust as a substitute for high cost malpractice insurance.

NEVIS APT FORMATION

Nevis has a small international bar and local trust experts who understand and can assist in furthering APT

---

objectives. The APT act has proven popular and a considerable number of trusts have been registered in Nevis.

Under the statute, the Nevis government does not require the filing of trust documents. They are not a matter of public record. The only public information needed to establish an APT is a standard form or letter naming the trustee, the date of trust creation, the date of the filing and the name of the local trust company representing the APT. The fee is US$200 upon filing and an equal annual fee to maintain the filing.

BROAD TRUST POWERS

Under the Nevis International Trust Ordinance the same person can serve in the triple role of grantor, beneficiary and protector of the APT. This allows far greater control over assets and income than U.S. domestic law permits. Generally, American law forbids the creation of a trust for one's own benefit. The basic structure of a foreign asset protection trust differs little from an Anglo-American trust.

The grantor creates the trust by executing a formal declaration describing the purposes, then transferring assets to be administered, according to the declaration, by the named trustees. Usually, there are three trustees named, two in the grantor's country and one in Nevis, the latter known as a "protector." Named trust beneficiaries can vary according to the grantor's estate planning objectives and under Nevis law, the grantor may be the primary beneficiary.

A word of caution: from the point of view of American courts and law, it's far better that a grantor not serve as a protector or trustee. That's because U.S. law (and the IRS) view a grantor in that capacity as having such a large degree of control over the assets as to call into question the validity of the trust. In many such cases, U.S. courts have ruled the entity to be an invalid "sham trust."

Nevis requires the appointment of a "trust protector" who, as the title indicates, oversees its operation and ensures legal compliance. A protector does not manage the trust, but can sometimes veto trustee actions. Nevis also allows a beneficiary to serve in the dual role as protector.

TAX AND LEGAL ADVANTAGES FOR AMERICANS

Under U.S. tax law, foreign asset protection trusts are tax neutral, as are domestic trusts. This means income from the trust is treated by the Internal Revenue Service as the grantor's personal income and taxed accordingly. Because the grantor retains some control over the transfer of his assets to any foreign trust, including those established in Nevis, U.S. gift taxes can usually be avoided. Although Nevis has no estate taxes, U.S. estate taxes are imposed on the value of trust assets for the grantor's estate, but all existing exemptions for combined marital assets can be used.

One device that a trust grantor can use to retain some control of trust assets is to form a limited partnership, then make the Nevis trust itself a limited partner. This arrangement allows you, as trust grantor, to retain active control over the assets you transfer to the Nevis trust/ limited partner. It also adds further protection to the trust from creditors and other legal assaults.

Aside from the undoubted protection offered by the Nevis International Trust Ordinance, this is a small nation, although indebted, with political stability, a highly reputable judicial system, favorable local tax laws, no language barrier and excellent international communication and financial facilities.

Nevis also has enacted comprehensive anti-money laundering laws, which are enforced. This has kept Nevis off the FATF blacklist of "dirty money" jurisdictions.

Contacts

Government of Saint Christopher (St. Kitts) & Nevis: Website: http://www.gov.kn/.

Nevis Government Information Service: Website: http://www.queencitynevis.com/.

Ministry of Finance, Nevis Offshore Financial Services, PO Box 882, Rams Complex, Stoney Grove, Nevis. Tel.: + (869) 469-0038; Email: info@nevisfinance.com; Website: http://www.nevisfinance.com/.

Official

Embassy of St. Kitts & Nevis, 3216 New Mexico Avenue, N.W., Washington, D.C. 20016; Tel.: (202) 686-2636; Web .site: http://www.stkittsnevis.org.

There is no American embassy in St. Kitts & Nevis. The nearest U.S. Embassy is located in Bridgetown, Barbados, Wildey Business Park, Wildey, St. Michael, Barbados.

Tel.: 246-436-4950, Website: http://barbados.usembassy. gov/.

Saint Vincent & the Grenadines

As an offshore financial center, Saint Vincent and the Grenadines has unusual European origins and more recently some questionable banking scandals. It's a great place for a vacation, but would you want to put your money there?

Saint Vincent and the Grenadines is a group of 18 small islands with 105,000 people that is part of the Windward Islands, 1,600 miles east of Miami, between the Caribbean Sea and Atlantic Ocean, north of Trinidad and Tobago. Included are the popular holiday islands of Mustique and Bequia. The islands average more than 200,000 tourist arrivals annually mostly to the Grenadines.

Resistance by the native Caribs prevented foreign colonization on St. Vincent until 1719. Disputed between France and the United Kingdom for most of the 18th century, the islands were ceded to the U.K. in 1783. The country gained independence from the U.K. in 1979 and has a parliamentary and common law system.

Most Vincentians are the descendants of African slaves brought to the island to work on plantations. There also are a few white descendants of English colonists, as well as some East Indians, native Carib Indians and a sizable minority of mixed race. The country's official language is English, but a French patois may be heard on some of the Grenadine Islands.

Recent years have seen important changes in the islands' precarious economy. Previously, St. Vincent and the Grenadines depended largely on agriculture, especially bananas that replaced the main sugar crop. The government has encouraged diversification, promoting other crops and supporting the development of tourism and financial services. The islands are vulnerable to external shocks, both natural (from weather changes such as droughts or hurricanes) and economic, from recession in the major tourism markets of the U.S. and U.K. In the 1990s, GDP growth variations ranged from a high of 8.3% to a low of 2.9%. In 2008, following two years of strong growth, the economic climate drastically deteriorated with the onset of the global financial crisis.

With jobless rates as high as 20%, persistent high unemployment has prompted many to leave the islands. In 2008, GDP amounted to $1.3 billion, with per capita GDP of $10,500. To put this in perspective, in 2003, the revenue from the local filming of the Walt Disney movie, Pirates of the Caribbean, starring Johnny Depp, surpassed that of the total income from the country's agriculture.

QUESTIONABLE BANKING

The country has a long tradition of international banking and finance but its current banking reputation is questionable at best. Its first bank was set up in 1837 by Barclays out of London and the first domestic bank opened its doors in 1909.

Kingstown, the capital, on the main island of St. Vincent, is the seat of the government and also the business and finance center, including an ever smaller offshore banking sector that claims to have adopted international banking and financial regulatory standards. In 1996, a major legislative overhaul of financial regulations was supposed to make financial services a focal point of the economy.

The twin objectives of the legislation were said to protect the right to financial privacy and for maximum asset protection. The government stated then that it would not help other countries collect taxes under the guise of "fishing expeditions" or prosecuting tax offenses. However the islands were soon embarrassed by banking scandals. In spite of what was claimed to be careful vetting, the licenses of three banks were revoked in 2005.

In 2002, the U.S. Treasury issued a formal warning to U.S. banks that the islands' banks were suspected of money laundering and the OECD Financial Action Task Force (FATF) placed them on their dirty money blacklist. The response was official adoption of an anti- money laundering law that was said to be "on a par with the highest of international standards." In 2003, FATF removed the islands from its blacklist.

The head of government of St. Vincent and the Grenadines boasted in 2008 that he had closed 34 of 40 banks since 2001, hardly a major confidence builder. In 2009, regulators took control of another island bank, Millennium Bank, which U.S. authorities linked to an alleged $68 million Ponzi scheme. As it happens, for several years I had warned people who were attracted to this bank by promises of unrealistically high gains that the bank was questionable. In 2009, questions were raised about another island bank that was accused of allowing two fraudsters based in Norway and New Zealand to use the bank to promote their Internet banking schemes.

INTERNATIONAL OFFSHORE CENTER

The concept of an international financial services sector here was first introduced by Swiss and Liechtenstein lawyers in 1976, three years before independence. As a result of this original foreign legislative inspiration, the same law firm in Liechtenstein (listed below) still specializes in applying St. Vincent's offshore laws.

A host of Swiss/Liechtenstein drafted offshore laws authorize various entities including international banks, international business companies, limited duration companies, international asset protection trusts, mutual funds and international insurance companies. Exempted companies and exempted limited partnerships receive a statutory guarantee of tax-free status for 20 years. At present, there are no corporate or individual income taxes or other taxes.

Until 2002, St. Vincent's law provided for strict financial privacy under the Confidential Relationship Preservation Act of 1996. This was repealed and replaced by the Exchange of Information Act of 2002. This Act allowed for the exchange or disclosure of information between island regulators and foreign regulatory/government and tax officials.

This was not enough to satisfy the G-20 and the OECD. In 2009, the islands were placed on the G-20/OECD "gray list" of countries allegedly failing to meet international standards concerning tax information exchange. At this writing, I have seen no reports that the islands have adopted a law containing the tax information exchange standard of OECD Article 26, allowing information to be provided in individual cases of alleged foreign tax evasion. My guess is that it will do so.

CONTACTS

Official

Embassy of St. Vincent and the Grenadines, 3216 New Mexico Ave. NW, Washington, D.C. 20016 Tel.: 202-364-6730; Email: mail@embsvg.com; Website: http://www.embsvg.com/.

The United States has no official presence in St. Vincent. The nearest U.S. Embassy is located in Bridgetown, Barbados, Wildey Business Park, Wildey St. Michael, Barbados, Tel.: + 246-436-4950, Website: http://barbados.usembassy.gov/.

TURKS & CAICOS ISLANDS

The Turks & Caicos Islands are an English-speaking British overseas territory that combines tax-free status, an idyllic climate and close proximity to the United States. They impose no income, corporate or estate taxes. There are no exchange controls and the U.S. dollar is the country's legal tender. There is a wide range of financial and other professional services readily available. Unfortunately, self-government has not gone well here in recent times.

In 2009, the Foreign Office in London deposed the elected head of government and the parliament for corruption. Control of the islands was temporarily placed with Her Majesty's appointed Governor General.

Until recently, the Turks & Caicos Islands were a British self-governing territory, a chain of more than 40 islands, only eight of which are inhabited. (As you will learn, self-government was temporarily suspended by the U.K. in 2009). The inhabited islands of Providenciales, Grand Turk, North Caicos, Middle Caicos, South Caicos, Parrot Cay and Pine Cay long have attracted those who love pristine beaches, as well as shrewd investors. The Islands are in the Atlantic Ocean 575 miles southeast of Miami at the southern end of The Bahamas chain. They have non-stop air services from Miami, New York, Boston, Charlotte, Atlanta, Philadelphia, Toronto and London.

The Turks & Caicos are called the "Isles of Perpetual June" because they enjoy a year-round comfortable climate cooled by trade winds, but with lots of sunshine. The have 230 miles of sandy beaches and have become a major stop for eco-tourists and divers who discover some of the finest coral reefs in the world. In recent times, celebrities such as movie actor Bruce Willis and author Jay McInerny have taken up residence.

In 1512, Europeans first visited these islands but no settlement resulted. In the late 17th Century, British settlers from Bermuda came in search of salt. Gradually the area was settled by U.S. planters and their slaves, but with the local abolition of slavery in 1838, the planters left. Until 1848, the Islands were under the jurisdiction of The Bahamas. In 1873, they became a dependency of Jamaica and remained so until 1959. In 1962, Jamaica gained independence and the Turks & Caicos became a British Crown colony. Although independence was agreed upon for 1982, the policy was reversed and the islands remain a British overseas territory. Since 1976, it has had local autonomy, which, as I said, was suspended in 2009.

There has been a continuing political struggle between the islands on one hand and the colonial governors and the Foreign Office in London on the other. This was partially due to a strong pro-independence movement, but also because of alleged drug smuggling in the TCI. A low-key, but persistent movement has been afoot for some years seeking to have Canada annex the Turks & Caicos and is still active today. Some members of the Canadian House of Commons even have championed annexation. Despite having adherents in both jurisdictions, this unusual proposal hasn't gained any serious momentum. The legal system is based upon English common law with a bend of laws from both Jamaica and The Bahamas.

ECONOMY

The economy is based on tourism, fishing and offshore

financial services. Most capital goods and food for domestic consumption are imported. The U.S. is the leading source of tourists — accounting for more than half of the 175,000 visitors per year. Major sources of government revenue include fees from offshore financial activities and customs receipts. Most tourist facilities are located on Providenciales (known as "Provo") and Grand Turk Islands. Provo is the tourist hub and scene of major developments including a Carnival Cruise ship dock, a Ritz-Carlton resort and numerous large condominium developments.

The offshore financial services sector began in 1981 with the adoption of the TCI Companies Ordinance, an innovative law that provides for formation of exempted companies (IBCs), as well as of local domestic companies, foreign companies, non-profit organizations and limited life companies. Companies can be formed by a local agent within 24 hours at a low cost between US$1,000-2,500, plus an annual maintenance fee of US$300 for exempt companies. A 20-year guarantee of tax exemption is available.

Offshore activity contributes 7% of GDP and ranks second to tourism as the main source of income. Since 2005 the government has conducted a sustained publicity campaign in the U.S., U.K. and other nations to attract offshore financial activities and investments.

The government encourages tourism, which pulls in nearly 200,000 visitors in some recent years. It has also created TCInvest (see below), to encourage inward investment with incentives. Financial services developed rapidly in the 1990s, and there are more than 20,000 offshore enterprises, mostly using the International Business (Exempt) Company form. The key offshore sectors are banking, insurance and trust management. The Islands have a popular yacht registry and also a registry for aviation ownership. There is a reasonable level of professional expertise on the Islands and costs are low by comparison with many jurisdictions.

No Taxes

The Turks & Caicos is a zero-tax jurisdiction. Government revenues come from various user fees, levies and duties on imported goods and services. Investors in approved projects get duty concessions, which are more generous in the lesser developed islands. The U.S. dollar is the local currency. There is no central bank or monetary authority and no restrictions on movement of funds in or out of the territory. The financial sector generates up to $20 million each year, about 10% of all government income.

There are five licensed banks with combined assets of about $900 million, 20 trust companies and about 3,000 insurance companies. The TCI has developed a niche market for captive insurance companies known as credit life or "producer owned reinsurance companies" (PORCS). These companies are typically owned by U.S. retailers and provide reinsurance for credit life and product warranty insurance.

If maximum financial privacy is important to you, keep in mind that the TCI are a British overseas territory and, ultimately, under the policing and political control of the Labor government of the United Kingdom. Banking confidentiality and secrecy were governed by the Confidential Relationships Ordinance 1979, which provided for penalties and terms of imprisonment for professionals, including government officials, who make unauthorized disclosure of confidential information. The Companies Ordinance

1981 contains similar provisions in relation to exempted companies. Additionally the common law also imposes civil liability for breaches of professional privilege.

In 2009, the Turks and Caicos were on the G-20 OECD "gray list" of tax havens judged to be deficient in tax information exchange policies. Now that the U.K. government has taken control of the islands government it will no doubt apply Article 26 OECD guidelines for tax information exchange. In 2008, British Prime Minister Gordon Brown had sent a letter ordering the TCI to sign TIEAs to share tax information with the U.K. and with other governments or face sanctions.

COLONIALISM RETURNS?

In May 2009, the British government took control of the Turks & Caicos Islands after a report pointed to widespread corruption in the territory, a move the islands' premier Michael Miscik, called "draconian." The "clear signs of political amorality and immaturity and of the general administrative incompetence, have demonstrated a need for urgent suspension in whole or in part of the constitution," a special investigator found.

The House of Commons in London approved handing over control to the Queen's appointed Governor General of the islands. At the center of the corruption claims was Michael Misick, who resigned as premier in March 2009. He is alleged to have built up a multi-million-dollar fortune since his election in part by corrupt acts. The 43-year-old London-educated lawyer and realty broker was elected in 2003 to lead the islands after eight years in the opposition. In 2007, he was sworn in for a second four-year term after leading his party to a sweeping victory, capturing all but two of 15 parliamentary seats.

The U.K. Foreign Office denied any colonial ambitions. "This would not be direct rule, nor would it be indefinite. It would be a smart, targeted, intervention for an interim period by the governor whose responsibilities not only include representing the Crown in the islands, but also the interests of the people of the Turks and Caicos Islands."

CONTACTS

Official

For information on the Turks & Caicos, contact the **British Embassy**, 3100 Massachusetts Ave NW, Washington, D.C. 20008. Website: http://www.britain-info.org.

Turks and Caicos Tourism Office, 11645 Biscayne Blvd, Suite 302, Miami FL 33181;Tel.: (786) 290 6199, Email: TCItourismMiami@cs.com, Website: http://www.turksandcaicostourism.com.

Turks & Caicos Islands Tourist Board, 175 Bloor Street East, Suite 307, South Tower, Box 22, Toronto, ON M4W 3R8 Canada Tel.: 416-642-9771 / 9772 / 9773 Toll Free: 866-413-8875, Email: rwilson.tcitourism@ allstream.net, Website: www.turksandcaicostourism.com.

There is no U.S. embassy or consular agency in the Turks & Caicos. The U.S. Embassy in Nassau, The Bahamas, has consular responsibilities over the territory.

U.S. Embassy, 42 Queen Street, Nassau, The Bahamas; Tel.: + (242) 322-1181 or after hours: + (242) 328-2206; E-mail: embnas@state.gov, Website: http://nassau.usembassy.gov/.

United States Virgin Islands

It's not well known, but under a unique special federal income tax arrangement applying only to the U.S. Territory of the Virgin Islands, it is possible for U.S. nationals and others who make the islands their main residence to enjoy substantial personal and business tax benefits. These lower taxes make the islands an offshore tax haven option for very wealthy U.S. citizens, entrepreneurs and foreign nationals seeking U.S. citizenship.

History

The Virgin Islands of the United States, as their name is officially styled, constitutionally are "an unincorporated territory" of the U.S.

With the Caribbean Sea to the south and the Atlantic Ocean to the north, the Virgin Islands offer a variety of deep sea and coastal fishing. Their tropical climate and minimal industrial development assure an abundance of unspoiled reefs for divers and snorkelers, with sandy beaches ringing deep coves. The large number of isolated, secure anchorages in the U.S. Virgin Islands and the British Virgins just to the east has made the chain a center for yachting. A thriving charter-boat industry in the Virgin Islands draws tens of thousands of visitors annually for crewed sailing adventures.

After their discovery by Columbus in 1493, the islands passed through control by the Dutch, English and French. In 1666, St. Thomas was occupied by Denmark, which, five years later, founded a Danish colony there to supply the mother country with sugar, cotton, indigo, and other products. By the early 17th century, Danish influence and control were established and the islands became known as the Danish West Indies. That political status continued until Denmark sold the islands to the U.S. for US$25 million in 1917.

The islands — St. Croix, St. Thomas and St. John — have a strategic value for the U.S. since they command the Anegada Passage from the Atlantic Ocean into the Caribbean Sea as well as the approach to the Panama Canal. U.S. citizenship status was conferred on the V.I. inhabitants in 1927. Although they do not vote in U.S. presidential elections, residents are represented by a non-voting delegate in the U.S. House of Representatives.

LITTLE-KNOWN U.S. LOW TAX PARADISE

The United States Virgin Islands (USVI) lie 1100 miles southeast of Miami, Florida — and it's one of the most impoverished jurisdictions under the American flag. But most Americans only know the islands as a vacation venue with beautiful resort hotels, white sandy beaches and blue lagoons.

The four principal islands —St. Croix, St. John, St. Thomas, and Water Island — have a population of about 110,000. Per capita income in the territory is only US$14,600. That's less than half the average in the conti-nental United States and $10,000 less than in Mississippi, the poorest state.

In addition to poverty, the USVI has another unusual distinction. They have been, until now, America's very own "offshore" tax haven. So much so, that the low-tax hating OECD denounced the USVI as the U.S. version of "unfair tax competition." What upset the OECD was the territory's prohibition against U.S. and local ownership of USVI "exempt companies," although this was required by the U.S. Congress in the U.S. Internal Revenue Code. The USVI was removed from the OECD "unfair tax" black list in 2002, but the OECD continued to criticize the islands for being America's own tax haven.

In 2009, when the G-20/OECD issued its list of tax havens allegedly deficient in tax information exchange, not surprisingly, the USVI appeared on the "white list" of "good" offshore financial centers. No surprise, because the United States, led by President Barack Obama, led the G-20 attack on all tax havens. More importantly, the U.S. finances most of the budget of the OECD black list writers.

The islands — St. Croix, St. Thomas, St. John, and Water Island — have been territorial possessions of the United States since they were purchased from Denmark in 1917. They are overseen by the U.S. Department of the Interior. The Naval Services Appropriation Act of 1922 (Title 48 U.S.C. § 1397) provides in part: "The income tax laws in force in the United States of America . . . shall be held to be likewise in force in the Virgin Islands of the United States, except that the proceeds of such taxes shall be paid to the treasuries of said islands."

USVI residents and corporations pay their federal taxes on their worldwide income to the Virgin Islands Bureau of Internal Revenue (BIR), not the U.S. IRS. Persons who are born in the USVI or those who become naturalized U.S. citizens in the USVI, for purposes of U.S. federal gift and estate taxes, are treated as nonresidents of the U.S. Since the USVI has no estate or gift taxes, this means that upon death the estates of such persons owe zero U.S. or territorial estate or gift taxes as long as they are domiciled in the USVI at the time of death or at the time of making a gift and have no U.S. assets. (Like any other nonresidents of the U.S. for gift and estate tax purposes, assets located in the U.S. are subject to federal estate and gift tax.)

GENEROUS PACKAGE

To attract outside investment, the USVI Economic Development Commission (EDC) grants generous tax relief packages that include a 90 percent credit against U.S. federal income taxes. This tax grant package, which is offered for a period of 10 to 30 years, depending on the business location within the USVI (with possible 10-year and then five-year extensions), is available to USVI chartered corporations, partnerships and limited liability companies. The tax credit applies to income from USVI sources, such as fees for services performed in the USVI, and certain related income, such as sales of inventory and dividends and interest from non-U.S. sources received by banking and finance companies based in the USVI.

For many years, a few U.S. investors with business activities ranging from petroleum production, aluminum processing, hotel and other tourism activities, to transportation, shopping centers, and financial services, have taken advantage of USVI tax laws and enjoyed income with very little taxes. As a result of the EDC marketing campaign to attract corporations, about 100 companies qualified for the program in between 2002 and 2004, and employing nearly 3,100 people.

The tax benefit program began paying dividends almost immediately after hedge fund managers started moving to the USVI in 1995. The islands' tax revenue doubled from US$400 million to US$800 million in a five-year period ending in 2005. The increase effectively erased a US$287.6 million deficit for the territory in 1999. The EDC program was worth about US$100 million annually to the local economy. A USVI government spokesperson said that the EDC was crucial in lifting the territory from a dire financial crisis seven years ago to a 2007 projection of a fiscal year surplus in excess of US$50 million.

Paradise Lost

All went well until the early 2000s when the IRS noticed a rapid increase in the number of high net worth individuals moving to the USVI — based on the increasing amount of taxes that the BIR counted as tax-exempt income the USVI. The IRS then received copies of what it perceived to be "marketing materials" from various EDC beneficiaries seeking additional investors — the federal and local statutes did not limit the number of investors to one beneficiary.

In 2003, the IRS raided a financial services firm, Kapok Management, in St. Croix, accusing the firm of sheltering income for dozens of partners who were living on the U.S. mainland, not in the USVI. In 2004, a Massachusetts life insurance executive who used this ruse pled guilty to federal tax evasion in St. Croix, although as of late 2007 he still had not been sentenced. But in 2009, after a two-month trial in the USVI federal district court, the IRS lost a big case when a jury acquitted the defendants of conspiracy, attempted tax evasion and fraud charges. The original indictment accused Kapok of fraudulently using the Virgin Islands' economic development program designed to promote local economic development and employment through the use of tax credits.

STRICT SIX-MONTH RESIDENCY REQUIREMENT

In 2004, U.S. Senator Charles Grassley (R-Iowa) drafted legislation to impose a strict six-month residency requirement and limited the territory's tax benefits only to income earned exclusively within the islands. (The 1986 legislation had provided that the territory's tax benefits applied to USVI and income connected with a USVI trade or business — but directed the IRS to issue special regulations to define "source" and "effectively connected income" for this purpose. But the diligent IRS went 18 years with no regulations.)

Grassley slipped his changes into a major tax bill without any hearings, and with no notice to the USVI delegate to Congress, the governor, or the U.S. Interior Department, all of whom were stunned to learn what had happened. This major change was imposed without any testimony, territorial input, and certainly without any consideration or understanding of the critical importance of the territory's Economic Development Program to its impoverished economy. The Congressional Joint Committee on Taxation estimated in a wild guess that Grassley's legislation would increase federal revenue by US$400 million over a 10-year period.

IRS Terror

In a reign of tax terror after the 2004 insurance executive case, the IRS opened about 250 audits on individuals who filed as USVI residents and on businesses that were beneficiaries of the economic development program. Many of these individual audits were of persons who had no economic development credits and made no tax exemption claims on their returns. The IRS and the U.S. department of Justice also brought the Kapok case mentioned above. At that point everyone who lived in the USVI had to wrestle with the six month residency requirements whether they were being audited or not. Since the 2004 changes were adopted, about 50 hedge funds managers and other financial services companies either halted activities temporarily or withdrew from the islands.

The islands' finance sector boom withered, crushed by the IRS and Grassley with a combination punch of the law and subsequent IRS rules that are still unclear with regard to income eligible for tax credits.

Residence Rules

The old, pre-Grassley rules required a person to be a bona fide USVI resident on the last day of the tax year, "looking to all the facts and circumstances," similar to the "domicile" test for estate and gift tax purposes. There was no "number of days" test and no requirement that a person be a resident for all or most of the year to file as a resident for that year.

The rules now require a resident to be present physically in the USVI at least 183 days, or roughly six months, every year. The IRS did set up four alternative ways to meet the physical presence test of the new residency requirement: 1) spend no more than 90 days in the United States during a taxable year; 2) spend more days in the USVI than in the U.S. and don't have more than $3,000 in earned income from the U.S.; 3) average 183 days a year over a rolling three-year period, or; 4) meet a "no significant connection" test. This last test means no house, no spouse, no minor kids, and no voting registration in the United States — and no days counting requirement.

The residency rules also require a "bona fide resident" to have a "closer connection" to the USVI than anywhere else — looking to where you vote, what address you use, where the closet is in which most of your clothes hang, where you have homes, where you bank, and where your family lives. Finally "a bona fide resident" must have a tax home in the USVI — which is usually your principal place of business.

The IRS claims authority to go back as far as it wanted and examine tax years without regard to the usual three-year statute of limitations. The number of financial firms and other service businesses that make the USVI their corporate home now has fallen to fewer than 40 from more than 80 several years ago.

The IRS also drafted an intrusive form for island residents it says is needed to prove valid residency. Form 8898 requires those who stop filing tax returns with the IRS, in order to file them in the USVI, to list where their immediate family lives, where their cars are registered and where they hold driver's licenses.

The former chief executive officer of the EDC has said, "In the States, they definitely see that they are losing taxes when some of their taxpayers move elsewhere. All of the people everywhere are competing for the same business. What's wrong with the Virgin Islands attracting some of those people?"

In fact, the betrayal of the USVI by the federal government, assures only one thing — that Americans seeking legal tax breaks will instead find them in secure tax havens such as Panama, Belize, the Channel Islands, Singapore and Hong Kong.

Something for Everyone

Notwithstanding all of the above, tax breaks could still be yours — but it is an absolute necessity that a person actually live and make their main residence in the USVI.

The USVI offers two types of benefit programs that are either fully or partially exempt from USVI taxes and U.S. federal income taxes as well.

One type is a USVI corporation (or partnership or LLC) that qualifies for the benefits of the Economic Development Program for its USVI business activities. Most beneficiaries of this program are in one of three areas — hotels, manufacturing, and service businesses serving clients outside the USVI. But benefits are also available for businesses engaged in transportation, marinas, large retail complexes, medical facilities, and recreation businesses. Most of the service businesses that have obtained benefits are engaged in fund management, general management, and financial services activities.

The beneficiaries that do qualify are fully exempt from most local taxes including the gross receipts tax (otherwise four percent), property taxes (otherwise .75%) and excise

---

taxes on raw materials and building materials. Beneficiaries also get a 90% credit against their USVI income taxes (although for C corporations the credit is equal to 89% of taxes). Beneficiaries also enjoy a special customs duty rate of one percent. They are exempt from U.S. federal income taxes on their USVI operations. The 90% credit also applies to dividends or allocations to a beneficiary's USVI bona fide resident owners — which is why it is so critical to meet the residency requirements.

STRICT REQUIREMENTS

To get these great benefits, a business must employ at least 10 persons full-time (32 hours a week) and must make a minimum capital investment of $100,000 (or more). Beneficiaries must also provide health and life insurance and a retirement plan to employees and must purchase goods and services locally — if possible.

For non-U.S. foreign persons, generous exemptions are available through the use of the second type of tax-free entity, a USVI exempt company. The USVI is the only jurisdiction in the world where a non-U.S. person can establish a tax-free entity under the U.S. flag. These exempt companies are used as holding companies for portfolio investments, for the ownership of aircraft that are registered with the U.S. Federal Aviation Administration, or as captive insurance companies. There are a number of other offshore tax-planning structures that can take advantage of USVI exempt companies. Up to 10 percent of the shares of an exempt company can be owned by U.S. residents and up to 10 percent can be owned by USVI residents.

The USVI also has a research and technology park at the University of the Virgin Islands, and technology businesses can also benefit from world-class connectivity through Global Crossing, AT&T's underwater cables on St. Croix.

CLOSE BY

Moving your residence to the USVI is no more difficult than moving from one U.S. state to another. The USVI has a well-developed infrastructure. The legal system is subject to the U.S. Constitution and is part of the Third Circuit Court of Appeals. The U.S. court system, postal service, currency, and customs and immigration agencies serve the islands. There is no restriction against maintaining a second home elsewhere inside or outside of the United States, as long as you maintain your principal residence in the USVI.

This American tax haven is limited but certainly worth considering for any high net-worth foreign person considering U.S. naturalization, or any current U.S. citizen willing to relocate to a warmer climate to legally avoid burdensome taxes. The benefits are particularly beneficial for businesses with a global, rather than a U.S., focus because certain foreign source (but not U.S.) dividends and interest are treated as effectively connected income for tax credit purposes and owners of such a business do not have to spend 183 days in the USVI as long as they are in the United States for no more than 90 days and have a closer connection to the USVI and a USVI tax home.

Obviously, the USVI tax exemptions are unique in that they require a foreign or U.S. person to reorder their personal and business lives in a major way. It means moving and establishing a personal residence and/or business headquarters in the USVI. However, this is a comparatively small price to pay to gain the substantial tax savings that can result from such a move.

CONTACTS

U.S. Virgin Islands: Website: http://www.usvi.net/usvi/.

U.S. Virgin Islands Economic Development Authority: http://www.usvieda.org.

U.S. Virgin Islands Taxes: http://www.usvi.net/usvi/tax. html.

V.I. Bureau of Internal Revenue, 9601 Estate Thomas, Charlotte Amalie, St. Thomas, V.I. 00802. Tel.: (340) 715-1040, Website: http://www.viirb.com/.

CHAPTER TEN

Emigrate to Canada, Leave Taxes Behind

*Canada is not an offshore tax or asset haven. But in
combination with several other factors, Canadian law
offers the possibility of the American dream — the end
to paying U.S. income and other taxes for the rest of
your life.*

*A process called "expatriation" that some may consider
drastic — even extreme — can accomplish this tax
freedom. It is both. Here I explain how expatriation is
done, legally and consistent with U.S. and Canadian
law. Expatriation requires professional advice and considerable preparation and planning. It also requires determination, will and a lot of courage. Read on.*

First, I must apologize for some of the lawyer-like
words and phrases I use in this chapter. (It gets even worse
in Chapter 12 because that one covers U.S. tax laws.)

Some of what you will read here may seem rather dry
and legalistic. But that's because the process described
must be done very carefully and thoroughly in accordance
with the laws of two different nations. I am going to walk
you through all the steps so that you will understand
exactly what must be done and how to do it.

As you go, keep in mind an absolute must — you must
obtain competent professional advice to guide you every
step of the way. Check the end of this chapter for the
names of professionals who can help you.

EXPATRIATE TO CANADA

A land of vast distances and rich natural resources, Canada became an independent, self-governing dominion in 1867 while retaining ties to the British crown. It is the second largest country in the world (after Russia) with 3,855,100 square miles covering 6.7% of the earth.

Canada is also one of the premier nations in the world for exercising the most effective wealth protection strategy — expatriation. But for a U.S. citizen (or anyone else), expatriation means eventually renouncing U.S. or other national citizenship, then becoming a foreign national — becoming a Canadian. Eh?

Radical? You bet.

Expatriation is an extreme measure meant for those who have the most to lose in continuing to pay high taxes in their home country.

First, understand that Canada is not a tax haven comparable to the many tax havens described in these pages. Except in the specific programs designed to entice new immigrants to Canada, which I will explain here, it doesn't offer tax breaks to foreigners. But these programs can be very important for you in saving, instead of paying, taxes.

Wealthy Americans stand to lose billions to the IRS. President Obama has pledged that for anyone who earns $250,000 or more annually, taxes will go up — and up. Without good estate planning, U.S. government death taxes could take up to 55% of the assets you wish to leave to your heirs when you pass on — and that final tax insult comes after having paid up to 40% of your earnings in federal income taxes every year — all your working life.

Throw in state and local income and sales taxes and you stand to lose well over half your earnings during your lifetime in taxes. For those with estates worth millions, the prospect of having their money enrich the bloated coffers of the IRS should be enough to force them to take drastic avoidance measures.

One of the options wealthy Americans are increasingly turning to is expatriation. Perhaps surprisingly, they are expatriating to America's friendly northern neighbor, Canada. Some immigrants are welcomed in Canada more than others for a variety of reasons — and you may be just the type of new citizen Canada welcomes with open arms.

Expatriation is a drastic measure, but it may be the only escape for the wealthy. This is definitely not a strategy for everyone, but it may make sense for you. There are certain trade-offs involved, each of which must be researched and considered carefully. Most importantly, you must do this correctly to make it work — so be sure you get qualified professional help if you choose to go down this radical path.

WHY CANADA?

Canada and the United States have long been staunch, if somewhat uneasy, allies. These friendly neighbors share the largest undefended border in the world, although post 9/11 anti-terrorist measures have made border crossing slower and more cumbersome. (Since 2009, citizens and residence of both nations must have official passports or the equivalent documents in order to cross the border, even for a day trip of a few hours.)

Every day, many thousands choose Canada as an excellent place to visit, do business, even to live — and with good reason. Economists at the United Nations researched the best nations in which to live and work. They judged Canada number one. Japan came in second, the United States only sixth and the United Kingdom tenth. Canada has a high standard of living, minimal social class divisions, low crime rate, a clean environment, beautiful scenery, economic opportunities, government support services, extensive infrastructure, comprehensive shopping and sports facilities, affordable housing and the generous hospitality of the Canadian people.

A distinct advantage that comes with this Canadian citizenship is the international official acceptance of the country's passport, one of the most respected in the world. And as citizens of a member nation of the British Commonwealth, Canadians are allowed to enter Britain without obtaining a prior visa, and entry to Britain allows travel access to all the nations of the European Union. It also allows visa-free travel to scores of British Commonwealth countries.

The downside includes long harsh winters and continuing English-French political and ethnic differences in the Province of Quebec.

But the major reason to choose Canada is because its laws allow its new citizens, those who have a certain level of wealth, to legally escape Canadian income and estate taxes.

IMMIGRATION

The virtues of Canada as the place to live are known around the world. Recent immigration figures attest to that fact. In recent years, Canada's population of nearly 34 million has increased annually by over 200,000 immigrants. In 2009, Citizenship and Immigration Canada proudly announced a record number of permanent and temporary residents had been admitted in 2008. The number of new permanent residents was 247,202; a total that was 70,000 more than in 1998. Also admitted were 193,061 temporary foreign workers and 79,459 foreign students, for a grand total of permanent and temporary residents for the year 2008 of 519,722.

A modern nation built by European settlers, Canada has increased its inflow of immigrants by three-fold in the last two decades. The top immigrant sources were the United States, India, Vietnam, Poland, the United Kingdom, the Philippines, Guyana and El Salvador. These increasing numbers have also included many wealthy Asians, especially residents of Hong Kong who came before Hong Kong was returned to Communist Chinese by the British in 1995. (Many of those new Canadians have since returned to Hong Kong as dual citizens.)

ABOUT CANADIAN TAXES

Before I get to the good news — the big tax breaks for new immigrants — you should know that the Canadian tax system is tough and comprehensive. Combined Canadian federal and provincial personal income taxes range from 45% to 54%, depending on the province. And the heavy Canadian tax burden has been a direct cause of capital flight, which is relatively unrestricted, although there is an exit tax for those citizens intending to leave permanently.

Canada's taxation system is based on residence. Residents of Canada are subject to taxation on their worldwide income, while non-residents are only subject to taxation on certain types of Canadian source income. When an individual ceases to be a resident, the provisions of the Canadian Income Tax Act attempts to tax the individual on all his or her income earned up to the date that residence terminates (called the "date of departure"), especially the income that will not be taxable once the individual becomes a non-resident. This tax is referred to as the "departure tax."

Canadian taxes are "territorial" — meaning taxes are levied for the most part only on earnings from within the country, not on offshore income. Although residents are hit with stiff taxes, unlike the U.S., Canada does not tax the worldwide income or foreign assets of its nonresident citizens. Canada taxes only the worldwide income of its resident citizens and resident aliens who live in Canada at any time during the calendar year. "Residents," by law, include individuals, corporations and trusts located in Canada.

Tax-Free New Resident Loophole

However, tough taxes may be for the average Canadian citizen, wealthy new immigrants can take advantage of a huge loophole available only to them. This major tax saving was deliberately written into law in order to encourage wealthy new arrivals. This preference for new citizens with substantial investment capital can translate into huge tax savings and far-reaching financial gains for you and your business.

High net worth immigrants who come to Canada have some useful and attractive options. Here are a few:

1) A qualified immigrant accepted for eventual Canadian citizenship is eligible for a complete personal income tax moratorium for the first five calendar years of residence in Canada — you pay no taxes if the source of your income is a previously existing offshore, non-Canadian trust, (known as an "immigrant trust") or an offshore corporation. Because of the costs of setting up and administering such a trust, it generally is only beneficial for immigrants who have in excess of CAD$1 million in assets that they can put into the offshore trust.

An offshore trust can be created in any of the many offshore havens I describe in this book before you move to Canada and become a citizen. The Bahamas, Barbados, Anguilla, Cayman Islands, Bermuda, Cook Islands, Isle of Man and the Channel Islands of Jersey or Guernsey all are appropriate. These havens all have little or no income tax, have common law legal systems that accommodate this type of trust planning and have suitable financial institutions that can act as trustees.

As a general rule, Canada has a three-year residence requirement after immigrant admission before citizenship is granted, but a five-year residence is required in order to be eligible for this very special tax break.

2) Canadian citizens and resident aliens employed by certain "international financial centers" are forgiven 50% of all income taxes.

3) Canada has abolished all national death (estate) taxes (but the provinces do have such taxes).

4) After living three to five years tax-free in Canada as a new citizen, you can move your residence (and your tax domicile) to another country and afterwards you pay taxes only on income earned or paid from within Canada. You pay no taxes on your worldwide income. But there is an exit tax paid after filing a notice of intent to live abroad.

5) If an individual, who has never resided in Canada and never plans to reside in Canada, creates a trust in an offshore jurisdiction for the benefit of Canadian resident beneficiaries, such a trust (known as a "Granny Trust") may never be taxable in Canada. A "Granny Trust" can be tax free in perpetuity for the trust's Canadian tax resident beneficiaries.

But beware: a naturalized Canadian citizen who lives 10 consecutive years or more outside Canada can be stripped of citizenship at the discretion of the government, although this is very rare and usually for cause.

How Americans Can Stop Paying U.S. Taxes

Let's suppose you, as an American citizen (or U.S. resident alien), wish to sell an established business, or convert fixed assets into liquid cash for investment or other purposes.

Depending on how long you have held the property and how the liquidation deal is structured, you may face U.S. capital gains taxes at the current maximum rate of 15% (or more, since President Obama has talked about increasing the CGT). Depending on your tax bracket, income taxes can be 40% or more. In either case, a major part of the cash proceeds from the sale or conversion will be devoured by the U.S. Internal Revenue Service and state tax authorities — before you ever see a dime.

How can you avoid this enormous tax burden?

What if you transfer the title of the U.S. business to a foreign trust (with the property owner — you — as the beneficiary) or to a corporation you control, conveniently located in a low or no-tax offshore jurisdiction?

And what if, after the trust or corporation receives title, you apply for and receive Canadian citizenship, later voluntarily end your U.S. citizenship and become a legal resident of Canada for at least five years?

As a new Canadian, that offshore trust or corporation can pay you benefits and income for five years — tax-free — if you carefully follow the regulations that govern this incredible tax break. You can be a free spirit with absolutely no income or capital gains tax liability in either the U.S. or Canada.

Think it sounds too good to be true? Read on.

TESTING THE WATERS

Maybe you would like to test the northern waters before making any major decisions about a future in Canada. Fortunately, Americans thinking about emigrating can explore life north of the border for an extended period. The U.S.-Canadian Free Trade Agreement allows reciprocal extended stays of up to one year, with no requirement to obtain a special visa. Plus, the number of one-year extensions is unlimited. Tourists are allowed to stay for at least 90 days without special permission.

Americans employed in certain occupations can enter, live and work in Canada without a work permit and without prior approval. Those welcome to work in Canada include Americans involved in research and designing, purchasing, sales and contract negotiation, customs brokering, financial services, public relations and advertising, tourism and market research, as well as professionals paid by U.S. sources.

Border Crossing

Since the 9/11 terrorist attacks, entry into Canada has tightened and now is solely determined by Canadian Border Services Agency (CBSA) officials in accordance with Canadian law, see http://www.cbsa.gc.ca for details.

Canadian law requires that all persons entering Canada must carry both proof of citizenship and identity. A valid U.S. passport or NEXUS card satisfies these requirements for U.S. citizens. The NEXUS program allows pre-screened travelers expedited processing by U.S. and Canadian officials at dedicated processing lanes at designated northern border ports of entry, at NEXUS kiosks at Canadian preclearance airports, and at marine reporting locations.

If U.S. citizen travelers to Canada do not have a passport or approved alternate document such as a NEXUS card, they must show a government-issued photo ID (driver's license) and proof of U.S. citizenship such as a U.S. birth certificate, naturalization certificate, or expired U.S. passport. Children under 16 need only present proof of U.S. citizenship.

U.S. citizens entering Canada from a third country must have a valid U.S. passport. A visa is not required for U.S. citizens to visit Canada for up to 180 days. Anyone seeking to enter Canada for any purpose besides a visit (to work, study or immigrate) must qualify for the appropriate entry status, and should contact the Canadian Embassy or nearest consulate and see the Canadian immigration web site at

---

> http://www.cic.gc.ca/english/index.asp.
>
> Anyone with a criminal record (including even misde-
> meanors or driving while impaired [DWI]) may be barred
> from entering Canada and must qualify for a special
> waiver well in advance of any planned travel for further
> processing, which may take some time.
>
> For information on entry requirements, contact the
> Canadian Embassy at 501 Pennsylvania Avenue N.W.,
> Washington, D.C. 20001; tel. (202) 682-1740, or the
> Canadian consulates in Atlanta, Boston, Buffalo, Chi-
> cago, Dallas, Detroit, Los Angeles, Miami, Minneapolis,
> New York, San Juan or Seattle. The Canadian Embas-
> sy's web site is http://www.canadianembassy.org/.

In the box above, it says US citizens can visit for up to
180 days, but two paragraphs above the box, it says US
citizens can visit for up to one year.

OPEN DOOR FOR IMMIGRANT INVESTORS

Before obtaining Canadian citizenship, you should first
explore any family ties you might have in the country.
The Canadian government will help you learn if you are
eligible for citizenship based on ancestry. Canadian consulates will provide a personal history information form to
be completed and submitted with copies of relevant birth
records to the Registrar of Canadian Citizenship in the
capital city of Ottawa. A "Certificate of Canadian Citizenship" is automatically issued to anyone who qualifies
for citizenship by family descent. If you are lucky enough
to qualify, this is the least complicated basis on which to
establish a new legal residence in Canada.

Independent applicants for permanent residence are

rated on a point system that takes into account age, education, fluency in English and French, financial standing, occupational or professional experience, local demand for certain types of workers, geographic destination and a personal assessment of the applicant. These factors comprise a 100-point scale; 70 points and over is passing.

Completely separate from the point system for admissions, Canadian law favors a special independent class of preferred immigrants, including investors, entrepreneurs, the self-employed and those who will add to the "cultural and artistic life" of the nation. With minor variations in each of the provinces, investor-immigrants generally must have a net worth in excess of C$500,000 (US$443,000) and be willing to invest at least C$250,000 (US$222,000) in some Canadian business for a minimum three to five-year period. Purchase of a residence usually does not qualify as an investment, although it may if you work from home.

With proof of sufficient assets and an attractive business plan (especially one creating new jobs for Canadians) your permanent resident status and eventual citizenship is almost assured. Government loan guarantees and other assistance may be available for immigrants willing to invest larger sums of C$750,000 (US$665,000) or more.

For potential investor visa applicants, the government rolls out the proverbial red carpet, officially known as the "Business Migration Programme." Business experience, marketing skills, contacts within Canada, an adequate credit rating and available funds all greatly increase your chance of success. Applicants are usually required to submit detailed business proposals or general business plans, which must accompany the application for permanent residence. Such plans must detail the nature of the business, operating procedures, key personnel (which may just be the applicant), a marketing plan and a financial strategy.

While Canada's national immigration laws facilitate the entry of certain foreign corporations and their key staff, the provinces offer their own investors and skills immigration programs. In British Columbia, for example, the province has a "Provincial Nominee Program" that offers expedited immigration solutions for international investors wanting to immigrate to Canada and wish to settle in that province.

CANADIAN IMMIGRATION PROCESS

The immigration process begins with a visit to the Canadian Embassy. It is located at 501 Pennsylvania Avenue NW, Washington, D.C. You can also try a Canadian Consulate, located in New York and other major U.S. cities.

There you can obtain an "Immigration Questionnaire" requiring basic personal information about you, your spouse and family. Within a few weeks, a more detailed questionnaire will be presented if the applicant is initially found acceptable. After this second document is reviewed, a personal interview and medical examinations are needed.

If all goes well, you will shortly receive a visa for entry into Canada as a landed immigrant: "Welcome, Bienvenue à Canada."

It is worth noting that Canada recognizes the principle of dual nationality. They allow successful applicants for citizenship to retain their nationality of origin. For reasons that will become obvious in a moment, that choice is not a viable option for an ex-American expatriating to Canada who wants to end U.S. tax obligations.

The Big Change — U.S. Expatriation

The potential immigrant from America will eventually have to give up United States citizenship in order to formally end his or her U.S. tax obligations. You may wish to review my comments in Chapter 2 concerning the U.S. "exit tax" that is now in effect to see if you come within the exit tax definition of a "covered person." If you are a covered person, the financial impact of the exit tax on you may outweigh any benefit to be gained by immigration to Canada.

Under this law, a person who is a "covered individual" falls within the clutches of the expatriation provisions if, on the date of expatriation or termination of U.S. residency:

(i)   the individual's average annual net U.S. income tax liability for the five-year period preceding that date is US$139,000 or more (to be adjusted for inflation);

(ii) the individual's net worth as of that date is US$2 million or more; or

(iii) the individual fails to certify under penalties of perjury that he or she has complied with all U.S. federal tax obligations for the preceding five years. Of course, if you're lucky and don't come within these definitions, the law may offer a very real opportunity to escape U.S. taxes, especially if you have a good prospect of becoming more prosperous in the future. You can leave now and escape the tax.

Do it the Right Way

Here's how to expatriate from the U.S. and avoid pitfalls along the way:

First, it is necessary to obtain proper legal advice on expatriation in order to be effective in surrendering citizenship. The worst outcome is to wind up with ambiguous dual nationality status. In that case, you go through an extended period retaining not only U.S. citizenship, but citizenship in another country as well. You may then find yourself within the potential grasp of two government taxing authorities.

Generally, an ex-American who properly surrenders citizenship is treated by U.S. law as a nonresident alien and taxed at a flat 30% rate on certain types of passive income derived from U.S. sources and on net profits from the sale of a U.S. trade or business at regular graduated rates. Expatriates can safely spend only about 122 days a year within the United States. After that, they expose themselves to IRS claims for full U.S. taxation based on alien residency.

Another strict caution: You must be certain to obtain valid foreign citizenship before you surrender your U.S. citizenship — if you fail to do so, you could become a "stateless" person, the proverbial "man without a country." A person without a passport and a nationality is legally lost in this world of national borders and bureaucratic customs officials and as such is not entitled to the legal protection of any government. Between 1995 and 2006 one poor soul who had no passport lived on a bench in the international waiting room area of DeGaulle Airport near Paris. He floundered in his "in transit" ambiguity while several governments and the UN Refugee Commission fought over the status of his nationality! He became so famous that the 2004 Tom Hanks movie, Terminal, was based on his predicament.

Valid surrender must be an unequivocal act in which a person manifests an unqualified intention to relinquish U.S. citizenship. In order for the surrender to be effective, all of the conditions of the statute must be met; the person must appear in person and sign an oath before a U.S. consular or diplomatic officer, usually at an American Embassy or Consulate. Because of the way in which the law is written and interpreted, Americans cannot effectively renounce their citizenship by mail, through an agent, or while physically within the United States.

Once the surrender is accomplished before an American diplomatic or consular officer abroad, all documents are referred to the U.S. Department of State. The Office of Overseas Citizens Services reviews them to ensure that all criteria under the law are met, but the State Department has no discretion to refuse a proper surrender of citizenship. This personal right is absolute. (If you do surrender your U.S. citizenship, in theory you could get it back, but only through a long and complicated process that any new U.S. immigrant applicant must undergo. And that takes years and involves attorney and other costs.)

Long before such a drastic final step is taken towards ending U.S. citizenship, the new Canadian immigrant should have his or her official Canadian citizenship in order, papers in hand and an established residence in their new homeland. This will most likely be in the metropolitan areas of Montreal, Toronto, or Vancouver, where the vast majority of immigrants decide to live.

Canadian Potential

One of the foremost benefits of becoming a Canadian citizen is the ability to take advantage of what is often called an "immigrant offshore trust."

The key to eligibility for this unusual tax-free "window of opportunity" is found in section 94(1) of Canada's Income Tax Act of 1952. This law ensures that an immigrant who has never been a Canadian resident can move to Canada and earn tax-free foreign source income from a nonresident trust or affiliated corporation for the first five calendar years of his new Canadian residency. But before you surrender U.S. citizenship, you must have already attained citizenship in Canada. As I said, this requires fulfillment of at least the first three of your five-year exemption period. As a U.S. citizen, during that time you are still subject to taxation on your worldwide income, including the trust income.

Beneficiaries

To qualify for this big tax break, the arrangement must include an immigrant residing in Canada plus either: 1) a foreign corporation or a trust with which the immigrant is "closely tied;" or 2) a foreign affiliate corporation controlled by a person resident in Canada. The essential factor is that the nonresident trust must have one or more beneficiaries who are Canadian residents, or the offshore corporation must be "closely tied" in some manner to one or more Canadian residents. The beneficiaries likely will be your family members and can include yourself. The foreign trustee will follow your instructions on how the trust assets should be invested and income disbursed.

A "beneficial interest" in a nonresident trust is defined as belonging to a person or partnership that holds any right — immediate or future, absolute or contingent, conditional or otherwise — to receive any of the income or principal capital of the trust, either directly or indirectly. It would be difficult to find a broader definition of "beneficial entitlement" than this — and the implications for tax avoidance are obvious and potentially huge.

Canadian tax officials and court cases have repeatedly stated that such immigration trusts and related businesses, when properly created and managed abroad, are not an abuse of the tax laws. That's because section 94 clearly is designed as a vehicle for exempting new immigrants from taxation for the stated period of five years. In the case of almost every other tax avoidance scheme, the Canada Revenue Agency would pounce. Here, the law does more than permit tax avoidance, it approves and encourages it.

Only a change in Canadian law by Parliament could remove this generous tax break and there is no current talk of removing the provision that has been so successful in attracting much needed capital and business to the nation.

TRUST PROPERTY SOURCES

In order for a nonresident trust or a nonresident corporation to qualify as a "controlled foreign affiliate," and to receive section 94 tax-free treatment, it must have acquired its property from a person who meets all of the following requirements:

1. the donor must be the trust or affiliate corporation beneficiary, or related to the beneficiary (spouse, child, parent), or be the uncle, aunt, nephew, or niece of the beneficiary;

2. the donor must have been resident in Canada at any time in an 18-month period before the end of the trust's first taxation year or before his or her death; and

3. if the trust property came from an individual, the individual donor eventually must be a resident in Canada for a period or periods totaling more than 60 months.

Section 94 applies regardless of the method by which the nonresident trust or corporation acquires its property including purchase, gift, bequest, inheritance or, exercise of a power of appointment by or from an individual. The law treats all such transfers as if you had transferred your property to the trust or corporation.

You must be careful to follow a few rules when donating assets to such a trust or corporation. You cannot retain any reversion right or power to designate beneficiaries after the trust is created. This is what is known in both U.S. and Canadian law as an irrevocable living trust. You cannot retain any control over how the trust property will be disbursed during your lifetime, nor can you retain more than 10% equity ownership in an offshore corporation to which you donate.

As a general rule, a trust donor should transfer only cash and title to intangible assets to an offshore trust. Portable assets, such as gold coins or diamonds, also can be used. Title to real estate or a business located in Canada or the United States definitely should not be made part of the trust property. Transfer of tangible property physically located in either nation does nothing to keep those assets away from Canadian or American creditors or tax authorities. Such action could even subject the trust to the jurisdiction of a Canadian court. By holding title to assets within Canada, the offshore trust could be deemed liable for Canadian taxes.

FOREIGN CONTROL A MUST

In order to determine if an offshore trust is "nonresident" from a tax perspective, the Canada Revenue Agency looks at who controls it and its ownership.

The residence of a trust is determined by where the managing trustees or the persons who control the trust assets actually reside. It is therefore important that the offshore trust have a majority of trustees living in the foreign jurisdiction where the trust is registered and where its operation is located. This requirement for majority offshore control does not diminish the ability of a trust beneficiary to serve as a trustee and to live in Canada. Neither status jeopardizes the offshore and therefore tax-free, status of the trust.

Canadian tax law specifically allows offshore immigration trusts to receive tax-free income from investment business conducted by a resident Canadian citizen during the five-year residency period. Thus, the new Canadian investor-citizen is free to roam the world by e-mail, phone, fax, telex, wire, courier, or letter, using his capital

and ability to produce profits for the trust and its beneficiaries. To maximize tax avoidance, the trust should
not carry on other active business in Canada or invest in
property located in Canada. Income from these sources
may subject the trust to certain domestic taxes because of
the Canadian source or location.

CREATING AN OFFSHORE TRUST

So where should you establish such an offshore trust?
You could conceivably set up shop anywhere in the world.

To do so effectively, you must look abroad for a
friendly national jurisdiction in which to locate your assets. The host government must impose little or no taxes
on foreign investors. Elsewhere in these pages, I describe
several such haven nations, some of them located in the
warm waters of the Caribbean, not too far from the U.S.
or Canada. One nation favored by Canadians is Barbados because it has a double taxation avoidance treaty
with Canada.

As covered in Chapter 2, an offshore asset protection
trust (APT) located in a tax haven is proven and effective
for offshore financial planning. The APT is the safety vehicle that places personal assets beyond the reach of many
irritants: your home country tax authorities, potential
litigation plaintiffs, an irate spouse, or unreasonable creditors — wherever such opponents may be located.

Even though an offshore immigration trust can guarantee five tax-free years for new Canadian immigrants,
the non-tax benefits are also important. The trust allows
Canadians asset protection, a high degree of financial
privacy, flexible estate planning and the ability to make

internationally diversified investments unrestricted by domestic Canadian law.

Case Study

Let's say you have C$3 million you wish to invest. Like any reasonable person, you want to avoid Canadian taxes on the income produced from your investment. The following strategy can help natural-born Canadian citizens and wealthy new immigrants.

First, you need a nonresident of Canada — a friend or relative — to act as manager of your offshore investment corporation. You also need a trust registered in an established asset haven. For this example, let's say you choose to set one up in Panama. You can't do it yourself, since the new Canadian immigrant must live in Canada for five years.

You transfer the C$3 million (US$2.6 million) to the Panama-registered trust, also administered by your friend as trustee, probably in the same Panama office. The trust manager invests that money in Canadian government treasury bills or public company stocks. The interest income this produces can be paid to you, your children, or any other named beneficiaries tax-free. At current interest rates, that means a savings of about C$100,000 (US$86,500) per year in taxes.

While this tax haven structure might be expensive to establish, the arrangement qualifies under section 94 for five years of tax-free income for trust beneficiaries. Even after the five-year period ends, this arrangement can continue to shield the Canadian beneficiary from taxes, so long as it is controlled by non-Canadians.

A Need for Caution

The objective of an offshore tax haven is the legal reduction of your tax obligations. Keep in mind that it

---

will do you no good to suffer the bother of restructuring your financial life, only to find yourself embroiled in years of complex and expensive court battles with the Canada Revenue Agency — or worse, facing criminal charges for tax evasion or a variety of other possible tax crimes.

Reasonable caution places a premium on pursuing the correct path from the very beginning. This means the assistance of competent tax experts from the very start. Cutting corners will only leave you and your financial advisors in deep trouble.

MECHANICS OF OFFSHORE BUSINESS

The country in which your Canadian immigration trust and the managing trustee are located should be, for obvious reasons, a nation with strong financial privacy laws. As I have said, most tax haven countries do emphasize such statutory privacy rights.

The ideal places for establishing asset preservation or tax avoidance trusts are tax haven countries such as Panama, Nevis, the Isle of Man, the Channel Islands or the Cook Islands. These are all countries with statutes tailored to asset protection needs.

TOUGHER OFFSHORE REPORTING

Creating an offshore immigration trust will affect your personal tax return, in that a taxpayer must disclose the existence of an offshore trust on his or her annual Canadian federal tax return. Generally, foreign trustees are not required to divulge information about assets held by a trust. They usually cannot be forced by Canadian courts to turn over trust assets. Canada Revenue Agency and other creditors must first go through the host country's judicial system at great expense.

Reporting laws require that all resident Canadian taxpayers must report the existence of their offshore assets that exceed the aggregate of C$100,000 (US$86,500). This includes offshore bank accounts, securities holdings and rental properties and interests in foreign trusts, partnerships, corporations, or any other offshore entities. Prior law required payment of taxes on offshore income by Canadian residents, but did not mandate a listing of assets as the new law does.

Commenting on the reporting law, a leading Canadian financial management company gave this opinion: "Revenue Canada seems to be following the U.S. Internal Revenue Service with respect to offshore entities and transactions. Some of the new reporting is tougher than the IRS, some less, but the intent is the same; the government wants to know everything."

Nevertheless,creditors must get a court to order you to reveal your tax return and the existence of the trust in any civil action. That takes time. If they do discover the trust's offshore location and file a collection suit in the haven country, local laws are hostile to nonresident creditors and the trustee can shift the trust and its assets to another country and another trustee in an emergency. Then, pursuing creditors must begin the process all over again.

TRUST ADVANTAGE

This protection in a civil suit gives trusts a distinct privacy advantage over corporations.

In most tax and asset haven countries, at least one person involved in organizing a corporation must be listed on the public record, along with the name and address of the corporation. In many countries, the directors must be listed on the original charter. In a few maximum privacy countries, only the organizing lawyer is listed, but even that reference gives privacy invaders a starting point for nosey investigators.

With a trust, nothing more than its existence is required to be registered in an asset haven nation — and often not even that. The trust agreement and the parties involved do not have to be disclosed and there is little or nothing on the public record. In privacy-conscious countries, the trustee is allowed to reveal information about the trust only in very limited circumstances.

The country chosen for such a trust must have local trust experts who can assist you in achieving your objectives. The foreign local attorney who creates your trust must be familiar with all applicable laws and tax consequences.

In its simplest form, the offshore immigration trust can be a trust account in a foreign bank. Many well-established multinational Canadian banks can provide trustees for such arrangements and are experienced in such matters. As an extra level of insulation from government pressure, however, use a non-Canadian bank.

With today's instant communications and international banking facilities, it is just as convenient to hold assets and accounts overseas as it is in another Canadian or U.S. city. Most international banks offer Canadian and U.S. dollar-denominated accounts, which often have better interest rates than Canadian institutions.

INTERNATIONAL BUSINESS CORPORATION

The offshore corporation is best suited for the needs of Canadian business owners who seriously desire to run a legitimate international business. Establishing your corporation offshore can lower your taxes and increase profits immensely. Under section 94, income from "affiliated" offshore corporations qualifies for the five-year tax exemption. The company can also be for tax avoidance after the five-year moratorium ends, as I explain below.

But foreign corporations, as Canada Revenue Agency demands, must be more than a mere sham. A full-scale company, complete with working offices, staff, international fax and telecommunications facilities, bank accounts, a registered agent, board of directors, a local attorney and an accountant can cost upwards of US$50,000 annually.

Members of your board of directors and associates of the local tax specialists who help you form the company, may be paid about US$2,500 a year. There will be annual taxes to pay and reports to be filed with the local government and with Canada.

As the Canadian owner, you will want to visit your company offices once or twice a year, a pleasant enough activity if you locate your business in one of the tropical venues specializing in such corporate arrangements. January is an excellent month for Canadians to head south for a visit.

How It Works

Let's say as a new investor-immigrant, you purchase a Canadian manufacturing business that exports products worth C$5 million (US$4.3 million) each year.

Because it is a legitimate business with established foreign transactions, your Canadian company can incorporate an offshore affiliate, in say, Barbados. Like Canada, Barbados is a member of the British Commonwealth. More importantly, it is a place where international companies pay only 2.5% corporate income tax and benefit from credits and inducements for foreign-owned businesses. Compare that to Canada's 45% corporate tax.

You can set up your affiliate with offices in the capital, Bridgetown (population 8,000). It has eight major international banks including branches of the Royal Bank of Canada, the Canadian Imperial Bank of Commerce, Chase Manhattan and Barclays. Regular air service is offered by Air Canada, British Airways, American and other major carriers.

Your Bridgetown affiliate will handle all foreign sales and international marketing for your Canadian company. For these services, it will charge a 15% mark-up on the value of the goods it sells. This will amount to about US$750,000 a year at your current export levels.

What you have done is legally transfer the profits from your Canadian company to an offshore affiliate where taxes are much lower — 2.5% vs. 45%! After gladly paying US$18,750 in local corporate income taxes, the rest of the money, US$731,250, can be sent back to Canada as a dividend from exempt surplus income. This is paid to your company — tax-free! During the first five years of your citizenship, you personally can share in that corporate income — again, tax-free!

Even after your five-year tax-free period ends, Canadian taxes on the income can be deferred indefinitely. You can do so until the parent company's shareholders need the money for their own use, or until they sell the business. If the shareholders want payment immediately, it can be paid out as dividends. Dividends are taxed at 36%, well below the personal income tax rate of over 50%.

Investment Potential

The Barbados affiliate could also serve as an investment arm for your parent company. In this capacity, it can actively make international investments. All the earned income from such investments — dividends, interest and capital gains — will go to your Bridgetown affiliate. This will be taxed at the 2.5% rate that applies to offshore corporations. Investment profits can also be sent to the parent company tax-free. In order to follow this course successfully, all corporate investment decisions must originate with your Bridgetown money manager. The money manager must run your affiliate on a daily basis (i.e., you cannot dictate every move by phone from Montreal or Ottawa). As an added consideration, those with experience say that in order to be successful in using foreign affiliates for investment purposes, a minimum of US$1 million in capital will be needed to start.

In theory, this all sounds grand, but there are practical problems associated with an offshore corporation.

First of all, just as in establishing a domestic corporation, legal formalities must be strictly observed. Canada Revenue Agency will check this carefully. Moreover, the cost of starting up can be considerable. You will need a local legal counsel who knows the law and understands your business and tax objectives. Corporations anywhere are rule-bound creatures requiring separate books and records, meetings, minutes and corporate authorizing resolutions, which make it less flexible than many other arrangements.

But you can pay for a whole lot of recordkeeping with the money you will save in taxes.

When the Five Years End

After five, tax-free years, it won't be easy to face the Canada Revenue Agency. Your offshore trust can either be converted to a domestic Canadian trust (by passing majority control to trustees who reside in Canada), or its affairs can be terminated and the assets distributed to the beneficiaries. In this case, the beneficiaries will owe Canadian capital gains taxes on the fair market value at the time of distribution.

This is especially worrisome when you compare the outrageously high Canadian tax rates with those imposed in foreign tax havens. Luckily, prudent Canadians can take advantage of this wide international tax disparity by establishing an offshore tax shelter that can easily double after-tax disposable income.

This can be accomplished in full compliance with federal law. If you follow the rules, Canada Revenue Agency will not be able to mount a successful challenge, despite their recent efforts to go after anything they consider to be an "overly aggressive tax strategy."

Aggressive Tax Enforcement

The most dangerous attitude one can adopt when dealing with the establishment of offshore business arrangements is the cavalier approach — the stupid idea that "white collar" crimes are somehow less serious than violent crimes, or that the federal government is less concerned about financial offenses than they are about other civil wrongs.

Canadian courts display a stiff attitude towards tax scofflaws and the long arm reaches across oceans. For example, the Canadian Supreme Court held that the former manager of the Freeport branch of the Canadian Royal Bank could be forced to give testimony at a tax evasion trial in Canada, even though doing so would be a breach of the Bahamian bank secrecy law.

Powerful laws aimed at preventing tax evasion have aided the federal government's vigorous international enforcement efforts. By law, there is no statute of limitations on tax evasion, but a Canada Revenue Agency audit can only cover three prior years. CRA has power to obtain "foreign-based information or documents," and elaborate annual corporate reporting requirements were imposed on inter-company transactions between Canadians and any offshore entities. Failure to report, or false statements concerning such transactions, can result in fines of up to C$24,000.

The Canada Revenue Agency keeps an eagle eye on the tax shelter industry. Before the adoption of the new offshore reporting requirements, RC officials tracked the offshore business activity of individual Canadians as best they could. Now they have powerful new tools that place personal responsibility to report squarely on taxpayers.

In spite of these tough federal policies and an array of laws with sharp teeth, there are still many opportunities for profitable offshore financial activities. Offshore tax havens are legal and in selective circumstances, nonresident owned international investment and business structures can be used to reduce taxes.

CONCLUSION

There you have it. It may seem a difficult road to travel, but becoming a Canadian citizen investor can save a U.S. citizen millions of dollars that would otherwise go directly to the IRS.

Yes, these savings are predicated on major changes you must be willing to make, including surrender of your U.S. citizenship. You must move yourself, your family and your business to Canada and possibly to another country later on. Despite these drawbacks, the true bottom line measured in dollar savings can be enormous.

CONTACTS

Official:

Federal Government of Canada: http://www.canada.gc.ca/home.html.

Canada Revenue: http://www.cra-arc.gc.ca/menu-eng.html.

Citizenship & Immigration Canada: http://www.cic.gc.ca/english/index.asp.

U.S. Embassy, 490 Sussex Drive, K1N-1G8 Ottawa, Ontario; Tel.: + (613) 238-5335; Fax: + (613) 688-3082; Website: http://www.usembassycanada.gov.

Embassy of Canada, 501 Pennsylvania Avenue, N.W., Washington, D.C. 20001; Tel.: (202) 682-1740; Website: http://canadaembassy.org/.

For information about **Canada's Immigration Program**, consult the Websites of Citizenship and Immigration Canada: http://www.cic.gc.ca/english/immigrate/index.asp.

http://www.cic.gc.ca/english/citizenship/index.asp.

For visa information, see http://www.cic.gc.ca/english/visit/index.asp.

Chapter Eleven

The United States as an Offshore Tax Haven

Unbeknownst to most Americans, the complex tax laws of the United States make America one of the world's leading offshore tax havens — not for Americans, but rather almost exclusively for foreign citizens who invest in America. There are ways that U.S. persons can also get reduced taxes from U.S. tax laws that benefit foreigners, but those ways are highly complex, requiring costly professional advice and constant tax management.

In this chapter, I explain the intricacies of the U.S. Internal Revenue Code, so forgive me once again for the legalistic approach. It is much more complex than Chapter 10 on Canada and expatriation. But again, I urge you — get competent professional advice and realistic cost estimates before you embark on any plans this chapter may inspire you to attempt.

Tax Haven America

Few hard-pressed American taxpayers realize it, but the United States is considered a major tax haven for foreign investors.

There are a whole host of laws that provide liberal U.S. tax breaks that apply only to foreigners. While Americans struggle to pay combined taxes that can rob them of more than 50% of their total incomes, careful foreign investors can and do make lots of money in the United States — all tax-free.

The fact that the United States itself is a major tax haven exposes the rank hypocrisy of American politicians who rail against "offshore tax havens." That includes President Obama, who has made a major political and legislative issue out of the legal use of offshore tax havens by U.S. individuals and corporations, as I described in Chapter 3. These demagogic attacks portray Americans' use of tax havens as unpatriotic and akin to tax evasion. But these same politicians have no problem when foreigners use the U.S. as their offshore tax haven — they welcome the billions it brings into the U.S. every year.

Foreigners have more than US$4 trillion in passive investments in the form of bank accounts or brokerage accounts in the United States, according to U.S. Treasury figures. The U.S. government does not tax foreign persons on their interest income or passive capital gains earned in America. The government gives huge tax breaks to foreigners because the government wants and needs their money and their capital investments to keep the U.S. economy afloat.

However, foreign corporations operating within the U.S. do pay corporate income taxes on some of their U.S. earnings and, often, they pay plenty.

A haphazard array of complex provisions in the U.S. Internal Revenue Code (IRC), coupled with a host of international tax treaties, provide rich opportunities for the astute foreign investor. Assisting these investors is an elite group of high-priced American tax lawyers and accountants known as "inbound specialists." Their specialty is structuring business transactions so as to minimize taxes and maximize profits for their foreign clients.

The U.S. Treasury (and politicians) need this foreign capital to bolster the national economy, to finance huge government deficit spending, and to refinance the enormous national debt — as of this writing nearly US$11.6 trillion. With an estimated population of the United States at 306,434,603, each citizen's share of this debt is over US$37,800.

A large portion of foreign investment goes directly into short and long-term U.S. Treasury securities. This enormous cash inflow keeps the U.S. government afloat from day to day. (The debt increases by an estimated $3.7 billion each day.) Billions of dollars of the much talked-about "national debt" is owed directly to European and Asian investors. The communist government of the People's Republic of China is one of America's largest individual creditors by virtue of their investments in U.S. government debt securities. The old saying about government debt that "we owe it to ourselves" doesn't apply anymore — if it ever did.

Another scary fact is that the annual interest paid on the US$11 trillion government debt is now nearly a half a trillion dollars annually, a figure that exceeds all other federal budget program costs except that of the Defense Department. Some 38% of the entire budget is for interest payments alone, and much of it goes to foreign investors.

So we're talking very big money here!

As a consequence, these foreign investors have a lot of power over America and Americans.

When the U.S. Congress imposed a 30% withholding tax on all interest payments to foreign residents and corporations doing business in the U.S., foreign investors bluntly let it be known they would take their money elsewhere if the withholding tax remained. Not surprisingly, the IRC is now riddled with exceptions to the 30% tax.

The biggest U.S. tax break for many foreigners comes from a combined impact of domestic IRC provisions and the tax laws of the investor's own country. As Americans are painfully aware, the United States taxes its citizens and residents on their worldwide income. But non-citizens and nonresidents are allowed by their own domestic laws to earn certain types of income from within the U.S. tax-free. As you can guess, droves of smart foreign investors take advantage of this situation.

Foreign direct investment (FDI) in the United States declined sharply after 2000, when a record US$300 billion was invested in U.S. businesses and real estate. The cumulative amount, or stock, of foreign direct investment in the U.S. on an historical cost basis rose from US$1.8 trillion in 2006 to about US$2.1 trillion in 2007, an increase of 14%. But FDI fell by about 50% in the first quarter of 2009 compared to the final quarter of 2008, a reflection of the global recession. The U. S. defines foreign direct investment as the ownership or control, directly or indirectly, by one foreign person (individual, branch, partnership, association, government, etc.) of 10% or more of the voting securities of an incorporated U.S. business enterprise or an equivalent interest in an unincorporated U.S. business enterprise.

WHERE THERE'S A WILL

In a qualified, but highly circuitous way, and under the right circumstances, a U.S. citizen or resident alien also can benefit from this U.S. tax-free income that makes so many foreign investors wealthy. The qualifying process is complex, but the U.S. Tax Code does offer possibilities.

It is possible for an American to establish an offshore corporation to invest tax-free in U.S. securities and other property. Nevertheless, unfortunate things can happen if you don't structure these backdoor, offshore arrangements properly, due to the morass of IRS rules designed to keep Americans from benefiting from this reverse offshore tax avoidance route.

OFFSHORE CORPORATION LOOPHOLE

Years ago, a U.S. person could pay a pleasant, tax-deductible business visit to a tax haven nation, say The Bahamas, and form an IBC there.

You could then transfer some cash to the new company and have it put that money into selected U.S. investments. If you picked right and this triangle shot paid off, all the corporate income was tax-free. As long as your foreign corporation did not have an office in the U.S., the IRS treated it as a "nonresident foreign corporation" and most of its income was not taxed. As an owner, the company could pay your legitimate business-related expenses, and no income tax was imposed until you decided to pay yourself dividends. Meanwhile, assuming good management, profits could be deferred, ploughed back, and allowed to increase in value.

Part of that happy scenario remains true today.

As long as a foreign corporation does not maintain a U.S. office, or have sufficient contacts with the U.S. that would make it "effectively connected" to this country, the IRS considers it a "nonresident foreign corporation." Under the law, it can avoid taxes on certain U.S. source income as defined by law.

The very big difference today: the U.S. shareholder in an offshore corporation is taxed like a partner in a partnership. This means a controlling U.S. shareholder of a foreign corporation must pay annual income taxes on his or her pro-rata share of certain types of the foreign corporation's income when it is earned, even if that income is not distributed as dividends or in any other form, and even if the corporation retains these profits. No longer can the profits sit offshore out of the IRS tax collector's grasp. As you can guess, this has substantially reduced the incentive for Americans to create offshore corporations as a tax avoidance mechanism. If you abide by the law, most of the tax avoidance is gone.

Except — and there's always an exception when it comes to U.S. tax laws — for two remaining loopholes that still might allow tax-free investment possibilities for Americans using offshore corporations. You need to execute these strategies very carefully, with professional help, to make them both legal and effective.

But first, a little background history and some definitions that hopefully will broaden your understanding of what's going on here.

Controlled Foreign Corporations

The basic purpose of the complex rules governing controlled foreign corporations (CFCs) is to prevent U.S. taxpayers from avoiding or deferring taxes through the use of such offshore companies. Keep in mind as you read this that the object is to avoid having your offshore corporation being tagged by the IRS as a CFC because that status means higher taxes.

These rules can be found in IRC sections 951 through 964. Essentially, if a foreign corporation is controlled by U.S. taxpayers, those who own 10% or more of the corporation must report their respective share of the CFC income on their annual personal income tax return (IRS Form 1040). The effect is similar to the flow-through tax treatment of a domestic U.S. partnership or subchapter S corporation, but much more complicated.

The great ingenuity of the American lawyers and accountants who are inbound specialist tax advisors has produced numerous loopholes used to circumvent early versions of the CFC tax laws. Over time, the IRS and Congress have repeatedly revised the law, trying to close these loopholes. Undaunted, the tax experts found new loopholes, the IRS reacted, and Congress changed the laws again. The foreign tax area has become an ongoing battle of wits between the international tax experts and the IRS. Much of the Enron scandal came from the too-imaginative use of these offshore tax shelters.

We tell you this because no prudent investor or businessperson should venture into this offshore tax arena without being fully prepared. You need to be ready to cope with uncertainty and highly complex tax rules that are always in a state of flux. And don't forget the potential cost in accounting and legal fees required just to keep up with constant change. Unless the tax savings are significant, the cost of these arrangements may not be worth it.

Just so you understand how complex this area of tax law can be, I readily admit that most of what I say in this chapter is an oversimplification, a crude condensation of thousands of pages of IRS regulations, rulings and tax court cases. But persevere, for there's a potential for big profits, along with light at the end of the tunnel.

U.S. Shareholders

First, only a "U.S. shareholder" is affected by CFC tax rules.

A U.S. shareholder is defined as a U.S. person (including any legal entity), that owns 10% or more of the total voting power of the stock of a foreign corporation. This can mean a citizen or resident of the U.S., a domestic partnership or corporation, or a U.S. estate or trust that is not a foreign estate or trust. However, if a foreign trust is a grantor trust, or has U.S. beneficiaries, the U.S. grantor or beneficiary is treated as a shareholder of the foreign corporation.

In the case of a foreign estate, if a U.S. person is a beneficiary, then that beneficiary is considered a shareholder of the foreign corporation. In each instance, the IRS looks through the legal tangle and focuses on U.S. citizens receiving, directly or indirectly, income from a foreign corporation.

But there's another caveat: unless the corporation qualifies as a CFC under the second test described below, the U.S. shareholders are not required to report their share of the corporate income on their personal tax return unless the corporation is also a passive foreign investment company (PFIC — pronounced pee-fic).

Second Test

A foreign corporation is considered a CFC only if more than 50% of the total voting power or the total value of the stock is owned by U.S. shareholders having a 10% or greater stock interest on any day during the tax year. (Different rules apply to insurance companies.) If foreign persons (or entities) own 50% or more of the corporation stock, then it is not considered to be a CFC.

However, if a U.S. person is related to the foreign person or entity, then the U.S. shareholder is deemed to be a shareholder of the foreign corporation under the constructive ownership rules in IRC, section 318, (also called the attribution of ownership rules). These rules apply with respect to U.S. persons and foreign entities, but not to foreign individuals. Section 318(b) refers to section 958(b) with respect to the attribution rules for a CFC. IRC 958(b)(1) provides an exception to the constructive ownership rules in IRC 318. Thus, if a foreign relative (parent, child, grandchild, grandparent, or spouse) owns 50% or more of a foreign corporation, the U.S. owners are not subject to the CFC tax rules.

Third Test

If a corporation qualifies as a CFC for an uninterrupted period of 30 days or more during any tax year, then every U.S. shareholder (as defined above) who owns stock in such corporation on the last day of the tax year in which it qualified as a CFC must report as personal gross income, his or her pro-rata share of the CFC income.

Fourth Test

If the corporation is a CFC, its U.S. shareholders are required to report any CFC income that meets the definition of what is called Subpart F income. This includes most kinds of foreign source investment income, and foreign income derived from those related parties we just mentioned, but not income earned in the U.S.

The related parties means anyone who owns or controls (directly or indirectly) more than 50% of the stock of a foreign corporation, or one who is controlled by the foreign corporation, or a person (entity) who is, in fact, in a brother-sister affiliated corporate relationship. The related party can be individuals, corporations, partnerships, trusts, or an estate. These rules apply even though true ownership is masked by a long chain of interrelated controls. The IRS wants to know who controls the income source, and who gets the payoff. All of this legal jargon is laid out in IRC section 954(d)(3).

Subpart F income does not include any income earned in the U.S. because this income is taxable for the foreign corporation, just as it is for a domestic U.S. company. Thus, if a foreign company's domestic income is taxed by the IRS, it's not foreign-source income and is not subject to the CFC rules.

Generally, subpart F income does not include any income derived from doing business in a foreign country, so long as the buyer or supplier is not a related person. In plain language, the CFC rules are aimed at foreign corporations that buy or sell goods or services in a "sweetheart deal" from their related U.S. entities at a presumably favorable price. These underhanded firms then resell their goods or services abroad at a normal market price, thereby shifting the profit into the foreign entity.

Having said all this, we must point out that the specific rules applicable to subpart F income do not require that there be any actual shifting of profits to the foreign corporation in order for the IRS to rule that CFC status exists.

Additionally, where the foreign corporation is primarily an investment company that invests in foreign stocks, bonds or other *passive* income investments (as distinguished from an *active* trade or business), all of that investment income is treated as subpart F income. Also, note that the related party rules are not applicable to *investment* income.

TRIED BUT NOT TRUE

Now that I've tried to explain what a CFC and a U.S. person are in the tax context, let's look at some related schemes that the IRS has rejected.

Formally assigning title to half the offshore corporation's shares of stock to your offshore attorney, with his or her agreement to vote the shares as you instruct, will not avoid a CFC determination. The IRS looks at the reality of the situation, and easily sees through facades that use "straw man" ownership. The use of a foreign corporation with bearer shares that are held by any unrelated party on behalf of the real owner is treated the same as when an attorney holds the shares on behalf of the taxpayer.

Some slick offshore advisors will try to convince potential clients that a chain of legal entities putting lots of paperwork between you and your offshore corporation will fool the IRS into thinking there is no CFC. Of course, the more entities you set up, the more the costs and the more a promoter is paid.

Forget it! An interlocking chain of offshore trusts and corporations, usually with a trust holding the operating corporation's stock, is a dead giveaway to the IRS. It may even provide strong evidence of tax fraud, which is a criminal act. The IRS is likely to conclude that since the person who is ultimately responsible for creating the entities in the chain, is the beneficial owner of the stock. The only remotely attractive feature of this kind of tinker-toy legal arrangement is that it might be difficult for the IRS to uncover it. Once exposed, however, the sheer complexity would be seen as evidence of deliberate fraud. Don't do it!

What Does Work

Now let's examine some ways to avoid having your investment ruled a controlled foreign corporation. In other words, let's explore a few strategies to help minimize your tax burden. (By the way, you'll often hear a non-CFC called a "decontrolled foreign corporation" — they're the same thing.)

One way is to make certain that no U.S. citizen or resident alien owns more than 10% of the corporation.

Here's why: for purposes of the CFC rules, if any five or fewer U.S. persons or U.S. residents own 10% or more of an offshore corporation's voting stock, it's a CFC.

Suppose you and at least 11 of your associates (folks unrelated to you — see below) plan to divide ownership interests in an offshore investment company. Divide 100% by 11, and you get a 9.09% share for each U.S. shareholder. Your offshore corporation is not a CFC, because no one U.S. person owns 10% or more of the voting stock. Your group can invest its capital within the

United States with little or no tax cost, just as a foreign citizen does. The income can compound tax-free until you decide to pay yourselves dividends, which then become taxable personal income.

One caveat: Beware of the *attribution of ownership* rules mentioned above; if related U.S. persons are offshore corporate shareholders, they will be considered as constructive joint owners. Their shares will be added together for purposes of the CFC control test. Don't choose 11 associates who are your family members, and don't use your U.S. entities as owners. If you do, the offshore corporation probably will be ruled to be a CFC.

If you establish an offshore company with one U.S. person owning more than 50% of the voting stock, and other U.S. persons with less than 10% each, a CFC does exist because of the 50% U.S. shareholder. However, here's a twist; only the 50% shareholder is taxed on his pro rata share of the corporation's earned income each year. Because they have less than 10% of the voting shares each, the other U.S. persons are treated as though the company is a decontrolled corporation. They don't have to report their company income share annually, and are liable for taxes only when they actually do receive dividends or other corporate distributions. If a CFC also qualifies as a PFIC, then all U.S. shareholders are liable for their share of taxes on the income of the PFIC.

REAL FOREIGN PARTNERS

Another way to guarantee your offshore company will qualify as decontrolled is to invest along with one or more truly unrelated foreign partners. If the foreign person(s) own 50% or more of the voting power shares, the corporation is decontrolled. It then enjoys tax-free investments in the United States as a nonresident alien. Even though you are a partial American owner, you are taxed only as you withdraw money from the corporation, not each year. The foreign person can be a relative of the U.S. owner or owners.

Of course, the foreign persons must be the true owners of the stock. This sort of 50-50 ownership arrangement is particularly popular when foreign investors are from a country with similar tax rules, such as Germany. There have been many U.S.-German tax saving joint ventures in real estate that allow both halves to avoid a CFC designation by their respective national tax agencies.

WHAT KIND OF INCOME?

There's another way around the CFC designation, and that depends on the type of income the offshore corporation takes in; only subpart F income is counted as taxable and treated as though it passes through to U.S. shareholders. Non-subpart F income is not reportable annually on a pro rata basis. That income can accumulate and compound tax-free in the corporation until it is taken out as dividends.

Here are the *types of income that are counted as* subpart F income and are taxable for U.S. shareholders on a pro rata basis annually:

Foreign personal holding company income. All interest, dividends, royalties, and gains on securities, plus rents from related parties, are taxable. In other words, just about every kind of usual investment income is included in subpart F income. One exception is rent derived from the active conduct of a trade or business is not included, unless the rental income is received from a related party.

Example: suppose your foreign corporation owns an office building in The Bahamas. You occupy 15% for your own business, and your paid staff leases the remainder to unrelated parties and provides maintenance and other services. This would be considered the active conduct of a rental business in a foreign country, and rental income is not subpart F income.

Or, suppose your foreign corporation owns an oil drilling company in a foreign nation. When your equipment is idle, it is leased to other oil drilling companies. The rental from the leases is not considered subpart F income and can be accumulated in an offshore corporation. (Because there are special IRS rules for banking, insurance, shipping, or oil services income earned offshore, if that's your type of business, consult with an experienced international tax advisor who knows these rules.)

The IRS is so generous with the rent income exception because it knows that many tax haven countries prohibit nonresidents from owning land, so not many will be able to qualify for this rental income tax break.

Foreign-based company sales income: This is essentially income from the purchase of property from a related person, or the sale of property to anyone on behalf of a related person. Caveat: to avoid having this kind of income treated as subpart F income, you must purchase your goods or services from unrelated parties, and not sell your goods to a related party.

Foreign-based company service income: This is income from consulting services (legal, accounting, engineering, architectural, or management services) performed for, or on behalf of, a related person, but outside the country in which the foreign corporation is organized. Note: if your offshore corporation performs services for *unrelated* parties outside the U.S., that service income is not subpart F income.

De Minimis TEST GAMES

Yet another way to avoid offshore company subpart F income is to take advantage of the IRS' so-called *de minimis* rule. Here's the rule: If the sum total of the foreign-based company's service income, plus the gross insurance income, does not exceed 5% of the CFC's total income, or US$1 million (whichever is smaller), none of the income is considered foreign-based company income or insurance income.

For example, suppose that your offshore corporation buys some condominiums in Panama. You rent the condominiums to tourists who are unrelated to any corporation owners. Since rental income from unrelated persons is not subpart F income, this will not be passed through *pro rata* and taxed to U.S. shareholders. In addition, if the rental income makes up at least 95% of the offshore corporation's total income, it will keep the subpart F income from being passed through to the U.S. shareholders under the *de minimis* rule. (Get it? Five percent is considered as *de minimis*, an amount so small it gets you out from under the CFC taxes.)

If you have U.S.-based manufacturing or personal consulting services that can be moved offshore, you might be able to use non-subpart F income generated by these operations to shelter investments in the United States. Any importing and exporting of tangible products through a foreign corporation would escape the subpart F rules, so long as the products are not bought from or sold to a related party. In addition, offshore manufacturing and consulting income probably will not be subpart F income, so it is also sheltered from tax in the offshore corporation.

But be careful. There's a flip side, what might be called the reverse *de minimis* rule: if 70% or more of the offshore corporation's income is defined as subpart F income, then all income is treated as such. In that case, you really are stuck tax-wise. You can see how important the type of the income can be.

For clarity's sake (I hope), let's consider another example:

Suppose that your offshore business sells a product with very high production costs and low mark-up. Assume the product costs 90% of its selling price. As we know, investment income is considered subpart F income, but under the rules, if the gross income from the investment measures less than 5% of the gross product sales, then the offshore corporation won't be considered a CFC.

To make it more specific: If the offshore foreign corporation sells US$10 million of widgets, it can make up to US$526,500 of gross investment income without becoming a CFC (US$10,526,500 x 5% = US$526,325). However, in this example, the profit on the US$10 million of widget sales would be US$1 million, while the profit on the gross investment income might be close to US$500,000.

Now you know why foreign corporations need such good lawyers and accountants.

WATCH OUT FOR...

There's a trap that must be avoided when using the *de minimis* rule as a CFC designation avoidance tactic.

The rules say that if 50% or more of the foreign company's total asset value is used to produce passive income, or if 50% of those assets are being held for the production of passive income, the foreign corporation is treated as a *passive foreign investment company* (PFIC), which is discussed further below.

Take it from the experts: as a practical matter, it requires more assets to produce a 5% return in the form of passive investment income than to produce the same amount of net income from a business activity. A business might typically generate a return of 15% to 20% on its net assets, and about 10% to 15% on its total assets. Thus, in the example above, if the foreign corporation needs US$10 million in assets to produce US$1 million in gross profits from widgets sales, it cannot exceed a maximum of US$10 million in passive assets held to produce investment income. If it does, it is considered a PFIC. If the return on those investment assets is 5%, the example given above would work — but just barely

Before venturing into PFIC territory, we'll reiterate the obvious: subpart F income rules offer many possible avenues of tax avoidance. But after reading this, we don't have to tell you the rules are very complicated and riddled with exceptions. Even more discouraging, most of them were not even mentioned here. As always, consult an experienced U.S. international tax advisor before launching your offshore corporate career.

The PFIC (Pee-fik)

In yet another skirmish between offshore tax specialists and the IRS, Congress attempted to plug even more foreign corporate loopholes with the Tax Reform Act of 1986. This law established the concept of the *passive foreign investment company* (PFIC), and authorized the rules that govern such entities.

First, a definition: passive income is generally considered earnings from interest, dividends, capital gains, royalties, and a few other non-sales or service income types. The PFIC rules that apply to passive income are generally more difficult to avoid than other rules we already discussed.

Under the law, a PFIC is any foreign corporation that makes 75% or more of gross income from passive income sources. A corporation will also be considered a PFIC if at least 50% of the value of its assets produce passive income, or are being held for production of passive income. Unlike a CFC, there is no control test for a PFIC. Any offshore corporation that has the minimum amount of passive income, even if its ownership is only 1% American, qualifies as a PFIC.

Owning PFIC shares can be fairly costly. You may face a tax penalty or a loss of your tax deferral. Here are the two possible punishments:

- You pay a penalty tax either when you sell the PFIC shares, or when you receive an excess distribution.

The penalty tax assumes that the undistributed PFIC income and gains were actually paid to you annually, but that you didn't report the income and pay taxes owed on it each year. As penalty for your tardiness, you must pay the original tax owed plus interest based on the number of years you held the PFIC shares without paying the taxes. The shares of a PFIC are deemed to be sold at the date of your death, and your estate will be liable for the deferred taxes.

- The other option is to set up your PFIC as a *qualified electing fund corporation* (QEF) from the very beginning (the IRS has a name for everything). That means you report your *pro-rata* shares of the PFIC's income and gains annually, just as you would with a U.S.-based mutual fund. In other words, you lose any benefit that comes with tax deferral and compounding of profits. In order to make this election, the PFIC must be willing to provide you with annual information on your share of its income. Unless U.S. owners control the PFIC, this is not likely to happen. Another option is to use the mark-to-market election to compute your gains (or losses) each year based on the difference in the market value of the shares at the end of each year. However, this election is limited to widely held foreign fund shares sold through major exchanges.

Your foreign corporation can avoid the PFIC trap by reducing the percentage of the offshore corporation's gross income that is passive. On the other hand, you could increase the amount of the assets used to produce active business income. If the corporation is a PFIC because more than 75% of its gross income is passive income, then it's only necessary to change the percentage by generating more active business income, or less passive investment income. If the corporation is a PFIC because of the 50% asset test, then you can increase assets to produce more active business income, or you can reduce passive investment assets. To qualify, it's necessary to meet both of these tests. Failure to qualify on either ground could subject shareholders to the adverse tax treatment of a PFIC.

Another option is to combine the investment activities of an offshore corporation with an actual operating business. If you have manufacturing or consulting operations overseas, these can be used to avoid the PFIC penalty.

Another potential trap is the foreign *personal holding company* rules. In most cases, if you can avoid the CFC rules, or qualify as a decontrolled offshore corporation, you can also avoid the foreign personal holding company rules.

OFFSHORE CORPORATIONS OPERATING IN THE U.S.

Once your offshore corporation has done everything necessary to gain a favorable foreign business tax status under IRS rules, it is free to invest in the United States and reap the benefits of tax-free income just as a foreign citizen would.

But what you cannot do as a foreign corporation is "engage in a U.S. trade or business" as defined under U.S. tax law. Here are the guidelines to follow:

- No physical office or agent in the United States
- Books and records must be maintained outside the U.S.

- Actual management and control must be exercised elsewhere

- Directors' and shareholders' meetings must be held outside the U.S.

- The corporation cannot have a business located within the U.S.

Once your offshore corporation secures its status as a foreign business, some of the immediate benefits include no obligation to pay U.S. taxes on bank deposit interest, and no tax on capital gains earned on U.S. stocks and bonds. Although there could be tax liability for some dividends paid by American stock shares, these taxes often can be reduced or avoided by locating the offshore corporation in a country with a favorable U.S. tax treaty. Some bilateral U.S.-foreign tax treaties provide for a greatly reduced U.S. withholding tax rate on dividends paid to foreign corporations.

A good example of this dividend tax avoidance advantage became known during the so-called "junk bond" mess and the widespread collapse of insurance companies and savings and loan associations in the 1980s. When these faltering American companies tried to sell assets, many foreign corporations or partnerships submitted the best bids for their portfolios of junk bonds and shares. While potential U.S. bond buyers faced taxes on interest and capital gains, foreign investors, facing no U.S. taxes, could offer bids 10% or more above those of U.S. competitors. If these offshore companies were incorporated in tax-free havens like Panama or Nevis, they escaped dividend and interest taxes on these "fire sale" stock buys completely.

Warning — The Per Se List

For U.S. persons who control the shares in a foreign corporation, there are major limitations on U.S. tax benefits that would otherwise be available to a corporation formed in the United States. That is because the foreign corporation may be on what is known as the IRS "per se" list of foreign corporations, which appears in IRS regulations, section 301.7701-2(b)(8)(i).

The listed per se corporations are barred from numerous U.S. tax benefits. This means that U.S. persons cannot file an IRS Form 8832 electing to treat the corporation as a "disregarded entity" or a foreign partnership, either of which is given much more favorable tax treatment.

Under IRS rules, the foreign corporation that engages in passive investments is considered a "controlled foreign corporation," which requires the filing of IRS Form 5471 describing its operations. U.S. persons also must file IRS Form 926 reporting transfers of cash or assets to the corporation.

A U.S. person who controls a foreign financial account of any nature that has in it $10,000 or more at any time during a calendar year must report this to the IRS on Form TD F 90-22.1. There are serious fines and penalties for failure to file these IRS returns and criminal charges can also be filed. As a general rule, U.S. persons can be guilty of the crime of "falsifying a federal income tax return" by failing to report offshore corporate holdings.

Any eventual capital gains an IRS-listed per se corporation may make are not taxed in the U.S. under the more favorable capital gains tax rate of 15%, but rather as ordinary income for the corporate owners, which can be much higher. There is also the possibility of double taxation if the foreign corporation makes investments in the U.S., in which case there is a 30% U.S. withholding tax on the investment income. Under U.S. tax rules, no annual losses can be taken on corporate investments, which must be deferred by the U.S. owners until the foreign corporation is liquidated.

However, compared to these IRS restrictions, there may be offsetting considerations, such as complete exemption from foreign taxes, which may be more important in your financial planning. Therefore, it is extremely important that U.S. persons obtain an authoritative review of the tax implications before forming a foreign corporation for any purpose, including holding title to personal or business real estate.

U.S. REAL ESTATE A TAX BARGAIN

Investing in U.S. real estate used to be an easy avenue to tax-free income and gains for foreign citizens. However, the real estate tax rules were changed in 1980, and profits earned by foreign owners are no longer tax-free. Still, investment in U.S. real estate through a decontrolled offshore corporation can result in lower taxes on profits if the transaction is structured properly.

In the complicated and rapidly changing area of tax law, an offshore company should be incorporated in a country that has a favorable tax treaty with the United States. The Netherlands is an historic favorite. The offshore company then creates a subsidiary U.S. corporation, which buys the real estate. Sometimes, it makes sense to have one U.S. company hold title to the real estate, while another is created to receive property management fees. Don't forget that foreign investors can also enjoy U.S. stock market trading profits entirely tax-free. This applies whether or not their home country has a double tax treaty with the U.S. The IRS periodically issues revenue rulings attacking current schemes, so obtain up-to-date advice from an experienced U.S. tax advisor.

There is a 10% withholding tax imposed on the gross proceeds from the sale of a U.S. real estate property interest by a foreign person. This term includes an interest in the form of corporate stock, partnerships, trusts, etc. In a case where there is no depreciation taken, a gain on U.S. real estate of 67% of the gross sales price would be subject to a 15% tax, resulting in a tax equal to 10% of the gross sales proceeds. Where the gain is less than 67%, the foreign investor would be paying too much tax with a 10% rate of withholding. Where the property is subject to depreciation, the accelerated depreciation is subject to a 25% rate of tax instead of 15%. This is an extremely complicated subject and one that I have not gone into in any real depth.

SUMMARY

The major points you should remember are those that apply to the offshore ownership structure (decontrolled corporation vs. CFC), and the type of income to be earned (either subpart F or not).

In evaluating any offshore tax planning proposal, be especially wary of:

- schemes involving chains of foreign entities, all of which ultimately are controlled by the same person;

- foreign-based agents who offer to act as accommodation agents to establish proxy control of a foreign entity;

- any plan that depends on secrecy, non-reporting and hindrance of IRS oversight;

- poorly capitalized, low asset corporations. The IRS and the courts often simply ignore such corporations when determining tax liabilities on any specific transaction. They view them as dummy or sham corporations with no continuing business purpose, set up mainly to avoid taxes.

This information overload is not meant to deter you, but to educate you about the risks of haphazard planning. The most disturbing aspect of studying offshore foreign corporations is the large number of Americans who are unaware of the tax saving possibilities that do exist. If you take the final step and explore these strategies, you won't regret it as long as you are careful to play by the rules.

Also, have an expert on costs "run the numbers" before you create a foreign corporation. It takes a net profit of about US$100,000 in a foreign-based business to justify the added operating expenses with the potential tax savings. Each foreign venture will involve different facts and costs, so that each one will need to be evaluated in terms of whether the potential tax savings is worth the cost and the complexity of operating offshore.

If you want to establish any offshore trust or corporation, your financial future will be determined in large part by attorneys and accountants and their professional abilities. It is vitally important that these professionals be both qualified and experienced in practical offshore business and legal operations.

Pending IRS Proposal

One last word: in January 2001, outgoing President Bill Clinton tried to pull a last minute trick on behalf of the Internal Revenue Service. He formally proposed U.S. regulations that would require all U.S. banks to report annually to the IRS all interest they pay to nonresident alien individuals, so that the IRS could pass on this information to the tax collectors in the many countries with which the U.S. has tax treaties.

The IRS proposal was advanced at the specific request of the tax hungry European Union, led by high-taxing France and Germany.

As I have noted, unlike the U.S., which taxes the worldwide income of its citizens and residents aliens, most other countries have a territorial system of taxation that only taxes income earned within the country or when foreign income is repatriated back to the country. Thus, so long as earnings from dividends, interest and capital gains remain outside these countries, there is no tax liability.

Of course, Europe's welfare states want to know what their citizens are earning offshore, how they spend their cash, all the better for EU tax collectors to squeeze out every last dollar or euro they can find. The noted offshore lawyer, Marshall Langer, has shown that the IRS proposal would cause major harm to the American economy by diverting billions in needed capital away from America.

Earlier in this chapter, I noted the trillions of investment dollars have flowed into the US, much from Europe, especially from France and Germany, where taxation and regulation are especially onerous. This capital flow has enabled U.S. businesses to expand plant and equipment, increase productivity, create new and higher paying jobs, and enjoy higher rates of economic growth than in Europe.

At a time when the U.S. economy is straining to end the recession, the last thing needed is a major policy change that would seriously hurt capital investment and jobs. During the eight years under the administration of President George W. Bush, this proposal was put aside and never finally approved. However, it will be interesting to see what the anti-tax haven President Obama will do about this IRS informant proposal. He and Democratic legislators in Congress have proposed all sorts of increased reporting and restrictions that will harm Americans who dare to invest and do business offshore. It remains to be seen if the same principles will be applied to foreigners who invest trillions in America.

GLOSSARY

acceptance — unconditional agreement by one party (the offeree) to the terms of an offer made by a second party (the offeror). Agreement results in a valid, binding contract.

arbitrage — simultaneously buying the securities in one nation, currency, or market and selling it in another, to take advantage of the price differential.

assets — items that have earning power or other value to their owner. Fixed assets (also known as long-term assets) are things that have a useful life of more than one year, for example buildings and machinery; there are also intangible fixed assets, like the good reputation ("goodwill") of a company or brand.

asset protection trust (APT) — an offshore trust which holds title to, and protects the grantor's property from, claims, judgments, and creditors, especially because it is located in a country other than the grantor's home country.

attachment — the post-judicial civil procedure by which personal property is taken from its owner pursuant to a judgment or other court order.

basis — the original cost of an asset, later used to measure increased value for tax purposes at the time of sale or disposition.

bear market — in a bear market, prices trend downwards and investors, anticipating losses, tend to sell. This can create a self-sustaining downward spiral.

bearer share/stocks — a negotiable stock certificate made out only to "Bearer" without designating the shareowner by name. Such shares are unregistered with the issuing company and dividends are claimed by "clipping coupons" attached to the shares and presenting them for payment. Bearer shares are illegal in most countries.

beneficiary — individual designated to receive income from a trust or estate; a person named in an insurance policy to receive proceeds or benefits.

bequest — a gift of personal property by will; also called a *legacy*.

bond — a debt security, or, more simply, an IOU. The bond states when a loan must be repaid and what interest the borrower (issuer) must pay to the holder. Banks and investors buy and trade bonds.

bull market — a bull market is one in which prices are generally rising and investor confidence is high.

capital — wealth (cash or other assets) used to fuel the creation of more wealth; within companies, often characterized as working capital or fixed capital.

capital gain — the amount of profit earned from the sale or exchange of property, measured against the original cost basis.

captive insurance company — a wholly owned subsidiary company established by a non-insurance parent company to spread insured risks among the parent and other associated companies. Bermuda is the leading jurisdiction where such entities are registered.

carry trade (currency) — the borrowing of currency with a low interest rate, converting it into currency with a high interest rate and then lending it. One common carry trade currency is the yen, as traders seek to benefit from Japan's low interest rates. The element of risk is in the fluctuations in the currency market.

civil suit — a non-criminal legal action between parties relating to a dispute or injury seeking remedies for a violation of contractual or other personal rights.

civil forfeiture — laws that allow the U.S. and state governments to seize private property allegedly involved with a crime without charging anyone with the crime; the burden is on the property owner to disprove the alleged criminal association.

Chapter 11 — a term from U.S. bankruptcy law that describes court-supervised postponement of a company's obligations to its creditors, giving it time to reorganize its debts or sell parts of the business.

collateralized debt obligations (CDOs) — a financial structure that groups individual loans, bonds or assets in a portfolio, which can then be traded.

commercial paper —unsecured, short-term loans issued by companies; funds that are typically used for working capital, rather than fixed assets, such as a new building.

commodities — products such as agricultural products or iron ore that, in their basic forms, have a market price and are bought, traded and sold. See also *futures*.

common law — the body of law developed in England from judicial decisions based on customs and precedent, constituting the basis of the present English, British Commonwealth, and U.S. legal systems. See also *equity*.

community property — in certain states in the U.S.,

property acquired during marriage jointly owned by both spouses, each with an undivided one-half interest.

contract — a binding agreement between two or more parties; also, the written or oral evidence of an agreement.

corporation — a business, professional or other entity recognized in law to act as a single legal person, although composed of one or more natural persons, endowed by law with various rights and duties including the right of succession.

corpus — property owned by a fund, trust or estate; also called the *principal*.

creator — See also *grantor*.

credit default swap — a swap designed to transfer credit risk, in effect a form of financial insurance. The buyer of the swap makes periodic payments to the seller in return for protection in the event of a default on a loan.

creditor — one to whom a debtor owes money or other valuable consideration.

currency — official, government issued paper and coined money; hard currency describes a national currency sufficiently sound so as to be generally acceptable in international dealings.

dead cat bounce — a phrase long used on trading floors to describe a short-lived recovery of share prices in a bear market.

debtor — one who owes another (the creditor) money or other valuable consideration, especially one who has neglected payments due.

decedent — a term used in estate and probate law to describe a deceased person.

declaration — a formal statement in writing of any kind, often signed and notarized, especially a document establishing a trust; also called an *indenture* or *trust agreement*.

deed — a formal written document signed by the owner conveying title to real estate to another party.

deflation — the downward price movement of goods and services.

derivatives — a way of investing in a particular product or security without having to own it. The value can depend on anything from the price of coffee to interest rates or what the weather is like. Derivatives can be used as insurance to limit the risk of a particular investment. Credit derivatives are based on the risk of borrowers defaulting on their loans, such as mortgages.

dividends — a payment by a company to its shareholders, usually linked to its profits.

domicile — a person's permanent legal home, as compared to a place that may be only a temporary residence. Domicile determines what law applies to the person for purposes of marriage, divorce, succession of estate at death and taxation.

due process — the regular administration of the law, according to which no citizen may be denied his or her legal rights and all laws must conform to fundamental, accepted legal principles.

equity — a body of judicial rules developed under the common law used to enlarge and protect legal rights and enforce duties while seeking to avoid unjust constraints and narrowness of statutory law; also, the unrealized property value of a person's investment or ownership, as in a trust beneficiary's equitable interest; also, the risk sharing part of a company's capital, referred to as ordinary shares.

equal protection — the guarantee under the 14th Amendment to the U.S. Constitution that a state must treat an individual or class of individuals the same as it treats other individuals or classes in like circumstances.

estate — any of various kinds or types of ownership a person may have in real or personal property; often used to describe all property of a deceased person, meaning the assets and liabilities remaining after death.

estate tax — taxes imposed at death by the U.S. on assets of a decedent except on the first US$3.5 million in value which is exempt during 2009. In 2010, the estate tax rate drops to zero percent; the heirs of those who die in that years will not pay any death tax. The U.S. Congress provided that the current estate tax law expires at the end of 2010. On January 1, 2011, the estate tax rate returns to 55% unless the law is changed before that date.

exchange controls — restrictions imposed by government on dealings in a national or foreign currency.

executor — a person who manages the estate of a decedent; also called an executrix if a female, personal representative, administrator or administratrix.

exemption — an tax law, a statutorily defined right to avoid imposition of part or all of certain taxes; also, the statutory right granted to a debtor in bankruptcy to retain a portion of his or her real or personal property free from creditors' claims.

expatriation — the transfer of one's legal residence

and citizenship from one's home country to another country, often in anticipation of government financial restrictions or taxes.

family partnership (also, family limited partnership) — A legal business relationship created by agreement among two or more family members for a common purpose, often used as a means to transfer and/or equalize income and assets among family members so as to limit individual personal liability and taxes. See *partnership* and *limited partnership*.

FATF — a subgroup of the OECD that claims to establish international anti-money laundering standards. See *OECD* and *G-20*.

Federal Reserve — (informally called "The Fed") is the quasi-public, quasi-private central banking system of the United States created in 1913.

fiduciary — A person holding title to property in trust for the benefit of another, as does a trustee, guardian or executor of an estate.

flight capital — movement of large sums of money across national borders, often in response to investment opportunities or to escape high taxes or pending political or social unrest; also called hot money.

FTSE-100 — an index of the 100 companies listed on the London Stock Exchange with the largest market capitalization; the share price multiplied by the number of shares. The index is revised every three months.

fundamentals — a company's assets, debt, revenue, earnings and growth. Fundamentals determine a company, currency or security's value.

futures — a futures contract is an agreement to buy or sell a commodity at a predetermined date and price. It could be used to hedge or to speculate on the price of the commodity.

future interest — an interest in property, usually real estate, possession and enjoyment of which is delayed until some future time or event; also, futures, securities or goods bought or sold for future delivery, often keyed to price changes before delivery.

G-20 — a formal association of 19 of the world's largest national economies, plus the European Union (EU). Collectively, the G-20 economies comprise 85% of global gross national product, 80% of world trade and two-thirds of the world population. Member countries are Argentina, Australia, Brazil, Canada, China, France, Germany, India, Indonesia, Italy, Japan, Mexico, Russia, Saudi Arabia, South Africa, South Korea, Turkey, United Kingdom and United States.

GDP — gross domestic product. A measure of economic activity in a country of all the services and goods produced in a year. There are three main ways of calculating GDP — through output, through income and through expenditure.

gift tax — U.S. tax imposed on any gift made by one person to another person annually in excess of US$13,000 (2009 exempted amount).

grantor — a person who conveys real property by deed; a person who creates a trust; also called a trust donor or settlor.

grantor trust — in U.S. tax law, an offshore trust, the income of which is taxed by the IRS as the personal income of the grantor.

gross estate — the total value for estate tax purposes of all a decedent's assets, as compared to net estate, the amount remaining after all permitted exemptions, deductions, taxes and debts owed.

guardianship — a power conferred on a person, the guardian, usually by judicial decree, giving them the right and duty to provide personal supervision, care, and control over another person who is unable to care for himself because of some physical or mental disability or because of minority age status.

haven or haven nation — a country where banking, tax, trust, and corporation laws are specially designed to attract foreign persons wishing to avoid taxes or protect assets.

hedge fund — a private investment fund with a large, unregulated pool of capital said to be managed by experienced investors using a range of sophisticated strategies to maximize returns including hedging, leveraging and derivatives trading.

hedging — making an investment to reduce the risk of price fluctuations to the value of an asset; for example, when one owns a stock and then sells a futures contract agreeing to sell that stock on a particular date at a set price. A fall in price causes no loss nor would there be a benefit from any rise.

indices of ownership — factors indicating a person's control over, therefore ownership, especially of trust property, including the power of revocability.

income beneficiary — the life tenant in a trust.

incorporation — the official government registration and qualification process by which a corporation is formed under law.

indemnity — an agreement by which one promises to protect another from any loss or damage, usually describing the role of the insurer in insurance law.

inflation — the upward price movement of goods and services.

inheritance tax — a tax imposed by government on the amount a person receives from a decedent's estate, rather than on the estate itself; also known as death tax.

insider dealing — selling or purchasing corporate shares for personal benefit based on confidential information about a company's status unknown to the general public.

interest — a right, title, or legal property share; also, a charge for borrowed money, usually a percentage of the total amount borrowed.

international business corporation (IBC) — a term used to describe a variety of offshore corporate structures, characterized by having all or most of its business activity outside the nation of incorporation, maximum privacy, flexibility, low or no taxes on operations, broad powers, and minimal filing and reporting requirements.

interbank rate of exchange — the interest rate which banks charge each other in their dealings. See also *LIBOR*.

insurance — a contract or policy under which a corporation (an insurer) undertakes to indemnify or pay a person (the insured) for a specified future loss in return for the insured's payment of an established sum of money (the premium).

irrevocable trust — a trust which, once established by the grantor, cannot be ended or terminated by the grantor.

junk bond — a bond (or loan to a company) with a high interest rate to reward the lender for a high risk of default.

joint tenancy — a form of property co-ownership in which parties hold equal title with the right of survivorship; a tenancy by the entireties is a similar tenancy reserved to husband and wife in some American states.

judgment — an official and authenticated decision of a court.

jurisdiction — the statutory authority a court exercises; also, the geographic area or subject matter over which a government or court has power.

Keynesian economics — economic theories of the late John Maynard Keynes; the belief that government can directly stimulate demand in a stagnating economy by borrowing money to spend on public works projects such as roads, schools and hospitals.

last will and testament — a written document in which a person directs the post-mortem distribution of his or her property. In the U.S., state law governs the specific requirements for a valid will.

legal capacity — the competency or ability of parties to make a valid contract, including being of majority age (18 years old) and of sound mind.

leveraging — also known as gearing, means using debt to supplement investment. The more you borrow on top of the funds (or equity) you already have, the more highly leveraged you are. Leveraging can maximize both gains and losses. De-leveraging means reducing the amount you are borrowing.

LIBOR — the London Inter Bank Offered Rate, the rate at which banks in the U.K. lend money to each other.

life insurance trust — an irrevocable living trust that holds title to a policy on the grantor's life, proceeds from which are not part of the grantor's estate.

life estate — the use and enjoyment of property granted by the owner to another during the owner's life, or during the life of another, at the termination of which, title passes to another known as the remainderman.

limited partnership — a partnership in which individuals known as limited partners have no management role, but receive periodic income and are personally liable for partnership debts only to the extent of their individual investment.

marital deduction — the right of the surviving spouse under U.S. law to inherit, free of estate taxes, all property owned at death by the deceased spouse.

mark-to-market — recording the value of an asset on a daily basis according to current market prices; also called marked-to-market.

marriage — the legal and religious institution whereby a man and woman join in a binding contract for the purpose of founding and maintaining a family.

money laundering — the process of concealing the criminal origins or uses of cash so that it appears the funds involved are from legitimate sources; a crime in most nations.

mutual legal assistance treaty (MLAT) — bilateral treaties between nations governing cooperation in international investigations of alleged criminal conduct.

numbered bank account — any account in a financial institution that is identified not by the account holder's name, but a number, supposedly limiting knowledge of the owner to a few bank officials. Often associated with Swiss banking, such accounts are more fiction than fact, since in every case the actual account owner is known to the bank.

nationalization — the act of bringing an industry, banks or other private assets like land and property under state control.

negative equity — a situation in which the current value of one's house or other mortgaged real estate is below the amount of the mortgage that remains unpaid.

OECD — the Organization for Economic Cooperation and Development, an unofficial international research group financed by the G-20 that has led attacks and blacklisting of tax havens. See FATF and G-20.

offer — a written or verbal promise by one person (the offeror) to another (the offeree), to do, or not to do, some future act, usually in exchange for a mutual promise or payment (consideration). See *acceptance and contract.*

option — a contract provision allowing one to purchase property at a set price within a certain time period.

partnership — an association of two or more persons formed to conduct business for mutual profit. See also *limited partnership.*

policy — in insurance law, the contract between insurer and insured. See also *insurance.*

Ponzi scheme — similar to a pyramid scheme, an enterprise in which, instead of genuine profits, funds from new investors are used to pay high returns to current investors. Named after the Italian-American fraudster Charles Ponzi, such schemes are destined to collapse as soon as new investment decreases or significant numbers of investors simultaneously seek to withdraw funds.

power of attorney — a written instrument allowing one to act as agent on behalf of another, the scope of agency power indicated by the terms, known as general or limited powers.

preservation trust — any trust designed to limit a beneficiary's access to income and principal.

primary residence —especially in tax law, a home place, as compared to a vacation or second home. See also *domicile*.

prime rate — a term used in North America to describe the standard lending rate of banks to most customers. The prime rate is usually the same across all banks, and higher rates are often described as "x percentage points above prime."

probate — a series of judicial proceedings, usually in a special court, initially determining the validity of a last will and testament, then supervising the administration or execution of the terms of the will and the decedent's estate.

property — anything of value capable of being owned, including land (real property) and personal property, both tangible and intangible.

protector — under the laws of some offshore haven nations, an appointed person who has the duty of overseeing the activities of an offshore trust and its trustee.

quit claim deed — a deed transferring any interest a grantor may have in real property without guarantees of title, if in fact any interest does exist.

real estate — land and anything growing or erected thereon or permanently attached thereto.

real estate investment trust (REIT) — an investment fund in trust form that owns and operates real estate for share holding investors who are the beneficiaries.

recession — a period of negative economic growth technically defined as two consecutive quarters of negative economic growth when real output falls. In the U.S., many factors are taken into account, such as job creation and manufacturing activity but this usually means that it can be defined only when it is well along or already over.

remainder — in testamentary law, the balance of an estate after payment of legacies; in property law, an interest in land or a trust estate distributed at the termination of a life estate. The person with a right to such an estate is the remainderman.

rescind — cancellation or annulment of an otherwise binding contract by one of the parties.

revocable trust — a living trust in which the grantor retains the power to revoke or terminate the trust during his or her lifetime, returning the assets to themselves.

right of survivorship — an attribute of a joint tenancy that automatically transfers ownership of the share of a deceased joint tenant to surviving joint tenants without the necessity of probate.

search and seizure — examination of a person's property by law enforcement officials investigating a crime and the taking of items as potential evidence; the 4th Amendment to the U.S. Constitution forbids unreasonable searches and seizures.

securitization — a recent process by which existing debt such as mortgages with their interest and principal payments are combined and converted into financial instruments backed by the cash flows from a portfolio or pool of mortgages or other assets. Securitization allows for an organization (such as a bank) to transfer risk from its own balance sheet to the debt capital markets through the sale of bonds. The cash raised is then used to issue new mortgages allowing the mortgage bank to increase its operational leverage. This type of securitization is known as a "mortgage backed security" (MBS). This type of activity contributed to the global banking melt down in 2008-2009 because buyers ultimately had no way of assessing the value of these debt instruments, which came to be known collectively as "toxic debt."

short selling — a technique used by investors who think the price of an asset, such as shares, currencies or oil contracts, will fall. They borrow the asset from another investor and then sell it in the relevant market. The aim is to buy back the asset at a lower price and return it to its owner, pocketing the difference; also called shorting.

spendthrift trust — a restricted trust created to pay income to a beneficiary judged by the trust grantor to be too improvident to handle his or her own personal economic affairs.

stagflation — the dreaded combination of inflation and stagnation; an economy that is not growing while prices continue to rise.

subchapter S corporation — under U.S. tax law, a small business corporation that elects to have the undistributed taxable income of the corporation taxed as personal income for the shareholders, thus avoiding payment of corporate income tax.

sub-prime mortgages — a mortgage with a higher risk to the lender (and therefore they tend to be at higher interest rates) because they are offered to people who have had financial problems or who have low or unpredictable incomes.

swap — an exchange of securities between two parties. For example, if a firm in one country has a lower fixed interest rate and one in another country has a lower floating interest rate, an interest rate swap could be mutually beneficial.

tax information exchange agreement — also known as a TIEA, a formal bilateral agreement between two countries governing tax treatment of its nationals by the other country; also providing methods of information exchange upon request.

toxic debt — debts that are unlikely to be recovered from borrowers. Most lenders expect that some customers cannot repay; toxic debt describes a package of loans that are unlikely to be repaid. See also *securitization*.

trust — a legal device allowing title to and possession of property to be held, used, and/or managed by one person, the trustee, for the benefit of others, the beneficiaries.

unit trust — in the U.K. and in Commonwealth nations, the equivalent of the investment fund known in the U.S. as a mutual fund.

U.S. person — for U.S. tax purposes, any individual who is a U.S. citizen or a U.S. resident alien deemed to be a permanent resident; a U.S. domiciled corporation, partnership, estate or trust.

warrants — a document entitling the bearer to receive shares, usually at a stated price.